KU-792-293

Praise for this book

Bernard Marr's latest book is an immensely valuable management handbook as well as a great read! The approach he takes in Strategic Performance Management *is accessible to anyone. The book includes tools, anecdotes, helpful hints and tips, and some fascinating case studies, making it a very practical guide for managers hoping to transform the performance of their businesses.*
Jocelyn Blackwell, Chief Executive Officer, Higham Group plc

This impressive book effectively melts the often disparate topics of strategic analysis, performance measurement, and performance management into a powerful framework for achieving strategic success. Using practical examples and tools, Bernard Marr provides fresh insights into the specific methods available to create a truly performance-driven organization.
Christopher D. Ittner, Ernst & Young Professor of Accounting, The Wharton School, University of Pennsylvania

At last, the definitive book on Strategic Performance Management! In this comprehensive guide to the discipline, Bernard Marr has distilled theory and practice into the essential information any executive needs to take their performance management initiative to the next level.
Steve Fluin, Chief Executive, performancesoft

In Strategic Performance Management *Bernard Marr provides trenchant insights into how organizations can design and use metrics to help maintain their dynamic capabilities in rapidly changing environments. The book is well written and will be insightful for both academic and executive audiences at the senior level.*
David Teece, Professor of Business Administration, Haas School of Business, University of California at Berkeley

Bernard Marr has written a practical, yet thoughtful, book on strategic performance management, which should provide a valuable point of access to the subject for all managers – whether in the private or public sectors. In a world of rapid and unpredictable change, the emphasis on how they can create a structured learning environment is particularly apposite.
Dr Reg Hinkley, CEO, BP Pensions Trustee Limited

Bernard Marr provides a concise, focused, and tightly-integrated approach to strategy analysis and performance management. The performance-oriented approach to strategy development and management he outlines is superior to balanced scorecard approaches

because it is firmly based upon the fundamental drivers of value creation.
Robert Grant, Professor of Management, Georgetown University

If you really want to improve the performance of your business read this book first! Adopting its clear and practical advice will help ensure success through visibility into what really matters and driving performance that has real impact. It's all here in one great book.
Nigel Youell, Business Performance Management Applications, Hyperion Solutions

Bernard Marr has written a very valuable, insightful and easy to read book on strategic performance management and value creation mapping. It will help to avoid that companies stay ignorant to this important issue. The book shows practical and illustrative cases and step-by-step guidance on how to go from management by numbers to management by insights. In this book Bernard Marr presents many well-designed templates for the identification of the value proposition and value drivers, for the design of meaningful performance indicators, and for the selection and adoption of software applications for a more efficient and effective strategic knowledge navigation and decision making.
Leif Edvinsson, Professor of Intellectual Capital, Lund University

By skilfully blending research insights and real life experience, Bernard Marr takes the reader on a journey through concepts, tools and methodologies which enable managers to develop and execute value driven strategies. He succeeds in creating a structured and straightforward approach that will help managers at all levels of any organization to become strategy focused leaders.
Fredrik Wastenson, President and CEO, Prodacapo AB

In a very pragmatic way this book outlines how to implement Strategic Performance Management. By doing so, Bernard overcomes the boundaries and shortcomings of the traditional Balanced Scorecard approach and takes Performance Management to the next level: true Strategic Performance Management!
Andreas Späne, Principal, Booz Allen Hamilton

Bernard Marr's work on value driver mapping at Novo Nordisk has been remarkably valuable. It allowed us to make transparent the impact of our intangible heritage (Triple Bottom Line business principle and Novo Nordisk Way of Management) on our overall business performance. It also enabled us to include indicators for our intangible performance drivers in our strategic planning and performance monitoring. I strongly recommend this book as a practical and inspirational tool to improve your strategic performance management.

Hanne Schou-Rode, Vice President, Business Strategy & Governance, Novo Nordisk A/S

Many organizations are still struggling to identify and manage the value driver, both tangible and intangible, that help to deliver value to their stakeholders. Unfortunately most books in this field are too narrow, focusing either on the strategic aspects, on the performance management issues, or on information technology matters. Bernard Marr has done a great job by presenting a really integrated and state-of-the-art approach to Strategic Performance Management *– linking together strategy and strategic planning, performance measurement, and performance management (including the role of PM software). This excellent book is a must read for everyone interested in performance management.*

Juergen H. Daum, CFO adviser, enterprise performance management expert, and Chief Solution Architect, SAP AG

Bernard Marr has authored another excellent book on measuring and managing organizational value drivers. Especially the Value Creation Map approach he has developed is a powerful tool to understand how value is created and how the tangible and intangible assets interact as value drivers. Bernard Marr's approach has provided us with invaluable insights about our business and allowed us to validate our business hypotheses.

Dr Holger Adelmann, Medical Science, AstraZeneca

Strategic performance management is high on the agenda of most managers and senior executives. A superficial or wrong understanding of performance management concepts often produces poor results and disillusionment. Real benefits are only created by designing an integrated system across the whole organisation based on common understanding of strategic objectives. In this book Bernard Marr provides clear guidelines of how to make strategic performance management work. Particularly insightful is his guidance on measuring intangibles, which represents one of the key challenges for all organisations. This book is entertaining to read, very comprehensible and is brought alive by numerous real-life case studies. It will prove to be of invaluable help in designing an efficient strategic performance management system for your organisation.

Norbert Büchel, Chief Executive Officer, Procos Professional Controlling Systems AG

Strategic Performance Management *is an exceptional book and the first strategic management book that focuses on measuring and managing intangibles as the key value drivers in today's organizations. I highly recommend it to top managers that are looking to build successful business recipes for a sustainable competitive advantage.*
José M. Viedma Martí, Professor of Business Administration Polytechnic University of Catalonia, Spain

Bernard Marr profoundly challenges many prevailing assumptions about measurement and management. It is your chance to be enlightened. If you feel that you are measuring the wrong things, if you feel you haven't identified all your intangible value drivers, and if, like DHL, you think you should, then read this book. Value Creation maps are powerful tools to clarify your strategy by identifying and visualizing your tangible and intangible value drivers.
Gary Crates, Commercial Director, DHL

Bernard Marr's lucid and highly accessible book, filled with practical, real-life examples, is a pleasure to read and will greatly benefit any organization that takes his thinking to heart.
Kenneth Donaldson, Director of Pensions Strategy, Dunnett Shaw Ltd

Strategic Performance Management provides a great combination of tools, cases, and philosophies that have helped much-admired firms develop their performance management systems to deliver their strategy. This book is an excellent road map for managing for excellence in a format that is easy to understand and easier to implement.
Dr Yasar Jarrar, Executive Dean, Dubai School of Government

Do we need any more books on performance management, you might ask? Well, if these books are anything like Bernard Marr's book, keep them coming! With well chosen examples and anecdotes, often funny and always insightful, Strategic Performance Management *is a delight to read and even better it will entice the reader to act.*
André A. de Waal, Associate Professor, Maastricht School of Management, The Netherlands

This book provides invaluable insights on the approaches to linking different parts of an organisation to provide a coherent view on performance. I recommend it to professional accountants in business seeking a more sophisticated and practical approach to performance management.
Stathis Gould, Technical Specialist, Chartered Institute of Management Accountants

In Strategic Performance Management *Bernard Marr gives good examples of existing best practices and fresh insights into performance management. There is something for everyone to learn in this book.*
John Wilkes, Head of Performance Management, Capgemini UK

The book Strategic Performance Management *tackles one of the most important challenges corporations are facing today: the design of a system to measure and manage the tangible and intangible performance drivers. The book provides the reader with a great overview and sufficient details. What I particularly like about it is that it brings together scientific approaches with practical management needs. Bernard Marr has done great job in extracting, developing and describing sophisticated and applicable tools that will enable managers to make strategic performance management work.*
Professor Dr Klaus Möller, Technical University of Munich, Germany

With Strategic Performance Management *Bernard Marr provides clear guidance on how to overcome the challenge of effectively and efficiently connecting strategy to action. He avoids the common trap of proposing an all new 'silver bullet' strategy process or tool and instead provides the context within which to connect existing theories and methodologies in a simple and straightforward way.*
David McCormick, Corporate Strategy, Royal Dutch Shell plc

This book effectively communicates the core of modern thought on the management of intangibles in a strategic context. It is accessible and simple, but not superficial or simplistic. It is a good overview of the central themes in modern performance management and it integrates fields such as management control, strategy, and intangibles. Bernard Marr outlines a strong framework for the management of businesses in the modern economy.
Jan Mouritsen, Professor, Copenhagen Business School, Denmark

This book provides comprehensive guidelines of how to develop a strategic performance management system. With his step-by-step approach, illustrated by real life examples, Bernard Marr ensures that organizations identify, measure and manage the essential value drivers that really matter.
Professor Dr Péter Horváth, IPRI – International Performance Research Institute, Stuttgart, Germany

If you read only one management book this year, make it Strategic Performance Management *by Bernard Marr. This terrific book sets new standards of how to measure and manage what really matters in organizations today. In a thought-provoking manner, Bernard Marr*

demonstrates why many traditional approaches to performance management are doomed to failure. I believe every business leader can benefit from Bernard Marr's refreshing thinking on strategic performance management.
Roger Camrass, Director, Business Transformation Group, Fujitsu

This is an outstanding book! Bernard Marr provides leading edge thinking on strategic performance management presented in an engaging and practical way. This book is a milestone and a must read for every manager trying to manage strategic performance.
Eggert Claessen, Managing Director, Tolvumidlun Ltd and Chairman, GoPro Ltd

Excellent book! In Strategic Performance Management *Bernard Marr describes how managers can get a firm grip on their corporate performance. He shows remarkable insight into this topic and fresh ideas to make performance management work. With this book, Bernard will teach you how to put passion into performance.*
Frank Buytendijk, Research Vice-President Corporate Performance Management, Gartner

Bernard Marr has done it again! With Strategic Performance Management *he delivers a fascinating, refreshing, and actionable read. This book is not only a delight to read, it will open your mind, guide you through the distracting complications and traps of measuring and managing performance, and leave you with a clear vision of strategic performance management for the 21st century.*
Stuart Crainer, Editor, Financial Times Handbook of Management, Editorial Fellow, London Business School

Strategic Performance Management

I dedicate this book to the two most important people in my life my wonderful wife Claire and our daughter Sophia Kristina

Strategic Performance Management

Leveraging and measuring your intangible value drivers

Bernard Marr

AMSTERDAM • BOSTON • HEIDELBERG • LONDON • NEW YORK • OXFORD
PARIS • SAN DIEGO • SAN FRANCISCO • SINGAPORE • SYDNEY • TOKYO
Butterworth-Heinemann is an imprint of Elsevier

Butterworth-Heinemann is an imprint of Elsevier
Linacre House, Jordan Hill, Oxford OX2 8DP, UK
30 Corporate Drive, Suite 400, Burlington, MA 01803, USA

First edition 2006

Copyright © 2006, Bernard Marr. Published by Elsevier Ltd. All rights reserved.

The right of Bernard Marr to be identified as the author of this work has been
asserted in accordance with the Copyright, Designs and Patents Act 1988

No part of this publication may be reproduced, stored in a retrieval system or transmitted in
any form or by any means electronic, mechanical, photocopying, recording or otherwise
without the prior written permission of the publisher

Permissions may be sought directly from Elsevier's Science & Technology Rights Department
in Oxford, UK: phone (+44) (0) 1865 843830; fax (+44) (0) 1865 853333; email:
permissions@elsevier.com. Alternatively you can submit your request online by visiting the
Elsevier web site at http://elsevier.com/locate/permissions, and selecting *Obtaining permission
to use Elsevier material*

Notice
No responsibility is assumed by the publisher for any injury and/or damage to persons or
property as a matter of products liability, negligence or otherwise, or from any use or operation
of any methods, products, instructions or ideas contained in the material herein. Because of
rapid advances in the medical sciences, in particular, independent verification of diagnoses and
drug dosages should be made

British Library Cataloguing in Publication Data
A catalogue record for this book is available from the British Library

Library of Congress Cataloging-in-Publication Data
A catalog record for this book is available from the Library of Congress

ISBN-13: 978-0-7506-6392-2
ISBN-10: 0-7506-6392-8

For information on all Butterworth-Heinemann publications
visit our web site at books.elsevier.com

Printed and bound in Great Britain

06 07 08 09 10 10 9 8 7 6 5 4 3 2 1

BLACKBURN COLLEGE
LIBRARY
Acc. No. BB04015
Class No. 658.402 MAR
Date July 2006

Working together to grow
libraries in developing countries

www.elsevier.com | www.bookaid.org | www.sabre.org

ELSEVIER   BOOK AID   Sabre Foundation
            International

Contents

About the author

Bernard Marr is one of the world's leading experts on strategic performance management. He specializes in the identification, measurement, and management of value creation and strategic performance drivers. In this capacity he has worked with many leading organizations including Accenture, AstraZeneca, BP, DHL, Fujitsu, Gartner, HSBC, NovoNordisk, the Home Office, and Royal Dutch Shell. He has extensive work experience across the United States, Europe, Africa, the Middle East and Asia, which makes him an acclaimed keynote speaker, consultant, teacher, and award-winning writer.

Having gained management experience in consulting, manufacturing and international trading corporations, Bernard Marr moved to the University of Cambridge to become a management researcher at the Judge Institute of Management Studies. Since 1999 he has been a Research Fellow at the renowned Centre for Business Performance at Cranfield School of Management, he also holds multiple visiting professorships.

Bernard Marr has contributed to over 100 books, reports, and articles on topics such as Corporate Performance Management, Balanced Scorecard, Strategy Maps, and Intangible Value Drivers. His recent books include *Perspectives on Intellectual Capital: Managing, Measuring and Reporting Intangibles*, *Weighing the Options: BSC Software*, and *Automating your Scorecard*.

Currently, he is chairman of the international PMA IC Group, Intangible Assets Editor of the journal *Measuring Business Excellence*, and a member of the editorial board of *The Handbook of Strategic Management* and serves on the editorial boards of many leading journals in the field. In its recent article 'wise guys' the *CEO Journal* recognized Bernard Marr as one of today's world-leading business brains.

For more information please see: http://www.cranfield.ac.uk/som/cbp/
Or e-mail: *bernard.marr@cranfield.ac.uk*

Preface

The term 'Strategic Performance Management', sometimes also called 'Corporate Performance Management' or 'Enterprise Performance Management', has entered the agenda of most senior executives around the globe. It is frequently used to refer to the processes of managing and measuring organizational performance. Today's interest in the management and measurement of performance is driven not only by new compliance and corporate governance regulations, but also by the urge to identify, measure, and manage the organizational value drivers. Whereas identifying and managing traditional financial and physical value drivers is difficult enough, identifying and leveraging the intangible value drivers is still seen as the holy grail of management.

Whereas executives and managers clearly recognize the vital importance of intangibles as key drivers of performance, their measurement and management is one of the weakest links in their strategic performance management initiatives. I have been talking to many senior executives, of both corporations and not-for-profit organizations, over the past years, and everyone shares the same frustration that the existing measures are of little value. Even though record numbers of performance measures are being collected, often driven by the desire to provide better and more useful insights about the strategic value drivers, few valuable insights are produced.

What everyone aspires to is to clearly understand how the strategic value drivers – tangible and intangible – help to provide the competencies needed to deliver value to all stakeholders. Following this understanding, managers want relevant performance indicators that help them to extract worthwhile management insights. These insights should then be shared, discussed, validated and acted upon. Strategic performance management is therefore used for strategic decision-making and learning, not only at the executive level, but also throughout the entire organization. In a performance-driven culture, strategy becomes everyone's everyday job. Relevant performance data is used to learn, to validate or challenge strategic assumptions, to assess risks, to evaluate the suitability of mergers and acquisitions, and most importantly to facilitate decision-making and actions.

This book is about how to put strategic performance management into practice. It is about how to identify, visualize and describe the tangible and intangible value drivers and the way they create core competencies, performance outputs, and value. And it is about establishing relevant and meaningful performance indicators, which will then be used by everyone to extract insights, make decisions, validate and challenge assumptions, assess risk, evaluate future directions, and to continuously learn.

The ideas, concepts and tools presented in this book are grounded in fields including strategic management, organizational learning, theory of measurement, and psychology. The tools and concepts have proven to be powerful enablers of strategic performance management initiatives not only in world-leading corporations, but also in not-for-profit organizations, as well as central and local government institutions. The book is deliberately designed to be applicable for any organization, be it an international corporation, a small or medium-sized business, a business unit, department, a not-for-profit organization or a government institution. Throughout this book I will use the term 'organization' to refer to all of the above.

Organizations that have successfully deployed many of the tools and concepts described in this book include Astra Zeneca, BP, DHL, Fujitsu, Novo Nordisk, The Executive Office in Dubai, Royal Dutch Shell, as well as banks, insurance companies, manufacturing firms, and various local and central government institutions around the world. Without these organizations it would have been impossible for me to create my insights and tools and I would like to thank all of the many executives, managers, and employees I have worked with over the years. All of them have helped to shape my thinking.

The second major source of influence has come from my colleagues at the Centre for Business Performance at the Cranfield School of Management. This group of leading experts in measuring and managing performance has been an incubator for ideas and concepts on the topic. It is impossible to create a book like this in a vacuum and many of the ideas presented in this book have their roots in this great reservoir of knowledge. However, this book is my cut of this joint pool of expertise. I would like to thank every single member of the Centre for Business Performance for providing me with a continuously stimulating and challenging environment, for their support and friendship as well as the many valuable insights they provide. I would like to mention Mike Bourne, Monica Franco, Dina Gray, Mike Kennerley,

Veronica Martinez, Steve Mason, Pietro Micheli, Karim Moustaghfir, Andy Neely, Göran Roos, and J. C. Spender. I would also like to thank my colleagues who work 'behind the scenes', in particular Angela Walters, Eva Barton, Sue Gregory, and Sue Gow and Jacqueline Brown.

Colleagues from other institutions who have been inspirational and significantly shaped my thinking on strategic performance management include Chris Argyris, Robert Grant, Chris Ittner, Robert Kaplan, Baruch Lev, Jan Mouritsen, Giovanni Schiuma, and David Teece. There are so many other individuals who have also influenced my thinking and I hope they know who they are and how much I have valued any input and dialogue over the years. Special thanks go to Chris Adams for editorial support and to Tim Goodfellow for providing the opportunity of turning my intangible ideas into a tangible book.

The other force that consciously challenges me, supports me, and gave me the space and time to write another book is made up of my family, my brother Marc Andre Marr, Julie and Alan Parkins, and especially my beloved wife Claire and our daughter Sophia Kristina.

Introduction

Today's business world requires new approaches towards Strategic Performance Management. The wrong approach will often drive dysfunctional behaviour and jeopardize performance. Three key components of this problem are an incomplete picture of the strategy (the strategy trap), the wrong performance measures (the measurement trap), and the wrong approach towards managing performance (the Performance Management trap). This book will outline how you can avoid these traps and provide you with the necessary tools to become a truly performance-driven organization.

Imagine an organization with people who don't really understand the strategic goals and the direction where the organization is heading. The executive team of this organization believes that the noted downturn in performance is in fact caused by this lack of strategic understanding. They believe that they have a quite well-formulated strategy but need to improve its execution. To better align business unit performance and employees' activities with corporate objectives, the organization decides to initiate a Strategic Performance Management project. Key elements of this are performance measures, which are developed by managers of each business unit. The managers hold brainstorm meetings and create sets of measures based on the existing strategy. The teams are careful to come up with measures for each of the different organizational functions and departments. It was quite easy to produce a set of measures and targets for most areas. These measures with targets are then given to each functional manager and regular performance evaluations are put in place to measure progress against targets. A bonus pool is created for all managers and therefore achieving their targets will result in better pay.

Nine months pass by and the regular performance evaluations reveal that alignment has improved. Most measures have moved towards the targeted performance levels and some business units have already met their annual targets. The executive team sees this continuous progress and deems their Strategic Performance Management project as successful. However, when after twelve months the overall performance data is brought together it reveals that organizational performance has fallen, even though the measures and targets of the different business units were met. In addition to this, some key people within the organization have decided to leave, and the employee and customer surveys reveal sharp deterioration in performance.

What happened here? First of all, this organization didn't really have a well-formulated strategy; secondly it fell into both the classic measurement trap and Performance Management trap. The wrong things were being measured, and where the right things were measured the wrong metrics were used. These metrics were then imposed on people who didn't want to be measured and couldn't see how these metrics would be useful for them. They were not able to see how the measures were linked to the strategy. This in turn frustrated people immensely and caused dysfunctional behaviour. Since people knew that their performance was being judged on their achievements of hitting their performance targets, this is what they concentrated on. The consequence was that it eliminated cross-departmental collaboration as everyone was only interested in their own performance. Performance measurement became a game of providing numbers to someone who would collate them and then prepare reports. People stopped caring about overall strategic objectives and were only interested in what was being measured. Human beings are extremely creative and very quickly devise ways of delivering a good measure result without necessarily delivering good performance – especially if they believe that the measures are not really providing them with any interesting insights.

Consequences of poor Performance Management

There are countless examples that illustrate the dysfunctional consequences of poor Performance Management. One example I particularly like comes from an airport – a complex organization with different business units. Here, key performance measures were developed for the different functional areas of the airport. On the arrivals side, customer satisfaction is equated to channelling passengers through the airport as quickly and conveniently as possible. What customers want is that once the plane has landed it quickly reaches its final parking spot, passengers get off the plane and swiftly pass through passport control, collect their luggage, and easily reach their transport links for their onward journey. A key factor for success therefore is the amount of time it takes to get the luggage off the plane and onto the conveyor belt in the luggage reclaim area. Luggage handlers were therefore given a measure and a target of fifteen minutes. The way it was measured was easy since data was available about landing times as well as operational data from the conveyor belts. The measured time therefore started once the plane landed and stopped once the luggage reached the conveyor belt and it started moving.

Instead of focusing on customer satisfaction – the overall objective – the baggage handlers saw hitting the measurement target as a game. They wanted to look good in their performance review and therefore ensured that one of the baggage handlers took their emergency vehicle and raced up to each plane once it reached its final parking spot, then grabbed the first piece of luggage off the plane, raced back to the terminal, put it on the conveyor belt and started the belt. This explains why this team, on paper, outperformed all other teams at the airport. It also explains why we see so many single pieces of luggage going round on the conveyor belts of airports. Overall, it illustrates some of the dysfunctional consequences often caused by not understanding Strategic Performance Management and its behavioural implications.

What is Strategic Performance Management?

Strategic Performance Management is about creating an environment in which organizational performance becomes everyone's everyday job. This involves a clear understanding by everyone in the organization of the strategic direction and competitive advantage as well as their accepted responsibility for continuous refinement of this strategic direction. In such an environment employees use performance indicators to test and challenge the strategic assumptions that underlie performance. Relevant performance indicators are collected to inform strategic decision-making at all organizational levels, and not merely to put them into reports that no one really cares about.

> Strategic Performance Management (SPM) is therefore defined as the organizational approach to define, assess, implement, and continuously refine organizational strategy. It encompasses methodologies, frameworks and indicators that help organizations in the formulation of their strategy and enable employees to gain strategic insights which allow them to challenge strategic assumptions, refine strategic thinking, and inform strategic decision-making and learning.

The strategy trap

One of the essential premises of this book is that strategy formulation (or, more commonly, reformulation) is a layered process and an essential pre-requisite for successful Strategic Performance Management. A three-step pathway is required in order to build the essential 'information stock' that is needed in order to make effective decisions about strategic directions.

A sound strategy should be developed with the aid of a reasonably thorough analysis of the environment in which the organization operates so that it can develop its value proposition more precisely. Using different tools to identify opportunities in the markets has been the traditional approach of strategy formulation. Here, organizations choose a market or consumer segment and then align the organization with its value proposition, internal processes, and capabilities to the opportunity in the market.

However, organizations have realized that they need to match external opportunities with their existing competencies. One strategy thinker made a point when he said that 'opportunism without competence is a path to fairyland'.[1] Over the past decade the Strategic Management field has seen a shift towards more internally focused approaches, where organizations exploit their internal strengths and competencies. The reasoning is summarized by Strategy Professor Robert Grant, who argues that

> in a world where customer preferences are volatile, the identity of customers is changing, and the technologies for serving customers' requirements are continually evolving, an externally focused orientation does not provide a secure foundation for formulating long-term strategy. When the external is in a state of flux, the firm's own resources and capabilities may be a much more stable basis on which to define its identity. Hence, a definition of a business in terms of what it is capable of doing may offer a more durable basis for strategy than a definition based upon the needs which the business seeks to satisfy.[2]

In this view, markets are selected based on the exploitation of core competencies, which are based on the organizational resources. Here, the term 'resources' is used in the widest sense to include not only physical and financial resources, but also intangible resources such as knowledge and skills, image and relationships, processes, intellectual property, organizational culture or intellectual property. Companies such as 3M, Honda, The Walt Disney Company, or Wal-Mart have demonstrated how they based their strategies on their resource architecture and core competencies.[3] In 3M's case, for example, it allowed them to understand that they had shared competencies in substrates, coatings, and adhesives.[4] Identifying the various ways to combine these core competencies has allowed them to enter businesses as diverse as sticky tape, photographic film, magnetic tape, and 'Post-it' notes.

Market-based versus resource-based viewpoints

The various academic pundits of strategy formulation tend to position themselves in one of two camps: market-based theorists and resource-based theorists. Yet to practitioners either one seems intuitively to be too narrow a view to understand the future potential of the enterprise. Increasingly, attempts are being made to unite these two views of strategic management. This book will consider both points of view, since they complement each other and only together provide a comprehensive understanding of the strategic situation of any organization.[5]

An analogy might help to illustrate how these ideas fit together. Think of the organization as a tree.[6] Its foliage is how it presents itself to the external world and its fruits (say, apples) are the products or services it offers to its customers. The major branches of the tree represent the set of businesses in the portfolio of an organization. The tree's hidden roots, on the other hand, represent the tangible and intangible resources it needs to have in place in order to provide the sustenance it requires to grow the apples that people will buy. The tree's trunk then represents the core competencies that give it its strength and connects the resources with the delivery of the products and services. The trunk therefore provides the channel leveraging the resources to create value. Similar to companies, all trees are made up of the same components and share the same biological processes of photosynthesis and nutrient extraction, but the shape of the trees and their fruits differs widely.[7] See Figure I.1.

What apple trees cannot do of course, that organizations usually must do, is grow a blend of red and green apples at the same time in different quantities according to the demand for each type. Nevertheless, defending this slight snag in the analogy, the owner of an orchard can plant a mixture of trees that provide a supply of both green and red apples. The organization might then perhaps be better considered as an orchard rather than a single tree.

The purpose of this analogy is simply to highlight the point that organizations create value not only by understanding their markets and the wants and needs of their customers, but also by having a

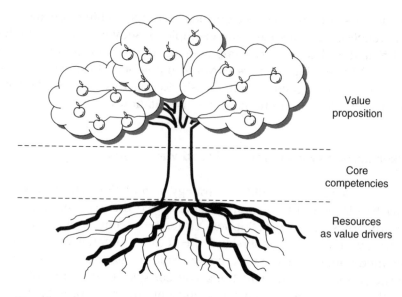

Figure I.1   Tree analogy

deep understanding of the nature of their competencies, capabilities and resources that are critical to their success. Organizations need to understand how they can get the best out of these and, in the commercial sector at least, in a way that makes them distinctively different from competitors. Organizations embarking on any Strategic Performance Management initiative, therefore, need to analyse information not only about their external markets but also about their internal resources. In other words, the market-based views must be reconciled with the resource-based views (or vice versa).

I acknowledge that the starting point is rarely a blank piece of paper and it is not always possible for organizations to redefine their market segments – especially for public sector organizations or most organizational business units, since they generally have a clearly defined external stakeholder environment they need to serve. However, I have worked with many public sector organizations around the world as well as business units and found that even though their 'markets' might be fixed, they often severely lack a clear understanding of how they deliver value to their customers or communities. And without such understanding it is impossible to design a good Strategic Performance Management approach.

Organizations fall into the Strategy trap when they develop a one-sided view of strategy that does not connect external opportunities and value propositions with their internal core competencies and resource structure. In Part I of this book I will outline the strategy development process from both views, which then allows you to pick your appropriate starting point. In the end it doesn't matter where we start as long as we create a comprehensive view of our strategy that includes the defined value proposition, the specific core competencies, and the underlying resource architecture. This comprehensive understanding of strategy can then guide the development of relevant performance indicators.

The measurement trap

Performance measures are vital aspects of our organizations and Performance Management. In the words of the fifth century BC philosopher Philolaus – without measures we can understand nothing and know nothing. Once organizations have defined and clarified their strategy, measures can be used to gauge performance in comparison to, for example, their expectations, targets or competitors. Measures enable us to define future goals like a certain market share or shareholder value, and they should help us understand whether we are on the right track towards delivering our strategy. Indicators should allow us to challenge our business assumptions and provide us with insights that will guide our everyday decision-making. Without indicators we can't assess our success, we don't know whether our assumptions or decisions were correct, and we don't see whether we are moving in the right direction.

However, this is not what happens in most organizations. What I see is often a very narrow use of measurement. Common reality is that there are too many metrics; no one knows why they are being collected, and most people agree that the measures that are used are not measuring what they are supposed to measure or what really matters. Organizations have become obsessed with measuring everything that walks and moves but often fail to measure what really matters. In many cases measurement has become an administrative burden where we spend a lot of our time collecting and reporting metrics, which we know is of little or no value. As a consequence, few strategic insights are extracted from the measures we collect and little or no learning takes place.

Also, too many organizations are making the mistake of only measuring everything that is easy to measure. For example, they often tend to focus on efficiency measures with the hope that these will somehow equate to customer satisfaction or better financial performance. However, it has long been established that it is dangerous to measure one thing while hoping to achieve another. It is important to remember that measures focus our attention and drive behaviour.[8] A classic example comes from call centres, where measures such as number of calls and call duration are automatically produced by the system and therefore easily reported. The result is that because they are measured and reported people assume that they are important and relevant metrics for the business. This is all okay until we find out that front-line agents continuously transfer customers or even cut them off to meet their measures – while the efficiency targets are being achieved, customer service and with it overall performance is not. Call centres, like most departments and business units, are rarely detached operations with a solitary goal of driving down costs. They are integral parts of organizations and their service or product offerings. Therefore, performance measures need to reflect the strategic direction of the entire organization. To avoid the measurement trap organizations need to put efficiency measures into the context of overall performance. This can only be achieved by clearly understanding the strategy of the organization.

As outlined above, strategy for today's organizations involves not just corporate objectives such as shareholder value but also an understanding of how this can be delivered. Measures have to be developed for the customer value proposition, the core competencies, and the underlying resources. These then become leading indicators for future performance and important components of Strategic Performance Management. One of the problems is that many of these leading indicators are intangible in nature and therefore intrinsically difficult to express in simple metrics. When it comes to concepts like 'intellectual capital', 'reputation', or 'organizational culture' it is impossible to 'measure' those in a traditional measurement sense. The reason for it is that the word 'measure' is often associated with accounting and mathematics. It therefore works in the simplified world of financial numbers, where we can clearly define things and then reduce them to a number. However, businesses operate in a social context that is more complex and we therefore have to realize that by measuring things we will only capture part of the reality behind them.

A great example to illustrate our measurement limitations is measuring human intelligence. The 'measure' we would traditionally use is IQ (Intelligence Quotient). However, the questions that arise are: what is intelligence and what do IQ scores actually measure? Whereas the details of the answers to these questions are still subject to an ongoing debate, on the whole IQ tests focus on our analytical and mathematical reasoning. However, Dr Howard Gardner, Professor of Education at Harvard University, has shown that there are multiple facets to our intelligence.[9] His studies have identified eight different forms of intelligence – of which IQ only measures a small subset.

The forms of intelligence identified by Gardner are linguistic intelligence ('word smart'), logical-mathematical intelligence ('number/reasoning smart'), interpersonal intelligence ('people smart'), bodily-kinesthetic intelligence ('body smart'), spatial intelligence ('picture smart'), musical intelligence ('music smart'), naturalist intelligence ('nature smart') and intrapersonal intelligence ('self smart'). This suggests that someone can be classed as intelligent when he or she, for example, has great hand–eye coordination and awareness of space – and therefore becomes a great basketball or football player. Someone can have great emotional intelligence and therefore be able to connect with other people and become a great leader.[10] Others might have great musical ability and become composers or musicians. All of these people wouldn't necessary need a high score on an IQ test, since it only assesses linguistic and logical-mathematical skills.

The above example hopefully illustrates that measures cannot capture the entire truth when it comes to intangibles. However, they can indicate the level of performance. They are therefore indicators, rather then measures, and have to be treated as such.

Organizations fall into the measurement trap when they don't link their indicators to the strategy of the organization and when they attempt to quantify the unquantifiable or measure everything that is easy to measure without focusing on the relevant and meaningful indicators in order to use them for strategic decision-making and learning. Part II of this book will outline how, based on the strategy of the organization, relevant indicators can be developed.

The management trap

Once we have identified the strategy and derived relevant performance indicators we need to use them. Too many organizations believe that, once they have collected the measures and put them into spreadsheets or reports, this will by magic lead to better decision-making. Unfortunately this is not the case. I often use a short story to illustrate this point. Imagine three frogs sitting on a leaf in a pond. One of the three frogs decides to jump away – how many frogs are left on the leaf? Still three! The one frog initially decided to jump but then changed his mind. Similar to this story, we put metrics in place to help us make better decisions. However, unless we use these measures and actually make better decisions nothing changes and no value is added. Instead, the opposite is the case; it becomes an additional administrative burden with negative value that causes a lot of frustration.

Today's organizations have evolved and subsequently we need to evolve our Performance Management approaches. Management Professor Charles Ehin writes that over the past hundred years or so we have deliberately chosen to design our social institutions with almost one single purpose in mind – to control the behaviour of people within them. However, he continues, success in the knowledge age demands that we let go of the top-down, command-and-control framework.[11] What we used to do in firms was specify the tasks someone had to perform and then put measures in place to control whether this was achieved.

This approach was pioneered by Frederick Taylor at the beginning of the twentieth century, who called it 'Scientific Management'.[12] According to Taylor, it is only a matter of matching people to a task and then supervising, rewarding and punishing them in accordance with their performance. In Taylor's view, there was no such thing as skill required since all work could be analysed step-by-step, as a series of unskilled operations that could then be combined into any kind of job.[13] This control-driven Performance Management approach treats people rather like machines and it infers that someone else knows best how they should perform their job. Scientific Management worked for Taylor in the mass production world of the industrial revolution, where the only reason that people were working in factories was because they couldn't yet be replaced by machines. The effect was that it made people not only stupid but ignorant.[14] But then no one expected them to be clever or innovative. In such a world it didn't matter that people stopped developing intelligence or imagination to look for ways of improving processes or overcoming difficulties.

In today's organizations, we generally want more from people than just for them to perform simple and repetitive tasks at a conveyor belt. And more importantly we can't afford for anyone to be ignorant. We rely on their insights in order to create innovative products and processes, we rely on their ability to build relationships with customers and other stakeholders, and we rely on their ability to integrate into teams and make performance their day-to-day job. And as we have seen, these are the things we can't really 'measure' in a controlling sense. Applying the machine-like command-and-control model is not only inhumane but also goes against the increasing need for organizations to be more adaptive to ever-changing customer needs in the knowledge economy.[15]

If we therefore use measures to treat people like machines and try to control them like robots we will not get any of their intellectual capital or intangibles. We will get just what we measure, which is not what we want! If we fail to acknowledge these facts then we also get the dysfunctional behaviour and the gaming of measures. Instead, we need to create what I call an 'enabled learning environment'. Here, people understand the strategy of the organization they are working in and use indicators that are aligned to this strategy to make better-informed decisions as well as to refine and challenge the strategy. The organization, in turn, understands and acknowledges the limitations of measurement and empowers people to become accountable for strategic performance. In this culture we engage everyone in Performance Management, instead of ignoring their inputs and so creating a culture of apathy, lethargy, and anti-learning.[16]

Organizations fall into the Performance Management trap when they either collect too many irrelevant measures or when they use the measures in a command-and-control fashion; both situations mean that measures will not be used for any strategic decision-making or learning. Part II of this book will also describe how to create an enabled learning environment so that strategy and performance become everyone's everyday job.

IT support for Strategic Performance Management

Once strategy, indicators, and management approaches are in place, we need to implement them and ensure that they become embedded into the organization. And here is where software applications represent vital enablers for those organizations that are serious about implementing Strategic Performance Management. Today, there are still too many organizations that rely on spreadsheets to manage their performance without understanding their severe limitations. Nowadays, many specially designed software applications are on offer. These so-called Performance Management software applications are designed to enable data integration, analysis and communication in order for us to extract real management insights from our performance information.

Part III of this book will provide an overview of what these software packages can deliver. It will provide an insight into the role of such automation tools and an understanding of the different capabilities and limitations of such tools. The problem we face today is that there are over thirty application providers to choose from, each of them claiming that their solution offers unique and important features. Selecting the wrong solution can undermine the entire development effort and the credibility of the Performance Management system.[17] Here you will be given a starting point as to how to select the appropriate automation solution for your organization.

Structure of the book

The book has been structured in a way that reflects the key elements of Strategic Performance Management and is split into three major parts (see Figure I.2). The first part the book explores the strategic context. This part is divided into four chapters. Chapter 1 discusses the strategic boundary conditions and how they can influence the strategic direction of an organization. Chapter 2 looks at the analysis of the external environment and how to identify the stakeholder value proposition. This involves identifying who the organization is delivering value to and a definition of what this value could be. Chapter 3 looks inside the organization to identify the key value drivers, capabilities, and core competencies. Chapter 4 looks at how the three views of strategy can be brought together in a 'value creation map', that visualizes the organizational value creation logic and a 'value narrative', which describes the value creation logic. This part also includes many real life case studies of how this has been achieved in practice.

The second part of this book is concerned with Performance Management. The strategic business model captured in a value creation map is the starting point for this phase. Part II is split into three chapters. Chapter 5 looks at how to create meaningful and relevant performance indicators and at methods of how performance can be assessed and reported in organizations. Chapter 6 looks at how to create

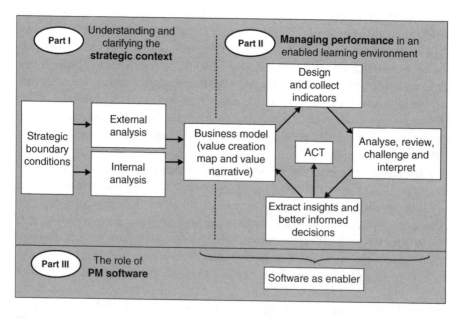

Figure I.2 Elements of Strategic Performance Management

an enabled learning environment in which performance information is used for forward-looking learning. It also looks at how to align performance review meetings to this environment in order to extract more valuable strategic management insights. Chapter 7 looks at more sophisticated ways of using the strategic business model and indicators. It discusses double-loop learning to challenge current strategic assumptions, as well as how to test and validate causal models, how to assess risks in your organization, and how to evaluate possible business extensions, mergers, and acquisitions.

The third and final part of this book will look at software-based automation of Strategic Performance Management. It will explore what the latest Strategic Performance Management software applications can deliver and how this can be used to leverage the full potential of Strategic Performance Management. An Appendix to Part III provides an overview of the software market, a list of the leading vendors, and a framework to facilitate the software selection process.

References and endnotes

1 Andrews, K. R. (1971). *The Concept of Corporate Strategy*. Dow Jones-Irwin: Homewood, IL.

2 Grant, R. (1998). *Contemporary Strategy Analysis*. Blackwell: Oxford, p. 181.

3 For case studies see: Collis, D. J. and Montgomery, C. A. (1997). *Corporate Strategy – Resources and the Scope of the Firm*. McGraw-Hill: Boston; and Stalk, G., Evans, P. and Shulman, L. E. (1992). Competing on Capabilities: The New Rules of Corporate Strategy. *Harvard Business Review*, Vol. 70, No. 2, Mar/Apr, p. 57.

4 Prahalad, C. K. and Hamel, G. (1990). The Core Competence of the Corporation. *Harvard Business Review*, Vol. 68, No. 3, May/Jun, p. 79.

5 For a further discussion about the complementarities of the resource-based and market-based approach of strategic management see also: Conner, K. R. (1991). A Historical Comparison of Resource-Based Theory and Five Schools of Thought Within Industrial Organization Economics: Do We Have a New Theory of the Firm? *Journal of Management*, Vol. 17, No. 1, p. 121 or Spanos, Y. E. and Liokas, S. (2001). An Examination into Causal Logic of Rent Generation: Contrasting Porter's Competitive Strategy Framework and the Resource-Based Perspective. *Strategic Management Journal*, Vol. 22, No. 10, pp. 907–34.

6 This analogy has been used on various occasions, one of the most convincing was by Prahalad, C. K. and Hamel, G. (1990). The Core

Competence of the Corporation. *Harvard Business Review*, Vol. 68, No.3, May/Jun, p. 79. However, tree diagrams can be traced back to the third-century Syrian philosopher's diagram named after its developer, 'Tree of Porphyry' based upon the work of Aristotle.

7 Collis, D. J. and Montgomery, C. A. (1997). *Corporate Strategy – Resources and the Scope of the Firm*. McGraw-Hill: Boston, p. 130.

8 For a classic, but still very relevant article on the behavioural consequences of wrong measures see: Ridgway, V. F. (1956). Dysfunctional Consequences of Performance Measurements. *Administrative Science Quarterly*, Vol. 1, No. 2, pp. 240–7.

9 To learn about multiple intelligences see for example: Gardner, H. (1993). *Multiple Intelligences: The Theory in Practice*. New York: Basic; and Gardner, H. (2000). *Intelligence Reframed: Multiple Intelligences for the 21st Century*. New York: Basic.

10 To find out about emotional intelligence see for example: Goleman, D., Boyatzis, R. and McKee, A. (2001). Primal Leadership: The Hidden Driver of Great Performance. *Harvard Business Review*, Vol. 79, No. 11, pp. 42–51; and Goleman, D. (1996). *Emotional Intelligence: Why It Can Matter More Than IQ*. Bloomsbury: London.

11 Ehin, C. (2000). *Unleashing Intellectual Capital*. Butterworth-Heinemann: Boston, p. 179.

12 Taylor, W. F. (1913). The Principles of Scientific Management (Reproduced by Lightning Source UK Ltd, 2005).

13 Crainer, S. (1998). *Key Management Ideas*, 3rd edition. FT Prentice Hall: London.

14 Ibid. Adam Smith is quoted to have commented on the potential problems of mass production (p. 30).

15 Haeckel, S. (1999). *Adaptive Enterprise: Creating and Leading Sense-and-Respond Organizations*. Harvard Business School Press: Boston.

16 See: Preskill, H. and Torres, R. T. (1999). *Evaluative Inquiry of Learning in Organizations*. Sage: Thousand Oaks, CA, p. 63.

17 Marr, B. and Neely, A. (2003). *Automating your Scorecard: The Balanced Scorecard Software Report*, Gartner and Cranfield School of Management, InfoEdge: Stamford, CT; or Marr, B. and Neely, A. (2003). Automating the Balanced Scorecard – selection criteria to identify the appropriate software application. *Measuring Business Excellence*, Vol. 7, No. 3, pp. 29–36.

Part I

Understanding and clarifying the strategic context

Introduction to Part I

Strategic Performance Management is about challenging strategic assumptions, refining strategic thinking, and facilitating strategic decision-making and learning at all levels of the organization. It is about engaging everyone in the strategy and its execution so that organizational performance becomes everyone's everyday job. The starting point for Strategic Performance Management is therefore a shared understanding and clarification of the strategic context of the organization. We cannot expect people to implement and challenge our strategy if they don't know what this strategy is.

Understanding the realistic context of an organization's strategic direction might seem intuitive to the managers and executives involved in determining its strategy. However, my experience has taught me differently. Far too often organizations embark on their Performance Management initiatives without clarifying their strategy. Ignoring the thorough examination of the context of an enterprise's strategy is a mistake that we tend to make time after time. And if companies do understand the strategic context then it is often a one-sided view where they either look at external opportunities or internal competencies. The main reason for this is that we are too often deeply submerged in the everyday micro-detail of the organization's workings. However, if we want to make Strategic Performance Management a success then we need to come up to the surface, take a deep breath and have a realistic look at where we are.

While some managers and executives may feel that they clearly understand their organization's strategy, my experience is that this understanding is often their interpretation of the strategy and that others have a significantly different interpretation of what the strategy is. Developing a common and shared understanding of the organization's direction is one of the most valuable and rewarding exercises. This shared understanding can then be translated into a visual and narrative

summary of the organizational business model. A so-called 'value creation map' can be created to bring together on one piece of paper the
key components of the organization's strategy, namely the stakeholder
value proposition and the core competencies required to deliver the
value proposition, as well as the key resources (tangible and intangible)
that underlie the core competencies. This is then accompanied by a
brief one-page narrative summary of this business model called the
'value narrative'.

The value creation map and value narrative describe the business
model and therefore a shared understanding of the strategy. This in turn
helps to create a common purpose, a shared identity, and a sense of
community. This understanding of strategy can then be used to guide
the development of meaningful and relevant performance indicators,
which can then be used to challenge and refine the business model
and its assumptions.

A comprehensive understanding of the strategic context therefore
starts with an understanding of the boundary conditions that delimit
the confines in which an organization operates. These boundaries are
usually set by the overall purpose, the visionary goals, and the organizational values. In most cases these are already defined. Chapter 1
describes what they are and their role in the organization. Chapters 2
and 3 then look respectively at the critical external environment as
well as the vital internal competencies and resources. Organizations
tend to have a better insight into the changes in the external environment that pose both the biggest threats to and the best opportunities
for the future of their enterprises. The key here is to translate these
into the right value proposition. However, before an organization is
able to do this it has to assess whether it has the vital internal competencies and resources needed to counter those threats or to capitalize
on those opportunities. Chapter 4 then describes how these insights
can be translated into a business model, visually represented in a
value creation map and described in a value narrative. The structure
of this part of the book will follow the diagram depicted on page 18.

Too many Performance Management approaches assume that the
strategic context and business models are well understood by everyone in the organization. From my experience this is not always the case
and this is often a key contributing factor to the failing of Performance
Management initiatives. The following chapters bring different components of Strategic Management together to form a template for what
needs to be addressed in order to understand the strategic context.
Depending on how well your organization's strategy is defined and
understood you can select the appropriate starting point. For many public sector organizations or many business units the external context is

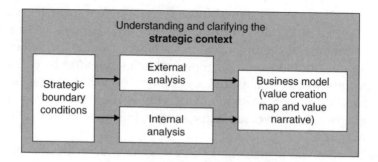

Understanding and clarifying the strategic context

a given and you could skip Chapter 1 and 2. Also, if you believe all the external contextual factors are understood, which is quite common since this has been the traditional approach towards strategy definition, you can go straight to the internal analysis (Chapter 3). If you believe both the external and internal contexts are understood (likely to be quite rare), you can go straight to the mapping of your business model (Chapter 4).

Understanding the strategic boundary conditions – purpose, values and goals

All organizations need to adapt over time – to either changes in their external competitive environments, to regulatory demands, to changing stakeholder wants and needs, or to evolving and changing internal competencies. Nevertheless, some aspects of 'what the enterprise is there to do and how it will go about doing it' remain relatively constant through time. These visionary 'mission statements' are created by organizations in order to provide the overall guiding principles for their strategic thinking and their employees' behaviour. The enterprise's founders often inaugurate them; although they can sometimes – but infrequently – change when the organization takes a fundamental change of direction, such as in a merger situation, where perhaps conflicting visions need to be harmonized. Essentially, what we are seeking here is the 'glue' that holds the whole organization together over quite a long period of time and sets the general boundaries in which an organization operates.

However, this should not be confused with the frequently changing platitudes iterated by successive chief executives, which purport to be visionary mission statements, but say much the same things that other firms in the same line of business expound because it becomes fashionable to emphasize certain characteristics. Usually such statements are, in fact, more like current strategic ambitions. Here we are looking for sound, long-lasting, and differentiated definitions of the very *raison d'être* of the enterprise. The questions I address in this chapter include:

- What are strategic boundary conditions?
- What is the fundamental purpose?
- What are core values?
- What are the visionary goals?
- How do boundary conditions set limits onto the forward strategy?

For a 'proper' visionary mission statement to achieve its ideological communication potential, it should include three essential components. These are:

- The fundamental **purpose** of the enterprise
- Core **values** that the enterprise commits to on the way to achieving its purpose
- Visionary longer-term **goals** that the enterprise will pursue towards achieving its aims.

Fundamental purpose

The fundamental purpose of the enterprise is the reason that it exists. It is normally expressed in brief, enduring and often loosely idealistic terms that nevertheless provide an over-riding focus for its ambitions. However, these ambitions are probably not new to the organization; they should already be existent within the culture of the organization, 'bubbling under the surface'. See Figure 1.1 for illustrative examples of its application within several commercial enterprises.

Core values

Core values should reflect the deeply held values that the organization espouses and should be totally independent of industry norms or topical management fads. Values can set an enterprise apart from the competition by clarifying its identity, limiting its strategic and operational freedom, and constraining the behaviour of its people.[2] The core values that the enterprise commits to on the way to achieving its purpose should be few in number (typically not more than five to seven, so

---

Core purpose is a company's reason for being

3M: To solve unsolved problems innovatively.

Cargill: To improve the standard of living around the world.

Fannie Mae: To strengthen the social fabric by continually democratizing home ownership.

Hewlett-Packard: To make technical contributions for the advancement and welfare of humanity.

Mary Kay Cosmetics: To give unlimited opportunity to women.

McKinsey & Company: To help leading corporations and governments be more successful.

Merck: To preserve and improve human life.

Nike: To experience the emotion of competition, winning, and crushing competitors.

Sony: To experience the joy of advancing and applying technology for the benefit of the public.

Wal-Mart: To give ordinary folk the chance to buy the same things as rich people.

Walt Disney: To make people happy.

Figure 1.1 Core purpose examples[1]

that they are memorable), but they can be expressed in lengthier prose than the purpose statements.

One core value that is receiving increasing attention and is finding its way into many organizational core value statements today is the notion of Corporate Social Responsibility (CSR). The issue of CSR addresses the ways in which organizations interact with the world around them – how their activities and practices impact on environment and society as a whole. The World Business Council for Sustainable Development produced the following definition:

> CSR is the continuing commitment by a business to behave ethically and contribute to economic development while improving the quality of life of the workforce and their families as well as of the local community and society at large.[3]

Many organizations are trying to become socially responsible companies. Shell, for example, has included sustainable development in their Statement of General Business Principles. Shell's aim is to make sustainable development part of the way it works by learning to look at all aspects of its business through a new lens. This lens lets Shell see the world through the eyes of its stakeholders and helps it to understand the many ways, good and bad, that its business activities affect and are affected by society and the environment.[4] Another example is BP, who placed sustainable development at the centre of what its brand stands for today. Its phrase 'beyond petroleum' is intended to encapsulate its sustainable long-term commitment to human progress and environmental leadership.[5]

Johnson & Johnson, the giant US pharmaceuticals and healthcare firm has, and continues to maintain, its core values in what it calls its 'credo'. This has been in place for over sixty years, with only very minor clarifications introduced in the meantime. First created in 1943 by General Robert Wood Johnson, it is a one-page document that sets out the firm's 'industrial philosophy' as to the corporation's responsibility to its various stakeholders. Sometimes seen as controversial, it puts customers first and shareholders last in its list of priorities. The company legitimately claims that its employees have made countless decisions that were inspired by the philosophy embodied in the credo and that these have succeeded in enhancing the company's reputation (not least during the company's well-known Tylenol product recalls in the 1980s). The full text of this philosophy is reproduced in Figure 1.2.

However, there are dangers lurking here too. Adopting blandly nice ideals that fail to differentiate an organization from its competitors is the most pressing one. As Patrick Lencioni, a leading consultant in this area says:

> Consider the motherhood-and-apple-pie values that appear in so many companies' values statements – integrity, teamwork, ethics, quality, customer satisfaction, and innovation. In fact, 55% of all Fortune 100 companies claim integrity is a core value, 49% espouse customer satisfaction, and 40% tout teamwork. While these are inarguably good qualities, such terms hardly provide a distinct blueprint for employee behaviour. Cookie-cutter values don't set a company apart from competitors; they make it fade into the crowd.[6]

Neither does the concept of core values include those corporate 'good behaviour' booklets that contain mounds of cant, such as the 123 rules created by JPMorganChase for its people to follow every day, or the 144 rules of 'leadership imperatives' issued by Cadbury Schweppes for its managers to 'live and breathe' (not to mention the further 82 principles that managers must *not* do). Moses had no such problems, and indeed how many people can remember all Ten Commandments?

Visionary goals

The visionary longer-term goals that the enterprise will pursue towards achieving its aims are clearly not the next year or two's results, but

---

J&J's credo

We believe our first responsibility is to the doctors, nurses and patients,
to mothers and fathers and all others who use our products and services.
In meeting their needs everything we do must be of high quality.
We must constantly strive to reduce our costs
in order to maintain reasonable prices.
Customers' orders must be serviced promptly and accurately.
Our suppliers and distributors have an opportunity
to make a fair profit.

We are responsible to our employees,
the men and women who work with us throughout the world.
Everyone must be considered as an individual.
We must respect their dignity and recognize their merit.
They must have a sense of security in their jobs.
Compensation must be fair and adequate,
and working conditions clean, orderly and safe.
We must be mindful of ways to help our employees fulfil
their family responsibilities.
Employees must feel free to make suggestions and complaints.
There must be equal opportunity for employment, development
and advancement for those qualified.
We must provide competent management,
and their actions must be just and ethical.

We are responsible to the communities in which we live and work
and to the world community as well.
We must be good citizens – support good works and charities
and bear our fair share of taxes.
We must encourage civic improvements and better health and education.
We must maintain in good order
the property we are privileged to use,
protecting the environment and natural resources.

Our final responsibility is to our stockholders.
Business must make a sound profit.
We must experiment with new ideas.
Research must be carried on, innovative programmes developed
and mistakes paid for.
New equipment must be purchased, new facilities provided
and new products launched.
Reserves must be created to provide for adverse times.
When we operate according to these principles,
the stockholders should realize a fair return.

Figure 1.2 J&J's credo

some future milestone that the enterprise will endeavour to achieve within perhaps 10 years' time. And this applies not only to commercial enterprises but to social service and not-for-profit organizations too. Essentially it is a statement of the organization's medium-term ambitions, either quantitative or qualitative goals, which are far beyond current performance levels.[7] For example, these might include 'stretch goals' such as becoming the dominant player in a particular field, reaching a certain size, becoming the best at something (that will still be valid in 10 years' time), beating a particular competitor, or becoming a role model in a different industry, and so on. The common theme is that they are a challenge that will not easily be achieved – along the lines of John F. Kennedy's inspirational exhortation to 'put a man on the moon'. When, eventually, these ambitions are reached, then of course they have to be replaced with a new challenge in order for the organization to renew itself. It is extraordinary how many commercial enterprises and public services omit to do this and so become vulnerable to complacency.

Strategic boundaries

These three factors then are important because they set the *boundary conditions* for the enterprise's contemporary forward strategy (see Figure 1.3). But as Jim Collins and Jerry Porras, authors of *Built to Last: Successful Habits of Visionary Companies*, point out:

> Many executives thrash about with mission statements and vision statements. Unfortunately, most of those statements turn out to be a muddled stew of values, goals, purposes, philosophies, beliefs, aspirations, norms, strategies, practices, and descriptions. They are usually a boring, confusing, structurally unsound stream of words that evoke the response 'True, but who cares?'[8]

What to do if your company is one of those? If these components are not properly in place already, then the enterprise in question has no guiding beacon or principles within which to operate. This means that it has no cohesive view of its over-riding objectives, no long-term policies, no view of how it should interact with its various stakeholders, and no guidance as to how its employees should behave. Where that is the case, then moving forward with Strategic Performance Management decisions is by all means possible but should be approached with greater care. I have worked with various organizations where these guiding principles were in place but not made explicit, or others where these principles were developed and then forgotten or buried somewhere in the organizational databases. It sometimes makes sense to either dig them up or try to make them explicit.

On a lighter note, another option might be to visit the games section of the dilbert.com website, which provides the wonderfully humorous

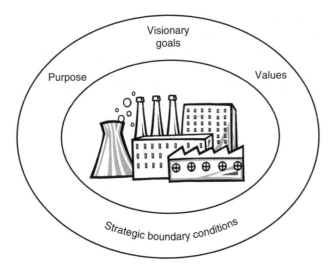

Figure 1.3 Components of vision: strategy's boundary conditions

facility of a random 'mission statement generator'. How about these: *'The customer can count on us to collaboratively utilize world-class intellectual capital and professionally administrate performance-based resources to exceed customer expectations'* or *'We envision to professionally customize emerging data so that we may endeavour to interactively build economically sound resources to stay competitive in tomorrow's world'?* These admirably satirize the sheer vacuousness of the vast majority of mission statements. A tad cynical perhaps, but amusing nonetheless.

The output of this initial stage should be a clarification of the boundary conditions within which the new strategy must be set. It simply sets out the essential basis for the enterprise to move forward without harming the central premises to which it aspires.

References and endnotes

1 Adapted from Collins, J. C. and Porras, J. I. (1996). Building Your Company's Vision. *Harvard Business Review*, Sept–Oct, pp. 126–48.
2 Lencioni, P. M. (2002). Making Your Values Mean Something. *Harvard Business Review*, July, pp. 113–17.
3 Please see the report *Making Good Business Sense* by Lord Holme and Richard Watts, World Business Council for Sustainable Development, www.wbcsd.org
4 See: The Shell Report, www.shell.com

5 See: www.bp.com
6 Lencioni, P. M. (2002). Ibid (see note 2 above).
7 Referred to, in late 1990s-speak, as 'Big, Hairy, Audacious Goals' by Collins & Porras (1996).
8 Collins, J. C. and Porras, J. I. (1996). Building Your Company's Vision. *Harvard Business Review*, Sept–Oct, pp. 126–48.

External strategic analysis – market-based view

The second piece of analysis that needs to be completed in order to understand the strategic context is to take a hard look beyond the boundaries of the enterprise. This involves an external analysis of both the macro-environment in which the enterprise operates and the micro-environment in which it competes with other providers of similar products or services. One would expect most companies to understand this part of their strategic context relatively well. The key outcome from the external analysis is the stakeholder value proposition – basically an answer to the questions of who are your key stakeholders and what do you have to do to deliver to them?[1] To follow my tree (or orchard) analogy and compare your organization with this metaphoric apple tree, the questions I believe you should try to answer include (see Figure 2.1):

- Who are our stakeholders and what do they expect from our tree (orchard)?
- What kind of product and service attributes (apples) do our customers what?
- What competitors do we face?
- What changes and discontinuities are there in the external environment?
- What are the different competitive forces in the market?
- How does the overall macro-environment (economic, social, political, etc.) impact our value proposition?

The tools presented in this chapter are individually well documented in other Strategic Management publications (which are referenced

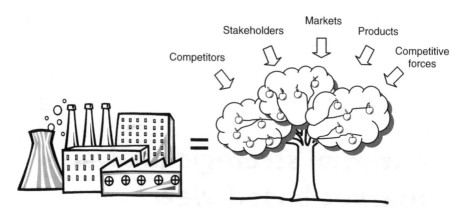

Figure 2.1 Understanding the external context

where appropriate). Individuals with a traditional strategy background will be familiar with these tools and I have therefore tried to keep this section to the bare minimum. However, many firms embarking on a Strategic Performance Management initiative might not be familiar with these tools. Applying them will provide the necessary information to clarify your stakeholder value proposition. Furthermore, the classical market-based tools are seldom brought together with the internal analysis (Chapter 3) to form a *cohesive* analysis of an enterprise's strategic context.

Identifying key stakeholders and their wants and needs

A good starting point is the identification of the key stakeholders of an organization. Here a key stakeholder is defined as a person, a group of people, or an institution that has an investment, share, or interest in your organization and who may significantly influence the success of your organization. Stakeholders can therefore be consumers, intermediaries (dealers, distributors, wholesalers, retailers, etc.) employees, suppliers, regulators, legislators, activists, or communities;[2] however, only those that can significantly influence the success of your organization are *key* stakeholders.

Knowing who these key stakeholders are and what their needs are will allow organizations to shape their value proposition better. Many traditional approaches often assume that shareholders,[3] or maybe customers, are the most important stakeholders. However, in today's interconnected business environment, other stakeholders can be very

Table 2.1 Stakeholder analysis

Stakeholder	Stakeholder's wants and needs	Assessment of influence on success
Consumer		
Regulator		
Community		
Etc . . .		

powerful with clearly identifiable needs that need to be addressed in an organization's strategy.

Instead of shareholders, communities are usually key stakeholders for public sector organizations. Regulators can become key stakeholders since virtually all business sectors today are regulated in some way or another. For example, in the financial services industry or the pharmaceutical industry regulators are very powerful and must be taken into account since they have the power to shut companies down or prevent them from taking products to market. In many countries telecommunications, electricity, water, or gas suppliers are also regulated, with regulators having the power to impose severe penalties or even price regulations on organizations. Pressure groups can become key stakeholders too. Shell experienced the power of Greenpeace when it campaigned for customers in Germany to boycott all Shell gas stations following a dispute about the best way to dispose of an oil platform in the North Sea. For manufacturing firms, some suppliers can become key stakeholders.

Companies can perform a simple analysis (see Table 2.1) that allows them to identify their stakeholders, define their wants and needs, and assess their potential influence on the future success of their organization.

Understanding the strategic macro-environment

A view of the strategic macro-environment in which an organization operates is typically analysed in terms of the following factors: political, economic, social, technological, environmental, and legal.

Political factors that influence an enterprise's strategic thinking include, for example, taxation policies, trade restrictions and tariffs, and investment incentives; the level of political stability may even be a significant issue in some markets. Economic factors – such as the rate of economic growth, interest rates, exchange rates, and inflation

Table 2.2 PESTEL analysis

	Market 1	**Market 2**	**Market 3**
Political conditions			
Economic conditions			
Social conditions			
Technological conditions			
Environmental conditions			
Legal conditions			

rates – influence both the firm's cost of resources and its customers' purchasing power. Social factors include the demographic (e.g. population growth, age distribution, ethnic diversity, etc.) and the cultural aspects of the environments in which the enterprise chooses to operate. Technological considerations would typically include the levels of R&D activity, automation achievement and potential, and the rate of technological change. Environmental regulations, disclosure requirements and employment legislation are also likely to be important macro-environmental considerations. Environmental and legal evaluations are frequently omitted from this type of assessment, but they are important contextual components for operating in different markets. These factors can be assessed and evaluated for different markets (see Table 2.2).

Understanding the strategic micro-environment

The classic approach to analysing the strategic micro-environment – that is, how the enterprise relates to its industry (rather than its geography) – was developed by Michael Porter in the late 1970s and early 1980s.[4] Since then, many organizations have applied his Five Forces framework (see Figure 2.2), which Porter describes as a model for industry analysis, when examining their competitive environment. However, it should be noted that it is not a particularly useful framework for analysis of many public services where the element of competition between rivals is absent.

Michael Porter's important contribution is to identify that competition is not only manifest in the industry's established combatants for market share, but is also present in customers, suppliers, potential new entrants and substitute products. They are all influences that may be more or less prominent or active depending on the industry.

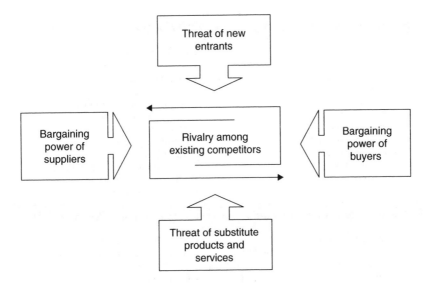

Figure 2.2 Porter's Five Forces framework

He says:

> The corporate strategist's goal is to find a position in the industry where his or her company can best defend itself against these forces or can influence them in its favour. The collective strength of the forces may be painfully apparent to all the antagonists; but to cope with them, the strategist must delve below the surface and analyse the sources of each. For example, what makes the industry vulnerable to entry? What determines the bargaining power of suppliers? Knowledge of these underlying sources of competitive pressure provides the groundwork for a strategic agenda of action. They highlight the critical strengths and weaknesses of the company, animate the positioning of the company in its industry, clarify the areas where strategic changes may yield the greatest payoff, and highlight the places where industry trends promise to hold the greatest significance as either opportunities or threats. Understanding these sources also proves to be of help in considering areas for diversification.[5]

Learning what makes the business environment tick, therefore, is a vital piece of analysis. Many of the key determinants are illustrated in Figure 2.3.

This combination of macro- and micro-environment analysis builds the external context in which strategy can be effectively devised, or, more commonly, revised.

Rivalry determinants	Entry barriers
• Industry growth • Fixed (or storage) costs/value added • Intermittent overcapacity • Product differences • Brand identity • Switching costs • Concentration and balance • Informational complexity • Diversity of competitors • Corporate stakes • Exit barriers	• Economies of scale • Proprietary product differences • Brand identity • Switching costs • Resources requirements • Access to distribution • Absolute cost advantages • Proprietary learning curve • Access to necessary inputs • Proprietary low-cost product design • Government policy • Expected retaliation
Determinants of supplier power	**Determinants of buyer power**
• Differentiation of inputs • Switching costs of suppliers and firms in the industry • Presence of substitute inputs • Supplier concentration • Importance of volume to supplier • Cost relative to total purchases in the industry • Impact of inputs on cost or differentiation • Threat of forward integration relative to threat of backward integration by firms in the industry	• Bargaining leverage • Buyer concentration versus firm concentration • Buyer volume • Buyer switching costs relative to firm switching costs • Buyer information • Ability to backward integrate • Substitute products • Pull-through • Price sensitivity • Price/total purchases • Product differences • Brand identity • Impact of quality/performance • Buyer profits • Decision-makers' incentives
Determinants of substitution threat	
• Relative price performance of substitutes • Switching costs • Buyer propensity to substitute	

Figure 2.3 Porter's elements of industry structure[6]

A look into the future

Another component that helps us to better understand the external environment is scenario analysis.[7] Scenario planning has been a recognized component of strategy formulation for a quarter of a century, since it became well-known that companies like Shell had successfully applied it as part of their portfolio of strategic planning tools in the 1970s. Shell is generally credited as the first company to use scenario analysis extensively for this purpose. However, Shell did not invent this approach; in fact, similar methods have been used for more like half a century. Herman Kahn developed the basic technique, which he initially called 'future-now' thinking, for the RAND Corporation in the 1950s.

At first, Shell applied scenarios to making better decisions about capital investment projects, which were more robust under a variety of alternative futures, before adapting them to strategic planning more generally. Shell of course is no stranger to the vagaries and impacts of volatile oil prices either then or today. Several practitioners from the company – including Pierre Wack, Kees van der Heijden and Arie de Geus – have described the art of applying scenario planning within organizations and what benefits can be accrued. Shell's former managing director André Bénard commented in 1980 that: *'Experience has taught us that the scenario technique is much more conducive to forcing people to think about the future than the forecasting techniques we formerly used.'*

The basis of scenario planning involves defining and visualizing alternative views of how today's *status quo* in the operating environment might evolve in the future. It distils the countless possibilities of the future state into a limited set of coherent views. And of course, what might happen in the future has a corollary: what to do about it?

Typically, scenario analysis asks 'what if' questions about the future direction of the 'ecosystem' in which the enterprise operates. So both the macro- and micro-climate analysis, described above, will normally be helpful towards informing this future-orientated analysis path. The power of scenario analysis, however, is in identifying the potential impacts of multiple events occurring simultaneously due to their interconnectivity. Each scenario needs a general theme that the organization's senior executives perceive as a potential threat – or opportunity – which needs to be addressed in the organization's longer-term strategic planning.

For example, Shell announced in June 2005 that the primary focus of its scenario planning to 2025 would switch from its previous (2001) assumptions about technological advances – that might see a shift in fuel consumption from oil to gas, nuclear and renewable energy – to one of national security and trust in the marketplace. Jeroen van der Veer, Chief executive, said:

Western societies now look to the state more than in recent decades to lead the restoration of physical security and market integrity. This brings into sharper focus the power of the state to regulate and coerce, in a role involving both the direct intervention to fight terrorism and police the market, and a more general emphasis on transparency, disclosure and good governance.

Seven criteria for good scenarios

1. *Decision-making power.* Each scenario in the set, and the set as a whole, must provide insights useful for the question being considered. Most generic or general scenario sets lack this power and needed to be complemented for decision-making purposes.

2. *Plausibility.* The developed scenarios must fall within the limits of what future events are realistically possible.

3. *Alternatives.* Each scenario should be at least to some extent probable, although it is not necessary to define the probabilities explicitly. The ideal is that the scenarios are all more or less equally probable, so that the widest possible range of uncertainty is covered by the scenario set. If for instance only one of three or four scenarios is probable, you only have one scenario in reality.

4. *Consistency.* Each scenario must be internally consistent. Without internal consistency the scenarios will not be credible. The logic of the scenario is critical.

5. *Differentiation.* The scenarios should be structurally or qualitatively different. Thus it is not enough for them to be different in terms of magnitude, and therefore only variations of a base scenario.

6. *Memorability.* The scenarios should be easy to remember and to differentiate, even after a presentation. Therefore it is advisable to reduce the number to between three and five, although in theory we could remember and differentiate up to seven or eight scenarios. Vivid scenario names help.

7. *Challenge.* The final criterion is that scenarios really challenge the organization's received wisdom about the future.

Figure 2.4   Seven criteria for good scenarios[8]

Like so many other fundamentally sound management techniques, this one is no different in that it can quite easily be abused. In the wrong hands, it can be used as a reason to procrastinate through over-analysis or, alternatively, the development of over-simplified scenarios can lead to underachievement in terms of its usefulness. Figure 2.4 illustrates many of the best practice factors that should be taken into consideration for its proper application.

There are other limitations to scenario planning and these usually derive from a paucity of human imagination about what the future might hold. Keeping an open mind about future development and thinking 'out of the box' is critical for good scenarios. What happens when we apply our current models and project these in the future is shown throughout history, where some of the biggest names in business have got the imagination of future scenarios totally and utterly wrong.[9]

In 1901, Daimler proclaimed, 'Worldwide demand for cars will never exceed one million, primarily because of a limitation in the number of available chauffeurs'. In 1915, Thomas Edison thought that fuelled motors would soon be replaced by nickel-iron batteries. In 1945, Thomas Watson, then IBM's chief executive, declared, 'I think there is a world market for five computers'. In 1968, the respected *Business Week* magazine reported, 'The Japanese car industry isn't likely to carve a big slice out of the US market'. A decade later, the chief executive of DEC was quoted as saying, 'There is no reason for any individual to have a computer at home'. And, as recently as 1995, Microsoft's Bill Gates famously commented, 'Internet is just a hype'. These misjudgements show that it is impossible to accurately predict the future. However, what we can use scenarios for is to identify possible and internally consistent developments in the external environment.

Clarifying the stakeholder value proposition

A stakeholder value proposition is a declaration of the way an organization proposes to use its resources and competencies to deliver a particular combination of values to its key stakeholders. A value proposition brings together elements such as customer needs and organizational capabilities. This means that a definitive value proposition cannot be created until the internal analysis (see Chapter 3) is completed.

The traditional three value propositions, seen as a promise an organization makes to its customers, are operational excellence, product leadership, and customer intimacy.[10] Operational excellence means that organizations market standard products to their customers, at the best price with least inconvenience. These organizations tend to offer the best price for their products within their competitors' radar. Product leadership means providing the very best products (new designs and/or new technology) to customers at the right time. Product leaders offer innovative products of exceptionally high quality, where price is not a significant barrier for their customers. Customer intimacy means proposing the best total solution to customers. These organizations focus on delivering the best expert advice and tailored service to their customers.[11]

Dr Veronica Martinez and her colleagues from Cranfield School of Management have extended these three traditional value propositions to build a value matrix.[12] The result of this combination is a matrix with six value propositions: innovators, brand managers, price minimizers, simplifiers, technological integrators and socializors (see Table 2.3).

Table 2.3 Value propositions[13]

Value proposition	Customers get	Company needs to do: Strategic objectives	Operational objectives
Innovators	New innovative designs, products never seen before.	Provide breakthrough through generations of continuous new designs, new features within technological basis.	Long-term vision, robust R&D and product development, capacity to innovate within short product life-cycles.
Brand managers	Status from the product; they get lifestyle, a feeling of superiority.	Expand the market reinforcing the solid brand image of the product and the company.	Superb brand recognition. Focus on market sector. Superior control over the product styles, quality and promotion.
Price minimizers	Ordinary, reliable products and services at lowest price possible. They get security on the product.	Production growth reaching high quality levels in the most cost-effective way and waste free.	Strong order fulfilment sustained by efficient and effective production processes within tight quality process controls.
Simplifiers	Convenience and availability of the products. Hazard-free experience.	Building streamlined processes to make life simple and uncomplicated for customers in a novel and profitable way.	Strong availability. Superb order fulfilment–distribution by conventional and unconventional resources (networking, IT, etc.).
Technological integrators	Tailored products and services. They buy total solutions.	Tailor specific and continuous solutions for carefully selected customers on the basis of permanent relationships.	Strong relationship with customer. Knowledge of customers' businesses, products and operations. Capacity to configure any specific need. Able to adopt the customer's strategy.
Socializors	Flexible services and inter-personal relationship because they trust in the company.	Build confidence and trust in the customers.	Sensitive fulfilment of customers' needs supported by careful delivery, reliability, and honesty. Excellent personal service.

Understanding the external environment

Using the tools and classifications outlined in this chapter allows organizations to clarify the external environment and develop a better idea about their stakeholder value proposition. They can do this by asking themselves who is it they are creating value for and what does value in the context of the environment and the boundary conditions look like. The next question is whether the organization is in a position to deliver this value proposition. To answer this question we move to the internal analysis in the next chapter.

References and endnotes

1 For a good overview of different stakeholder needs and how to measure them see Neely, A., Adams, C. and Kennerley, M. (2002). *The Performance Prism: The Scorecard for Measuring and Managing Business Success*. FT Prentice Hall: London.

2 Ibid.

3 Rappaport, A. (1998). *Creating Shareholder Value: The New Standard for Business Performance*. Simon & Schuster: New York.

4 See for example: Porter, M. E. (1980). *Competitive Strategy*. Free Press: New York; or Porter, M. E. (1985). *Competitive Advantage: Creating and Sustaining Superior Performance*. Free Press: New York.

5 Porter, M. E. (1979). How Competitive Forces Shape Strategy. *Harvard Business Review*, March/April, p. 137.

6 Source: Porter, M. E. (1985). *Competitive Advantage: Creating and Sustaining Superior Performance*. The Free Press, p. 6.

7 For an overview of how scenario planning can inform Strategic Performance Management please see Fink, A., Marr, B., Siebe, A., Kuhle, J.-P. (2005). The Future Scorecard: Combining internal and external scenarios to create strategic foresight. *Management Decision*, Vol. 43, No. 2. pp. 360–81.

8 Source: Lindgren, M. and Bandhold, H. (2003). *Scenario Planning*. Palgrave Macmillan, p. 31.

9 I borrowed these examples from my colleagues and friends Alexander Fink and Andreas Siebe, who have written a great book on scenario management (unfortunately only available in German): Fink, A., Schlake, O. and Siebe, A. (2001). *Erfolg Durch Szenario-Management*. Campus: Frankfurt.

10 Treacy, M. and Wiersema, F. (1996). *The disciplines of the market leaders*. Harper Collins: London.

11 I would like to thank Veronica Martinez for providing input for this section. For more information see also Martinez, V. (forthcoming). A Model for Managing the Creation and Operation of Organizational Value: The Value Matrix. *British Journal of Management.*
12 Ibid.
13 Ibid.

3

Internal strategic analysis – resource-based view

The third component of the contextual analysis requires looking inside the organization in order to make a critical appraisal of its competencies and key resources. Compared to the external analysis, this internal part of the strategic analysis is relatively new and many firms are struggling with the identification of their competencies and resources. In particular, organizations seem to have difficulties with the definition and identification of their intangible components. There is immense confusion among managers about the definition and classification of intangibles, as well as the difference between competencies, capabilities, and resources. I therefore aim to provide a detailed discussion and breakdown of organizational resources, and how they form the foundation for capabilities and competencies, before moving on to look at the tools to understand and map these. Staying with the tree analogy, this chapter therefore deals with the roots (the resources) and the trunk (the competencies). The questions we are trying to address include (see Figure 3.1):

- What kind of apples (products or services) is the tree or orchard (our organization) capable of producing?
- What are we good at? What are our competencies and capabilities?
- What does our root system (our resource architecture) look like?
- How do our roots (resources) combine to give us our capabilities?
- Which are the major roots (our key resources)?

Organizational resources

We start with the foundation and look at the roots of the tree – which represent the organizational resource architecture. Resources are critical

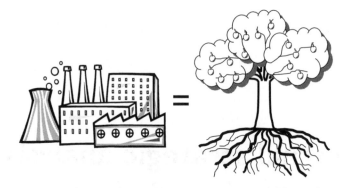

Figure 3.1   Understanding the internal context

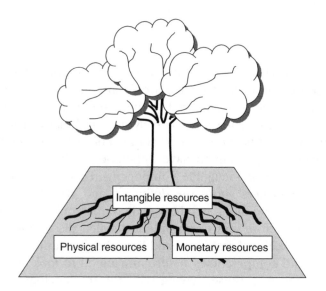

Figure 3.2   Organizational resources

building blocks of strategy because they determine not what an organization wants to do, but what it can do.[1] Even though economists started to make a strong case for the significance of intangible resources as an important production factor in the early part of the nineteenth century,[2] organizations have traditionally looked at only their financial and physical resources and, by doing so, often overlooked their intangible resources as a source of competitive advantage. Today, most executives do see the critical importance of intangible resources as the drivers of performance. Based on this, we can classify organizational resources into three principal categories (see Figure 3.2). These are: monetary resources, physical resources, and intangible resources.

Monetary resources are simply the amount of cash available – from various sources such as cash flows, borrowings, asset sales, equity stakes, etc. – to invest in the maintenance and development of either physical or intangible resources. Physical resources consist of such items as factories, information and communication technology infrastructure, R&D facilities, plant and equipment, premises or land, and, in some cases, owned natural resources. Intangible resources are non-physical sources of value such as knowledge and skills of employees, brand image, reputation, relationships with suppliers, organizational culture, best practices, or patents.

From a resource-based perspective, it is argued that resources are only valuable if they provide a unique competitive advantage for the organization and if they support the organization's core competencies.[3] In order for them to be strategically valuable, resources must therefore be inimitable, not substitutable, tacit in nature, or synergistic.[4] It is often argued that in today's economy most physical resources are transient and are therefore rarely sources of competitive advantage. With this in mind, one might argue that they could therefore be ignored. However, many intangible resources are only valuable in relationship with existing physical resources, or vice versa. Physical resources are often levers that enable companies to benefit from their intangible resources.

Wal-Mart's expertise in inventory replenishment, for example, is a key intangible element, but without physical resources such as the innovative physical distribution centres and store layouts it would be less, or not at all, valuable.[5] The fact that physical resources rarely create a competitive advantage on their own does not mean that they cannot be key drivers of competitive advantage and performance. One might think about DeBeers and its possession of diamond mines, or oil companies such as Exxon or BP and their oil reserves. We will come back to the interrelated nature of organizational resources, but before we do this we need to better define intangible resources and their important role in creating value.

The importance of intangible resources

A recent survey commissioned by the consulting firm Accenture revealed that most executives around the world believe that intangibles are critical for the future success of their businesses.[6] However, at the same time, most agreed that their approaches to managing intangibles were poor or non-existent. Indeed, it is estimated that the level of US corporate investment in intangible assets, around $1 trillion annually, almost matches investment in tangible assets.[7]

But not only commercial enterprises are seeing the value in intangible resources; other organizations and governments are recognizing the importance of them also. In the United Kingdom, for example, Prime Minister Tony Blair wrote in a recent Government White Paper that intangible resources such as creativity and inventiveness are the greatest source of economic success but that too many firms have failed to put enough emphasis on R&D and developing skills.[8] Patricia Hewitt, the UK's Secretary of State for Trade and Industry, added in a recent report that increasingly it is the intangible factors that underpin innovation and the best-performing businesses.[9] A report of the Brookings Task Force on Intangibles outlines that the large and growing discrepancy between the importance of intangible assets to economic growth and the ability to clearly identify, measure, and account for those assets is a serious problem for business managers, investors, and governments.[10] In order to identify intangibles we need to first define what we mean by them.

What are intangible resources?

The concept of intangible assets is frequently used, but not always well defined. Often different terms are used to describe the same concept, which means that intangible resources are also referred to using terminology such as 'intangible assets', 'intellectual capital', or 'knowledge assets'.[11] Since this book is about Strategic Performance Management, we use the terminology 'intangible resource', which is most closely associated with Strategic Management thinking.[12]

Many different classifications and definitions exist for intangible resources. It is important to stress that there is no right or wrong classification. Instead, what is important is that a classification is comprehensive, and doesn't leave out important forms of intangible resources. The classification provided below ensures that all critical intangible resources are included. The key objective of this classification is to facilitate the identification of the intangible resources within organizations. Debates whether one intangible should be put into one category or another are therefore not productive or particularly useful. What is important is that we identify all intangible resources that matter.

Here, intangible resources are defined as non-tangible resources that are attributed to an organization and which support an organization's competencies and therefore contribute to the delivery of the organizational value proposition to its various stakeholders. Intangible resources can be split into three component classes: these are human resources, structural resources, and relational resources (see Figure 3.3).

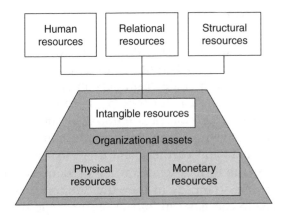

Figure 3.3 Classification of intangible resources

Human resources

The principal sub-components of an organization's human resources are naturally its workforce's skill-sets, depth of expertise and breadth of experience. Human resources can be thought of as the living and thinking part of the intangible resources.[13] These resources therefore walk out at night when people leave; whereas relational and structural resources usually remain with the organization even after people have left. Human resources include the skills and knowledge of employees, as well as know-how in certain fields that are important to the success of the enterprise, plus the aptitudes and attitudes of its staff.[14] Employee loyalty, motivation and flexibility will often be a significant factor too since a firm's 'expertise and experience pool' is developed over periods of time; for example, high levels of staff turnover mean that a firm is haemorrhaging these important resources. The importance of knowledgeable and experienced staff has been demonstrated by many studies. Heskett, Sasser, and Schlesinger from Harvard Business School report that the cumulative costs of replacing an experienced automobile salesperson with a novice are estimated to exceed $300 000 in lost productivity. They also find that:

> when Oracle loses a software engineer, the cost is several times that of hiring and training a replacement. This cost also includes the value of ideas and methods lost, as well as damage to the process by which knowledge is transferred in the organization. When Merrill Lynch loses a productive broker to a rival, the cost of the loss of clients more loyal to their broker than to the firm literally can be millions.[15]

Relational resources

Relational resources are the relationships that exist between an organization and any outside party, both with key individuals and other organizations. These can include customers, intermediaries, employees, suppliers, alliance partners, regulators, pressure groups, communities, creditors or investors. Relationships tend to fall into two categories – those that are formalized through, for example, contractual obligations with major customers and partners, and those that are more informal. While in the past, the former tended to be predominant, today the latter have a more important say in how the enterprise is managed. The type of relationship can have an impact on the value of these relationships; for example, they can determine the effectiveness of the information that is transferred between related parties.

In today's integrated economy and just-in-time supply chains, relationships with trading partners and suppliers can be crucial. The following example comes from the cell phone industry.[16] A fire in a Philips semiconductor plant in Albuquerque, New Mexico destroyed parts of the production facilities to produce a crucial cell phone chip which Philips supplied to both Nokia in Finland and Ericsson in Sweden, two major competitors in this area. Both companies were alerted to the fire at the same time, being told that production might be interrupted for a few days but should be resumed shortly. In the past, Nokia identified all strategically important suppliers and ensured that close relationships were established. This meant that Nokia's supply chain manager had a good relationship with the Philips plant in Albuquerque. They had daily communications and it soon became apparent that the production facility would not be up and running in a few days. Nokia therefore was able to launch its contingency strategy; it globally sourced and contracted alternative suppliers of this chip. Ericsson only found out about the real extent of the fire much later, with the consequence that Ericsson was unable to source sufficient chips to meet their demands, which probably contributed to the fact that Ericsson decided to discontinue the production of cell phones altogether.

Other factors that fall into this category are brand image, corporate reputation, and product/service reputation. Increasingly, this latter subcategory can be particularly important to the success or failure of organizations, and executives ignore this aspect at their peril. Research carried out by Richard Hall in 1992,[17] in a survey of 95 firms, identified reputation, both of the company and the products, as a critical contributor to overall success. A series of corporate scandals, the knock-on effects of which caused the rapid meltdown of several formerly respected companies (not least those of Enron, once the United States' seventh

largest company by market capitalization, and Arthur Andersen, one of
the 'big five' accountancy firms worldwide) have since put an even
higher emphasis on the relative importance of corporate reputation as
a critical strategic aspect of intangible resources and a vital resource for
development. Reputation is not only an important intangible resource
for companies but also for public sector organizations and governments.
In fact, a recent study found that perceived organizational reputation
is a key success factor in local authorities.[18]

Structural resources

A firm's structural resources cover a broad range of vital factors.
Foremost among these factors are usually the organization's essential
operating processes, the way it is structured, its policies, its information flows and the content of its databases, its leadership and management style, its culture and its incentive schemes, but they also include
the intangible resources that are legally protected. These resources can
be sub-categorized into culture, practices and routines, and intellectual
property.

Organizational culture can reinforce the achievement of the overall
goals, sometimes also referred to as social capital and context.[19]
Corporate culture gives each person in an organization a common
and distinctive method for transmitting and processing information; it
defines a common way of seeing things, sets the decision-making pattern, and establishes the value system.[20] Culture resources embrace
categories such as corporate culture, organizational values, and management philosophies. They provide employees with a shared framework to interpret events, a framework that encourages individuals to
operate both as an autonomous entity and as a team in order to achieve
the company's objectives.[21]

Practices and routines can be important organizational resources.
Shared knowledge in organizations is expressed in routines and practices.[22] Practices and routines include internal practices, virtual networks
and review processes; these can be formalized or informal procedures
and tacit rules. Formalized routines include process manuals providing
codified procedures and rules; informal routines could be codes of
behaviour or understood (but unstated) workflows. Practices and routines determine how processes are being handled and how work flows
through the organization. An example of a process that has become a
valuable strategic resource is the 25-minute airplane turnaround time
at Southwest Airlines. A process introduced as a necessity to start up the
business as a low-cost carrier, today has become a key differentiator. Any

additional minute at the gate would cost Southwest Airlines more than \$186 million in investments and about \$18 million in financing costs.[23]

Intellectual property – owned or legally protected intangible resources – is becoming increasingly important. Patents and trade secrets have become a key element of competition in high-tech organizations.[24] Here intellectual property is defined as the sum of resources such as patents, copyrights, trademarks, brands, registered design, trade secrets, database content and processes whose ownership is granted to the company by law.[25] Intellectual property is an element of organizational knowledge that is owned by the organization and can't walk out at night when everyone goes home. It represents the tools and enablers that help to define and differentiate an organization's unique offering to the markets in which it operates. Intellectual property includes trademark symbols such as the McDonald's Arches and the Nike Swoosh, or the patented '1-click' buying option at Amazon.com. Coca-Cola, for example, made a conscious decision to keep the formula for Coke a trade secret that is actively protected. Had they patented the formula instead, their patent protection would have run out many years ago, most likely destroying their market share.

Even though most organizations possess a wide stock of intangible resources not all of those are critical value drivers. The reasons for this are that the value of resources is context specific and that resources are not just static – they dynamically interact with each other to be transformed into capabilities and core competencies. For example, the know-how of creating light and durable composite materials so essential for successful Formula One motor racing teams is probably of little value to a telecommunications firm. On the other hand, the brand awareness and reputation of Amazon.com would fade rapidly without the efficient distribution network, the well-designed internal processes, and the strong supplier relationships it has developed. This is often referred to as the interconnectedness of resource stocks.

Capabilities and core competencies

No discussion about strategy and organizational resources would be complete without a view of how the individual resources interrelate with each other to create vital capabilities and core competencies. Similar to the definition of intangible resources, little consensus exists about what exactly constitutes a capability or a core competence. While people often use the words 'capabilities' and 'core competencies' interchangeably, I believe that some clear distinctions need to be made, which I outline below.

Capability refers to the quality of being capable – physically or intellectually. Capabilities are localized bundles of brilliance – sometimes called 'centres of excellence' – that shine within their organizations through a combination of the resources. They are activities that an organization is able to perform better than other activities. Capabilities can be defined as the combination of a set of organizational resources (physical, monetary, human, relational, and structural) that collectively enable that organization to perform well in specific areas. A number of combinations of different organizational resources can therefore yield many different capabilities that the organization is good at, but which may or may not be strategically vital.

A core competence, on the other hand, is an excellently-performed internal activity that is central, not peripheral, to a company's strategy, competitiveness, and profitability. The difference between capabilities and core competence is that an organization might have many potential capabilities resulting from the combination of their resources, whereas it will only have a very few core competencies. Core competence is therefore a capability, or a set of capabilities, that is linked to the strategic value proposition of an organization (see Figure 3.4).

The term 'core competencies' first became prevalent following an award winning article published in the *Harvard Business Review* by Gary Hamel and C. K. Prahalad.[26] Core competencies (sometimes referred to as 'strategic core competences') are therefore a distinctive combination of organizational resources, such as applied technologies, skill-sets, and/or business processes, which have evolved and been learned over a period of time in response to satisfying customer (and other key stakeholder) needs.[27] They uniquely define an organization

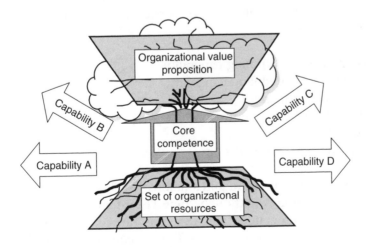

Figure 3.4 Capabilities and core competence

and provide a thread running through it, weaving their resources together into a coherent whole.[28] It is also the evolutionary learning process that gestates within the organization that makes it unique and, therefore, extremely difficult for competitors to replicate.

Often-quoted examples of core competencies are Sony's expertise in miniaturization to create 'pocketable' consumer products and Honda's ability to get the best out of internal combustion engines.[29] Honda's superior expertise in compact engine construction enabled it to build on this competence and become a major competitor to many established manufacturers of, for example, motorboat engines, lawn mowers and portable generators through its retail relationships, while continuing to sell automobiles and motorcycles through its own dealerships. Another company's management that has built its success on its understanding of the firm's core competencies is Wal-Mart, which transformed the company by building on its knowledge of 'cross-docking'. This supply chain management best practice – whereby incoming goods are immediately trans-shipped to delivery vehicles without expensive warehousing – was one of the factors that enabled Wal-Mart to outperform its rival K-Mart.[30]

Recognizing what capabilities an organization possesses and what core competencies are required to deliver the organizational value proposition is fundamental to strategy development. What can pose a challenge is harmonizing different capabilities that are required to deliver desired outcomes or core competencies, for example, excellent customer service. Consider a common business process, such as the order-to-cash fulfilment process in an electronics business for instance. The customer places an order, the company makes and delivers it, and then gets paid for it. To the customer it is a single process with multiple components, but it implies the presence of at least six different capabilities. These are:

- Customer order handling capability
- Planning and scheduling capability
- Procurement capability
- Manufacturing capability
- Distribution capability
- Credit management capability.

Each of these capabilities requires different skill-sets, different practices, different technologies (although some IT systems will likely be multi-functional and integrated) and different physical resources, such as offices, a factory, and warehouses. If each component capability does not dovetail effectively and cohesively with its peers within the same business process, then the customers will not be satisfied. The same applies to other similar processes, such as demand generation, product/service development, after-sales service, and so on. However, effectively joined-up capabilities can be an incredibly powerful means of creating a distinctive competitive advantage. So, capabilities work closely together not only to deliver immediate process outputs for the enterprise's stakeholders but also, consequently, they have longer-term outcomes that can dictate an enterprise's strategic options.

Hamel and Prahalad recommend three tests to help identify core competencies. These are that they must:

- Provide potential access to a wide range of markets
- Make a significant contribution to the perceived customer benefits of the end product (or service)
- Be difficult for competitors to imitate.

It is important to recognize too that core competencies often do not reside in a single strategic business unit and, therefore, head offices need to take ownership for them to ensure that they are properly nurtured so that they do not inadvertently wither, or even get outsourced. The notion of strategic core competencies requires that, over time, some existing core competencies will need to be abandoned, others strengthened, and some new ones created. This is done by reconfiguring the underlying resource architecture that shapes the core competencies – this could mean, for example, retraining people, updating the IT infrastructure, redesigning processes, establishing a new reputation, or building new strategic alliances.

The dynamic nature of resources

The above outline of organizational resources addresses the stock of resources and helps organizations to identify what key resource they have. This discussion highlighted that resources need to be bundled together to form either capabilities or competencies. Therefore, in order to be valuable, organizational resources have to be transformed, through core competencies, into products or services that deliver value. Resources are often referred to as performance drivers, which reinforces the notion of causal relationships between the resources and organizational value creation. Intangible resources such as employee skills and customer relationships often deliver customer satisfaction and loyalty, which in turn deliver shareholder value.[31]

Individual resources often impact performance with 'causal ambiguity'.[32] This means it is difficult to identify how individual resources, let's say a brand name, contribute to success without taking into account the interdependencies with other resources. For example, the value of a brand might rely on the quality of the production process, the order fulfilment, the product reputation, and/or the after-sales service. The latest technology could be an important resource in organizations, but it is worth little without the right knowledge and competencies of how to operate it. In turn, all the latest understanding and knowledge of how to operate technology is worthless if employees do not have access to the technology.

Baruch Lev, Professor at New York's Stern School of Business, notes that intangibles are frequently embedded in physical resources (e.g. the technology and knowledge contained in an airplane) and in labour (e.g. the tacit knowledge of employees). This leads to considerable interactions between tangible and intangible resources in the creation of value. He also emphasized that 'when such interactions are intense, the valuation of intangibles on a standalone basis becomes impossible'.[33] This is why a balance sheet approach to organizational resources does not provide information on the important interrelationships between them.[34] To gain strategic insights into the importance of organizational resources it is important to understand their interdependencies with other resources to form core competencies and thus products and services that deliver value.

In summary, organizational resources, both tangible and intangible, interact with and depend on each other to form the basis for capabilities and core competencies. Organizations, therefore, require tools to help them understand their resource architecture, capabilities, and core competencies.

Identifying strengths and weaknesses

One tool that has traditionally been used to understand the strengths and weaknesses of an organization is the SWOT analysis – simply an acronym for Strengths, Weaknesses, Opportunities and Threats.[35] Opportunities and threats are external factors and should be derived from the external analysis (Chapter 2). Here, the focus is on the strengths and weaknesses, since they can provide input for a contextual understanding of the internal environment. This analysis can play an important role in bringing together a first overview and consensus opinion of what really matters and what the organization is good at or not so good at. It can help to bridge the factions (e.g. technical *v.* marketing *v.* finance)

Positive	Negative
Strengths	**Weaknesses**
• Technological skills • Leading brands • Distribution channels • Customer relationships/loyalty • Production quality • Scale • Good management.	• Absence of important skills • Weak brands • Poor access to distribution • Low customer retention • Unreliable products/services • Sub-scale • Poor management.
Opportunities	**Threats**
• Changing customer tastes • Liberalization of geographic markets • Technological advances • Changes in government policies • Lower taxes • Change in demographics • New distribution channels.	• Changing customer tastes • Closing of geographic markets • Technological advances • Changes in government policies • Taxation increases • Change in demographics • New distribution channels.

Internal factors — (Strengths / Weaknesses)

External factors — (Opportunities / Threats)

Figure 3.5   Identifying strengths and weaknesses

which can exist within most large organizations. Figure 3.5 illustrates several of the typical components that might be brought together to summarize the internal and external views of the organization for strategic decision-making purposes. The content is intended to be illustrative rather than authoritative and other considerations may come into play.

Identifying the stock of key resources

The above categorization of resources that I have outlined can be used to facilitate a discussion about the current resource architecture. This can be conducted in individual interviews with key people in the organization; it can also be done in facilitated workshops, or even via a mail or online survey. From experience, doing individual interviews or surveys works best, as it means that everyone has their say, without their opinion being suppressed by stronger or more dominant participants in workshops. The resource categorization can be used to create a template that guides people through the different resources and prompts them to think about the different types of resources in their organization (see Table 3.1).

Table 3.1   Identifying resource stock

Resource category	Sub-categories	Resources with a significant presence in our organization
Physical resources	Property, plant, location of buildings, information and communication infrastructure, machines, equipment, natural resources, physical infrastructure, office design, etc.	
Human resources	Education, technical knowledge and expertise, skills, know-how, attitudes, experience, motivation, flexibility, commitment, creativity, etc.	
Relational resources	Customer relationships, supplier relationships, reputation, image, trust, contractual relationships, informal relationships, alliances, relationships with regulators, partners, etc.	
Structural resources	Processes, tacit routines, organizational structure, governance and management approaches, organizational culture, social capital, shared identity, patents, brand names, copyrights, trade secrets, codified information and knowledge, e.g. in databases or process manuals, etc.	
Monetary resources	Cash, investments, bonds, loans, budget, etc.	

It is important to emphasize again that the objective of this resource classification template is to address as many different resources as possible and facilitate a discussion. For this, it doesn't matter therefore if we classify a resource as relational, structural, or human. The aim here is to stimulate awareness of possible resources in order to identify the resource stock of an organization, rather than to put them into rigid categories.[36] For the purpose of identifying resources, it therefore isn't important if, for example, we put 'the ability to build customer relationships' into the human resources or the relational resources category. What matters is that we create a realistic picture of the existing resource architecture.

The individual responses can then be brought together and a list of all the resources can be presented in a facilitated workshop. Participants in this workshop are usually the senior managers; however, sometimes it is also advisable to include people from different hierarchical levels or even external stakeholders. This might depend on the complexity of the business. The more complex the business the better it is to involve as many people as possible. The outcome from this workshop is a list of key resources. At this point it is not important any more to use the categories, but rather the individual resources, presented in a language that is understood within the particular organization. Different organizations tend to have different names, or firm-specific terminology, to describe the same resources. It is always advisable to use the language that is used within the organization instead of the categories or examples provided in the template above. Using terminology such as 'human capital', for example, can cause misunderstanding or even cynicism, especially if this is not terminology that is usually used within the organization.

Identifying the relative importance of key resources

The relative strengths or importance of the identified key resources can only be assessed in the context of the existing organization. The questions to answer are: how important are our different existing resources to achieving our overall value proposition? Or, how strong are our existing resources and how can we utilize them more effectively? Here is where the market-based and the resource-based views come together from opposite sides. The former starts with the strategic value proposition identified by the external analysis (Chapter 2) and then identifies the relative importance of each resource to achieve the strategic objectives. The latter looks at the existing resource architecture and evaluates the strength of each resource in the organization independently of any value proposition or existing opportunities in the market.

The most realistic situation is that firms have an existing value proposition, and in the case of public sector organizations and many business units they even have a more or less prescribed list of products and services they have to offer. If you are in a situation where your value proposition is prescribed, or where you feel your existing strategy is good or can't be changed, you can start with the assessment of your resources with your current value proposition in mind. If you start with a blank piece of paper, which I have to admit I have never seen, you could then evaluate the strength of your resources without any context. In all other cases, you might want to do both.

Assessing the importance of the different resources to deliver your value proposition and to assess your resource strengths independently allows organizations to perform a gap analysis. This lets you understand

Table 3.2   Importance of resources

Identified key resources	Relative strengths of these resources in our organization 0 = not at all important 10 = vitally important	Relative importance of these resources to delivering our value proposition 0 = not at all important 10 = vitally important
Our marketing skills	7	7
Our website	8	8
Our supplier relationships	6	6
Etc.		

whether you are building the appropriate resource architecture for your value proposition, or whether you are under- or over-investing in certain areas (for a more in-depth discussion on this see risk assessment in Chapter 7).

This assessment is best done individually, either in interviews or by survey, or it can be completed as part of a workshop. The easiest way to do this is to produce a list with the resources identified above, and then to add columns for people to assess the importance (see Table 3.2). Here, both assessments are included which allows a gap analysis.

The results from the individual assessments can then be aggregated and visualized in a resource map. Such a map is the visual representation of the relative strength or importance of the different resources. It is also possible to include the two data sets (strengths and importance) and visualize the different size bubbles to indicate any gaps.

Figure 3.6 shows such a map that was created for a leading online retailing business.[37] Its aim was to understand the relative importance of its resources to deliver its existing value proposition. The value proposition for this well-known retailer was to become the world's preferred source for a particular type of goods by providing consumers not only with top level service, but also high quality of value-added information, excellent price, simple transactions, and an enjoyable shopping experience. In this example, structural resources and human resources were the most important value drivers for this firm, with particular emphasis on its know-how of the market and its customers, plus its processes and website. Other important resources were relational, especially with suppliers of the goods and with the lenders of the money, as the business is still in the growing phase and not making any profits. This map helped the firm to make sure that it is allocating its resources appropriately.

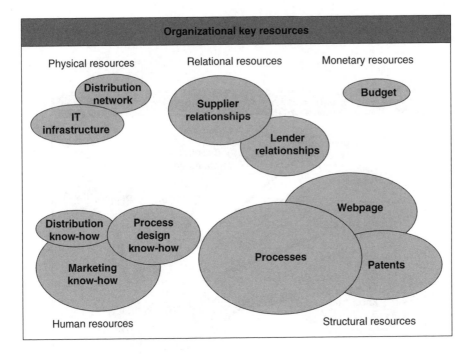

Figure 3.6   Visualizing the relative importance of the key resources

Understanding the interdependencies of resources

Resources depend on each other and interact with each other in order to create a core competence. This means that resource interdependencies can only be assessed in relation to the existing core competencies and value proposition of the organization. If you have defined your core competence, you can then use the resource list created above to understand how these interlink.[38] Individuals can use a matrix to rate how resource A is dependent on resource B to deliver the core competence, until all resource combinations are assessed.[39] The scale used for assessing the relationships could be between 0 and 5, with 0 indicating no relationship and 5 indicating a very strong dependency. Again, these matrices can be completed by individuals.

The results from the individual matrices allow a facilitator to create a resource map with interdependencies between resources (Figure 3.7). Here, thinner arrows indicate a weaker dependence and thicker arrows indicate a stronger dependence. In this example the processes, so vital for the core competence of this business (e.g. provision of a simple and enjoyable online shopping experience), strongly depend on the marketing know-how and understanding of the customer needs, as well as on the existing IT infrastructure, the distribution know-how and supplier

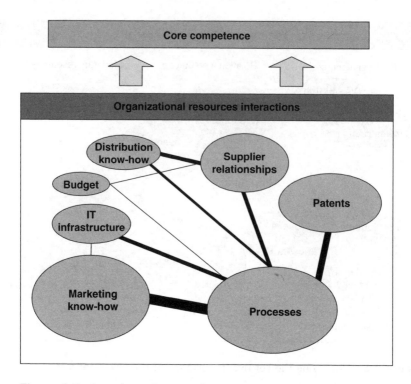

Figure 3.7   Interdependencies of resources

relationships. Once these processes are created this company aims to patent them to protect their competitive position.

The aim here is to display the key relationships. Often, these maps start as a 'spaghetti diagram' where all resources are related to every other resource. This is why it is important to assess the strength of the interdependencies. Once these are mapped, a workshop can be arranged with the aim of consolidating the interdependencies. The process involves jointly identifying the key dependencies and eliminating minor and unimportant dependencies. The objective is to gain consensus on the final map to represent the key resources and their key interdependencies that together deliver the core competence.

A look into the future

As discussed in Chapter 2, scenarios are traditionally used to describe possible alternative future developments in the external environment, which then inform current strategy assessment and future strategy development. However, with a shift in focus towards a resource-based view of strategy, scenarios can also be used to describe alternative internal development paths for an organization.[40] Internally, organizations have many options of how to react to external opportunities and threats. As outlined above, competencies are based on the resources which often depend on each other and are often path-dependent – that is, present choices about options are influenced by past choices.[41]

Within an organization there are often different perspectives on current problems, unsolved conflicts, different assumptions about the levers where changes could be initiated, different prioritizations of capability and resource development – and different interests. Considering these different views and accumulating diverse accounts about the possible developments of the internal resources can yield important information about the future direction of the organization. Holding a workshop to explore future developments of the organization allows managers to bring in their personal ideas and visions of the company's future and systematically link them to several strategy scenarios. Such workshops are best led by an external facilitator who is experienced in developing scenarios.

Understanding the internal environment

This chapter has emphasized the importance of understanding the internal resource architecture and core competencies of an organization. The outlined tools therefore allow organizations to clarify their internal context. Together with the external value proposition, be it a prescribed or market-based one, organizations can now use the insights gained to create their business model. This business model can subsequently be visually mapped into a value creation map and described in a value narrative. How to do this will be the focus of the next chapter.

References and endnotes

1 Collis, D. J. and Montgomery, C. A. (1997). *Corporate Strategy – Resources and the Scope of the Firm*. McGraw-Hill: Boston, p. 9.

2 See for example: Senior, N. W. (1836). *An Outline of the Science of Political Economy*. Longman: London; or Marshall, A. (1890). *Principles of Economics*. Macmillan: London. Volume I (1982): Knowledge and Knowledge Production, Volume II (1982): The Branches of Learning, Volume III (1984): The Economics of Information and Human Capital (Posthumous).

3 See for example: Wernerfelt, B. (1984). A Resource-Based View of the Firm. *Strategic Management Journal*, Vol. 5, No. 2, Apr–Jun, p. 171.

4 See: Barney, J. B. (1991). Firm Resources and Sustained Competitive Advantage. *Journal of Management*, Vol. 17, No. 1, p. 99; or Rumelt, R. P. (1984). Towards a Strategic Theory of the Firm. In *Competitive Strategic Management* (Lamp, R. B., ed.) pp. 89–102, Prentice Hall: New Jersey; or de Haas, M. and Kleingeld, A. (1999). Multilevel Design of Performance Measurement Systems: Enhancing Strategic Dialogue Throughout the Organization. *Management Accounting Research*, Vol. 10, pp. 233–61.

5 Stalk, G., Evans, P. and Shulman, L. E. (1992). Competing on Capabilities: The New Rules of Corporate Strategy. *Harvard Business Review*, Vol. 70, pp. 57–69.

6 Molnar, M. J. (2004). Executive Views on Intangible Assets: Insights From the Accenture/Economist Intelligence Unit Survey, *Accenture Research Note 'Intangible Assets and Future Value'*, Vol. Issue one, April.

7 Lev, B. (2002). Intangibles at a Crossroads: What's Next? *Financial Executive*, Vol. 18, No. 2, pp. 35–9.

8 DTI (2003). *Innovation Report – Competing in the Global Economy: the Innovation Challenge*. Department of Trade and Industry – UK Government White Paper, London; and DTI (1998). *Our Competitive Future: Building the Knowledge Driven Economy*. Department of Trade and Industry – UK Government White Paper, London.

9 DTI (2004). *Critical Success Factors: Creating Value From Your Intangibles*. Department of Trade and Industry: London.

10 Blair, M. M. and Wallman, S. M. H. (2001). *Unseen Wealth*. Brookings Institution Press: Boston.

11 Marr, B. (ed.) (2005). *Perspectives on Intellectual Capital: Multidisciplinary Insights into Management, Measurement, and Reporting*. Elsevier: Boston.

12 Ibid. The terminology of assets is mostly linked with the accounting discipline and knowledge assets, and intellectual capital is often linked to knowledge management work.

13 See for example: Roos, J., Roos, G., Dragonetti, N. C. and Edvinsson, L. (1997). *Intellectual Capital: Navigating the New Business Landscape*. Macmillan: London.

14 For additional reading see: Boisot, M. H. (1998). *Knowledge Assets: Securing Competitive Advantage in the Information Economy*. Oxford University Press: Oxford; and Itami, H. (1987). *Mobilizing Invisible Assets*. Harvard University Press: Cambridge, Massachusetts.

15 Heskett, J. L., Sasser, W. E. and Schlesinger, L. A. (2003). *The Value Profit Chain: Treat Employees Like Customers and Customers Like Employees*. Free Press: New York, p. 75.

16 See for example: Latour, A. (2001). A Blaze in Albuquerque Sets off Major Crisis for Cell Phone Giants. *Wall Street Journal*, 29 January.

17 Hall, R. (1992). The Strategic Analysis of Intangible Resources. *Strategic Management Journal*, **13** (2), 135–44.

18 Carmeli, A. and Tishler, A. (2004). The Relationships Between Intangible Organizational Elements and Organizational Performance. *Strategic Management Journal*, Vol. 25, pp.1257–78.

19 See: Ghoshal, S. and Nahapiet, J. (1998). Social Capital, Intellectual Capital, and the Organizational Advantage. *Academy of Management Review*, Vol. 23, No. 2, Apr, pp. 242; or Konno, N. and Nonaka, I. (1998). The Concept of "Ba": Building a Foundation for Knowledge Creation. *California Management Review*, Vol. 40, No. 3, pp. 40–54; or Brooking, A. (1996). *Intellectual Capital: Core Assets for the Third Millennium Enterprise*. Thompson Business Press: London.

20 Itami, 1987, p. 23 (see note 14 above).

21 Marr, B., Neely, A. and Schiuma, G. (2004). The Dynamics of Value Creation: Mapping Your Intellectual Performance Drivers. *Journal of Intellectual Capital*, Vol. 5, No. 2, pp. 312–25.

22 Nelson, R. R. and Winter, S. G. (1982). *An Evolutionary Theory of Economic Change*. Harvard University Press: Cambridge, MA.

23 As reported by Heskett, J. L., Sasser, W. E. and Schlesinger, L. A. (2003). *The Value Profit Chain: Treat Employees Like Customers and Customers Like Employees*. Free Press: New York, p. 203.

24 Grindley, P. C. and Teece, D. J. (1997). Managing Intellectual Capital: Licensing and Cross-Licensing in Semiconductors and Electronics. *California Management Review*, Vol. 39, No. 2, Winter, pp. 8–41.

25 See also: Clotier, L. M. and Gold, E. R. (2005). A Legal Perspective on Intellectual Capital. In *Perspectives on Intellectual Capital* (B. Marr, ed.) pp. 125–36, Elsevier: Boston; and Hall, R. (1989). The Management of Intellectual Assets: A New Corporate Perspective. *Journal of General Management*, Vol. 15, No.1, p. 53.

26 Hamel, G. and Prahalad, C. K. (1990). The Core Competence of the Corporation. *Harvard Business Review*, Vol. 68, No. 3, May/Jun, p. 79.

27 See for example: Adams, C. and Johnson, D. (1998). *The Concise Blackwell Encyclopedia of Management*. Blackwell Business, p. 624–5.

28 Ibid (see note 1 above), Collis and Montgomery (1997), p. 22.

29 Ibid (see notes 5 and 26 above, respectively); Stalk et al. (1992) and Hamel and Prahalad (1990).

30 Ibid (see note 5 above), Stalk et al. (1992).

31 See for example: Rucci, A. J., Kirn, S. P. and Quinn, R. T. (1998). The Employee-Customer-Profit Chain at Sears. *Harvard Business Review*, Vol. 76, No. 1, pp. 83–97; and Ittner, C. D. and Larcker, D. F. (1998b).

Are Nonfinancial Measures Leading Indicators of Financial Performance? An Analysis of Customer Satisfaction. *Journal of Accounting Research*, Vol. 36, pp. 1–35.

32 For a debate on causal ambiguity and interrelatedness of resources see: Lippman, S. A. and Rumelt, R. P. (1982). Uncertain Imitability: an Analysis of Interfirm Differences in Efficiency Under Competition. *Bell Journal of Economics*, Vol. 13, No. 2, Autumn, p. 418; and Dierickx, I. and Cool, K. (1989). Asset Stock Accumulation And Sustainability Of Competitive Advantage. *Management Science*, Vol. 35, No. 12, Dec, p. 1504; and King, A. W. and Zeithaml, C. P. (2001). Competencies and Firm Performance: Examining the Causal Ambiguity Paradox. *Strategic Management Journal*, Vol. 22, No. 1, Jan, p. 75.

33 Lev, B. (2001). *Intangibles: Management, Measurement, and Reporting*. The Brookings Institution: Washington DC, p. 7.

34 Roos, G. and Roos, J. (1997). Measuring Your Company's Intellectual Performance. *Long Range Planning*, Vol. 30, No. 3, Jun, p. 413.

35 Nobody really knows who invented SWOT analysis, though it was certainly being used by Harvard Business School academics during the 1960s.

36 Accountants have struggled with trying to categorize resources, especially intangibles, for many years, and their debate has yielded little insights. For an accounting view on intangibles see: Lev, B., Canibano, L. and Marr, B. (2005). An Accounting Perspective on Intellectual Capital. In *Perspectives on Intellectual Capital: Multi-disciplinary Insights into Management, Measurement, and Reporting* (B. Marr, ed.) pp. 42–55, Elsevier: Boston.

37 Due to strict confidentiality agreements the name of this business cannot be revealed.

38 Göran and Johan Roos have been instrumental in developing an understanding and mapping approach of resource interactions. For their insights on resource interactions see, for example: Roos, G. and Roos, J. (1997). Measuring Your Company's Intellectual Performance. *Long Range Planning*, Vol. 30, No. 3, Jun, p. 413; and Gupta, O. and Roos, G. (2001). Mergers and Acquisitions Through an Intellectual Capital Perspective. *Journal of Intellectual Capital*, Vol. 2, No. 3, pp. 297–309; and Pike, S. Roos, G. and Marr, B. (2005). Strategic management of intangible assets and value drivers in R&D organizations. *R&D Management*, Vol. 35, No. 2. pp. 111–24.

39 While Göran Roos et al., for example, use the Navigator Model to emphasize the influence and transformation from one resource to the next, here we assess the interdependence for creating a core competence. See, for example, Marr, B. and Roos, G. (2005). A

Strategy Perspective on Intellectual Capital. In *Perspectives on Intellectual Capital - Interdisciplinary Insights into Management, Measurement and Reporting* (B. Marr, ed.), Chapter 2, Elsevier: Boston; and Carlucci, D., Marr, B., Schiuma, G. (2004). The Knowledge Value Chain - How Knowledge Management impacts Business Performance. *International Journal of Technology Management*, Vol. 27, No 6/7, pp. 575–90; and Neely, A., Marr, B., Roos, G., Pike, S. and Gupta, O. (2003). Towards Third Generation Performance Measurement. *Controlling*, Vol. 15, No. 3/4, pp. 129–35.

40 See for example: Fink, A., Marr, B., Siebe, A., Kuhle, J.-P. (2005). The Future Scorecard: Combining internal and external scenarios to create strategic foresight. *Management Decision*, Vol. 43, No. 2. pp. 360–81.

41 See for example: Helfat, C. E. (2000). Guest Editor's Introduction to the Special Issue: The Evolution of Firm Capabilities. *Strategic Management Journal*, Vol. 21, No. 10/11, Oct/Nov, p. 955; and Pandza, K., Polajnar, A., Buchmeister, B. and Thorpe, R. (2003). Evolutionary Perspectives on the Capability Accumulation Process. *International Journal of Operations & Production Management*, Vol. 23, No. 7/8, p. 822; and Post, H. A. (1997). Building a Strategy on Competences. *Long Range Planning*, Vol. 30, No. 5, pp. 733–40.

4

Mapping and narrating value creation

The previous chapters have given you an understanding of your competitive external environment as well as of your internal strengths and competencies. Bringing these together allows you now to create a picture of your strategy and articulate it. This chapter will outline how the strategy can be visualized in a value creation map and described in a value creation narrative. Together, they allow organizations to make their strategic plans explicit and communicate them to everyone within the organization in order for the strategy to be executed, challenged and refined. Questions addressed in this chapter include:

- Why do we need maps and narratives?
- What are value creation maps and value creation narratives?
- How do we create value creation maps and value creation narratives?
- How do we cascade value creation maps in our organization?
- How have organizations applied these tools in practice?

Without an explicit understanding of strategy, Strategic Performance Management will never be possible. Today, one of the biggest barriers to successful Performance Management is that strategy is often communicated in cryptic or incomplete ways, with the hope that employees will understand how it all fits together. In most cases they don't! Organizational strategy has its roots in military strategy, and strategy execution in organizations is often compared with an army fighting a battle. Two and a half thousand years ago, Sun Tzu, a wise Chinese general, wrote that an army that both knows its enemy and knows itself can fight a hundred battles without disaster. He continues that once an army understands its enemy and knows its own strengths and weaknesses, it can lay out its plan.[1] This is exactly what we are trying to do here.

Chapters 1 to 3 have given readers the insights of understanding the external competitive environment and the internal strengths and weaknesses of an organization. Now we need to bring them together in order to lay out a strategic plan and communicate it to everyone. Back to the army analogy, we would expect a general taking his troops into battle to provide detailed maps of the terrain, telling field officers and troops exactly what the strategic objective is, and how he envisaged that it can be achieved.[2] Without a detailed plan, it would be difficult, if not impossible, to clearly communicate a campaign. The likely consequence would be that the field officers and troops won't really understand the strategic plan. However, in most organizations, leaders commonly communicate their strategy in cryptic and partial forms. Organizations regularly provide employees with lists of seemingly unrelated goals and targets, or budget forecasts in spreadsheets, without revealing how they fit together, thus providing very limited descriptions of the strategic objectives and how they could be achieved.

Why maps and narratives?

The primary function of value creation maps and value creation narratives is to communicate information so that it can become meaningful. Our human brain is there to interpret incoming information to create meaning. The work of Nobel Prize winners Roger Sperry and Robert Ornstein discovered that the brain is divided into two halves, or hemispheres, and that different kinds of mental functioning take place in each.[3] Thus, the left hemisphere operates sequentially and deals largely with 'academic' activities, such as reading, arithmetic and logic. By contrast, the right hemisphere operates holistically and deals more with synthesizing and 'artistic' activities, such as art, music, colour and creativity (see Figure 4.1). It is therefore easier for our brain to make meaning of complex information when it is presented in visual formats. Visual maps are processed in our right hemisphere which is better equipped to deal with complex and holistic information. This is why a picture can be worth a thousand words.

Left-brain-focused people, who are strongly text oriented, could lose out on important insights to be gained from images depicted in pictures and diagrams. The reverse may not hold true with the right-brain-focused people not necessarily being deprived of more linear

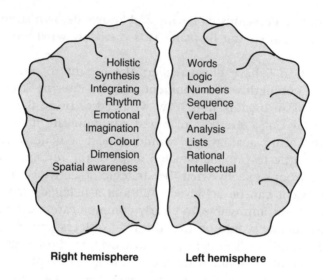

Right hemisphere   Left hemisphere

Figure 4.1   Left brain, right brain

and logical thinking. This may be due to our education, which already puts greater emphasis on 'left-brain thinking'. This early approach is then reinforced by the way we behave in business. Promotion of creative thinking into business activities can be seen as a means of counteracting our early and subsequent emphasis on linear thinking. Many great minds are believed to use both parts of their brains. A good example is Leonardo da Vinci who, in his time, was one of the most skilled men in a wide range of disciplines, such as art, sculpture, physiology, general science, architecture, invention, engineering, aviation and many more. As Mozart said, 'I can see the whole ... at a single glance in my mind, as if it were a painting or a handsome human being'. It is the role of value creation maps to focus everyone on 'the big picture'.

It is recommended that value creation maps are accompanied by a value creation narrative; here, a narrative means telling the story of value creation in writing. Dr Howard Gardner, Professor at Harvard University and author of *Leading Minds*[4], believes that stories constitute one of the most powerful tools in business. Narratives have proven to be useful tools for organizations in communicating how they function – and especially about how intangible resources help to deliver value.[5] However, narratives not only provide additional contextual information, they also engage the logical left hemisphere of the brain, and therefore ensure that both sides of the brain are engaged in understanding strategy.

Strategic mapping in business

Maps have long been used in strategic management to visualize relationships and knowledge.[6] Napoleon, for example, was advocate of their use. More recently, Robert Kaplan, Professor at H ...d Business School, and David Norton of the Balanced Scorecard Collaborative, have made strategic mapping part of their Balanced Scorecard (BSC) model, and thereby significantly contributed to the widespread usage of mapping tools in modern organizations.[7] Strategy maps are visual representations of the causal linkages assumed between strategic objectives in the following Balanced Scorecard perspectives: financial – traditional financial metrics; customer – customer value proposition (operational excellence, customer intimacy, product leadership); internal processes – manage operations, manage customers, manage innovations, manage regulatory and social processes; learning and growth – human capital, information capital, organizational capital. This visual representation of cause-and-effect relationships between distinct strategic objectives was first introduced into the BSC in 1996 and then extended in 2000. Kaplan and Norton argue that strategy maps show how an organization will convert intangible resources into tangible outcomes.[8] The Balanced Scorecard strategy map template is depicted in Figure 4.2.

However, generic strategy maps have been criticized for being too narrow and too prescriptive.[9] The overall goal of financial performance and shareholder value, for example, doesn't work for public sector or not-for-profit organizations, where finance is primarily an input resource that has to be managed as effectively and efficiently as possible, rather than as an outcome that has to be maximized.[10] Key criticisms of the Balanced Scorecard are that it mainly addresses the needs of shareholders as opposed to a broader set of stakeholders and that its resource classification is incomplete.[11] It is argued that the Balanced Scorecard fails to adequately highlight the contributions that, for example, employees and suppliers make to help the organization achieve its objectives, and that it fails to include monetary, physical and relational resources.[12]

In response to the limited stakeholder focus, a new scorecard framework, the Performance Prism, has been developed.[13] The Performance Prism adopts a stakeholder-centric view of strategy. The framework consists of five inter-related facets: stakeholder satisfaction; stakeholder contribution; strategy; processes; and capabilities. In doing so, the framework proves to be more comprehensive than many of the other existing measurement frameworks and is less limited in its definition of performance drivers. The Performance Prism model also includes a mapping approach. Here, a 'success map' is created to visualize the

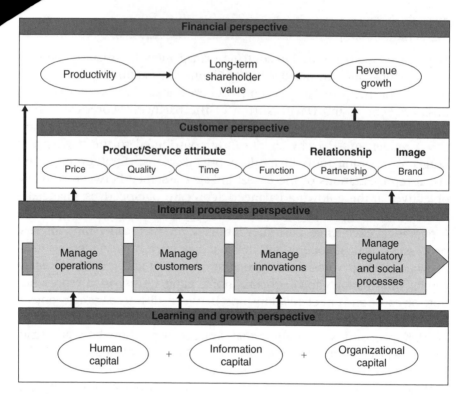

Figure 4.2 Kaplan and Norton's strategy map template

causal relationships between the different perspectives of the frame-work, and so delves into the vital operational workings of the organ-ization with the aim of creating value for its various stakeholders. A reverse process of developing a 'risk (i.e. failure) map' can also be applied; it is a less prescriptive approach than a BSC-based strategy map.

However, in order to map the organizational value proposition, the core competencies and the underlying resource architecture, as outlined in this book, a new tool is required. The value creation map outlined below builds on the important foundations laid by the Balanced Score-card and the Performance Prism models, but ensures that the three com-ponents of strategy, with their different components, are included.

What is a value creation map?

A value creation map is defined as a visual representation of the organ-izational strategy that includes the most important components that exist within this strategy (namely stakeholder value proposition, core competencies, and key resources) and places them in relationships with each other. It therefore establishes a shared understanding and facilitates communication of strategy.[14] Such shared understanding of the organizational strategy can then be the starting point to assess, implement, and continuously refine the strategy.

A value creation map brings together the key elements of an organizational strategy and visualizes them on one piece of paper. No two value creation maps should be the same since they represent the unique strategy of an organization at that point in time. Someone looking at a value creation map should be able to answer the following questions:

- Who are the key stakeholders of this organization and what value is the organization delivering to them? Basically, why does this organization exist and what are its roles and deliverables?
- What must therefore be the core competencies of the organization so that it can deliver the above value proposition? Basically, what are the few vital things the organization has to excel at?
- What are the key resources that underlie the above core competencies? Basically, what are the building blocks of these competencies in terms of monetary, physical, and intangible resources?

The basic template of a value creation map is shown in Figure 4.3. The top box shows the stakeholder value proposition or the output deliverables. As discussed earlier, these are either prescribed in the case of public sector organizations or business units, derived from the external analysis outlined in Chapter 2, or developed based on the core competencies and resource architecture. In the middle, are the core competencies. In this template, I have depicted three core competencies; usually organizations would have between one and five core competencies. In the bottom box, are the organizational resources. Here, the different types of resources are shown with their relative importance for the core competencies identified. The way the resources are visualized can vary depending on preferences, levels of understanding, and available data. The most basic visualization is shown here, which does not show any causal relationships or individual interdependencies between individual resources. By showing overlap between the relatively sized bubbles, it indicates that these different resources are interdependent and, as a bundle of resources, provide the outlined core competencies.

More sophisticated visualizations will be discussed below. The bottom box also includes capabilities, but these are optional to include. Some organizations I have worked with preferred to include certain capabilities that they felt were important to include in the map for 'political' reasons. In those cases, important functional capabilities (such

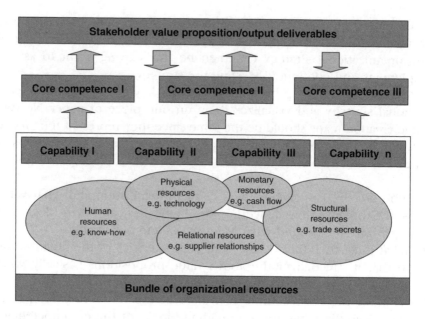

Figure 4.3 Value creation map template

as 'marketing' or 'production') were included. Whereas, in my view, this should not be necessary in most cases, it has proven useful to help senior managers of these functional areas to buy into this process.

Organizations with a better understanding of their resource architecture might want to move to more sophisticated mapping approaches within the value creation map. The outlined approach above provides a holistic first step to understanding an existing pattern of relationships between resources. The next level of sophistication is to highlight specific relationships between the individual resource bubbles as outlined in Figure 3.7. To achieve this, organizations can follow the methodology outlined in Chapter 3. I outlined in Chapter 3 that organizational resources depend on each other and dynamically interact. However, in order to make value creation maps more operational many organizations create cause-and-effect or dependence (also called 'influence') diagrams.[15]

Figure 4.4 shows the different types of relationships between resources that could be visualized. The first is a simple arrow that indicates that there is a cause-and-effect relationship between the two resources – meaning that A leads to B. This is the level of sophistication seen on success maps and some strategy maps.[16] In the most sophisticated visualizations, organizations can differentiate between the levels of dependence between the different resources. This allows organizations to see that, for example, the dependence of resource B on resource A is

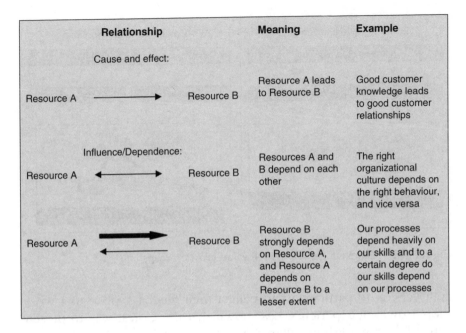

Figure 4.4 Possible causal relationships between resources

stronger than the dependence of A on B. Furthermore, the difference in strength of dependence of two resources on each other can be visualized. For example, resource B might heavily depend on resource A, but resource A only moderately depends on resource B.[17]

Whereas 'bundled' value creation maps correspond with the systems dynamics view,[18] which indicates that all resources are interdependent and reliant on each other, the 'causal' value creation map takes a more pragmatic view and visualizes the most important causal dependencies between the different resources (see Figure 4.5). This makes value creation maps easier to interpret and analyse, and also provides the possibility to verify and test the assumed causal relationships and interdependencies (see Chapter 7).

How to construct a value creation map

A value creation map is best drafted by a facilitator who brings together the insights from both the external analysis and the internal analysis. The findings from individual interviews or surveys, as well as from workshop sessions, can be mapped into a first version of a value creation map. This first draft is best presented in a workshop with the senior management of the organization. Some firms have preferred to mail a

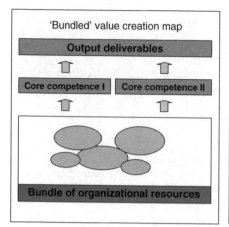
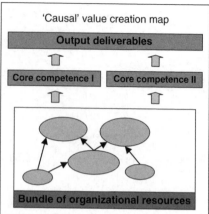

Figure 4.5 'Bundled' versus 'causal' value creation maps

draft version to participants to collect their feedback prior to a workshop. However, experience has shown that the easiest way to present a map is in a workshop, where immediate questions and feedback can lead to quick consensus. It is recommended, that these workshops should not have more than about 15 participants.[19] Their aim is to gain consensus about the final map, and with too many participants this can be difficult. Also, every participant needs to have his or her say in order to achieve buy-in.

There are advantages if this workshop is facilitated by an experienced facilitator and, if possible, someone external to the organization. This is especially recommended if there are any dominant participants who might be able to impose their view of reality on other participants. In the workshop, some linkages might be deleted and others might be emphasized and wordings need to be finalized. It is always good to give the map a 'corporate' feel to it by using familiar language, colours and formats. A good tip also is to draw the map with a dry-wipe-marker pen on a whiteboard and use Post-it notes for the different components of the map. This way, the linkages can be easily erased and redrawn, and the different components can be moved around. Good practice is then to draw the finalized map and mail it out to all participants after the workshop for consideration and comments. This gives people some time to think about the final map and compare it with the reality of everyday business. Feedback can then be collected and if necessary a final workshop can be arranged to agree on the final layout of the map.

A value creation map visualizes the strategy of an organization at a single point in time. Organizations continuously evolve and change.

The external and internal environments evolve and so the strategy needs to evolve too. This means that the value creation map needs to be revised on a regular basis in order to ensure that it reflects a current view of the strategy. How often these revisions take place depends on the speed of change in the industry the organization is part of. It is usually a good idea to align the revisions of the value creation map with the strategic planning cycles and, for many organizations, an annual revision is adequate. However, in some emerging or fast-moving industries this revision cycle can be accelerated.

What is a value creation narrative?

A value creation narrative is defined as a concise piece of written work that describes the organizational strategy and tells the story of how that organization intends to create value by specifying its value proposition, required core competencies and key resources. A value creation narrative is there to accompany a value creation map and provide additional contextual information and allow organizations to explain the chain of events in a story format.[20] Stories are the way we, as human beings, have communicated over thousands of years and our brain is predisposed to absorb information in narrative form.

The format of a value creation narrative is not prescriptive. It very much depends on organizational preferences and should be aligned with the corporate look and feel. However, a value creation narrative should not be longer than about 500 words. The story should be clear and readable, and written in a conversational style.[21] It is recommended that jargon or technical terms which readers of the narrative might not be familiar with are avoided as this may interfere with their understanding. At the same time, it is important to use language and terms that are usually used and understood within the organization. Clarifying the strategy in a concise narrative is a powerful way of clarifying the organizational strategy.

How to construct a value creation narrative

A value creation narrative provides contextual information of the strategy that is visualized in a value creation map. The value creation map is therefore the starting point for writing a value creation narrative. Based on the map, an individual or a small group of people can produce a draft version of the narrative. This draft is then circulated to a wider group of people, usually the senior management team, who then review the document and submit comments and suggested edits. These are then collected by the individual or group that produced the draft to create the final version of the narrative. Alternatively, and possibly for best results, the draft version of the value narrative is circulated and subsequently a group session is arranged with the senior management team to edit the report in an interactive workshop. This process can produce over-long narratives – please remember that it *must* be concise.

Cascading value creation maps

A frequently raised question is when and how to cascade a value creation map. A value creation map is supposed to be a management tool that clarifies the strategy and therefore creates a shared identity and engages people in assessing and evolving this strategy. If this strategy is too distant and hence too abstract to people, it fails in its role. Employees need to be able to relate to the elements on the value creation map – it must reflect their reality in order for them to identify with it. It therefore becomes clear that a corporate value creation map of, for example, a large and diverse international corporation will not be meaningful for someone working as a middle manager in one of the many businesses or business units. It becomes too generic, too abstract; and similar in many ways to corporate mission statements that are often no more than a set of well-meaning words that have little operative value for people working further removed from corporate centres. For that reason, value creation maps have to be cascaded and translated to a meaningful local perspective.

How many value creation maps an organization needs depends on its size and diversity. Let's take, for example, a company like Royal Dutch Shell plc. Shell is a group of diverse companies that includes 'Exploration and Production' – responsible for finding and producing oil and gas; 'Renewables' – building commercial scale wind parks and selling solar photovoltaic panels; 'Shell Trading' – trading of crude oil, refined products, gas, electrical power; and 'Shell Global Solutions' – providing business and operational consultancy, technical services and R&D expertise to the energy industry worldwide, among other corporate entities.[22]

It is clear that all of these businesses have different stakeholder value propositions, unique core competencies, and very dissimilar resource architectures. As a consequence, each of the different businesses would require their own value creation map and there would be little similarity between them (but, I would argue, there should be elements of connectivity between them). For more homogeneous organizations, a similar value creation map can be used. Take, for example, companies such as Burger King or Hilton Hotels. Their individual restaurants or hotels might have much the same generic value propositions, as well as an almost identical set of core competencies and resources but, potentially, substantially different product or service ingredients and pricing arrangements that reflect different customer expectations in different parts of the world.

Each business usually has a diverse set of functional business units, such as operations, HR, marketing, finance, logistics, IT, etc. These functional business units all contribute to delivering the overall value proposition of the business as a whole, but each of them has a value proposition of its own. Various books and articles have been written about how to strategically align functions, such as HR or IT, with the overall strategy of the business.[23] It is important that all functional business units understand how they contribute to the overall value proposition.

The business level value creation map is often too abstract and general. Business units therefore need to cascade the value creation map of the business as a whole into a map that reflects their reality, but which is aligned with the strategy of the business. Any cascade needs to be based on the value creation map of the business as a whole. Business units need to understand where and how they are contributing to the delivery of the overall strategy. In the case of an IT function, for instance, its key contribution might be to one of the resource 'bubbles' on the value creation map, e.g. an innovative technology base, whereas the HR function, for example, might be contributing to various 'bubbles' (see Figure 4.6). It is important that the link to the business strategy is kept explicit and I suggest that the different maps with their specific linkages are visualized. Also, the value creation narrative plays an important role in this as it has the ability to provide the contextual information of how the strategies integrate.

In terms of number of employees, it is more difficult to provide a definite answer on when to cascade a value creation map. Cascading based on number of employees is more of an operational consideration than a conceptual issue. The map might look the same or very similar for a large number of people in the organization, but some of the underlying indicators and objectives might vary significantly between different groups or departments. Let's take Hilton Hotels again as an example. The structure of the value creation map might look the same for each hotel; however, there are clearly differences in the issues and underlying measures. Another example is provided by local governments. A central agency might provide a value creation map template to be used in each local government office; however, the issues they are facing will vary and cannot be generalized.

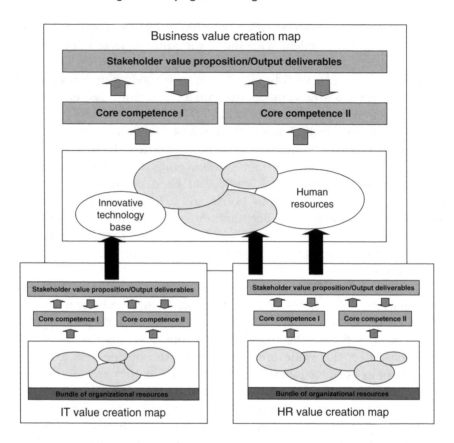

Figure 4.6 Cascading a value creation map

If a value creation map is to become a tool that facilitates strategic decision-making and learning at every level of the organization, then it is critical that the information provided is relevant to its people. The field of anthropology has found that humans have a limit to the number of people with whom we can retain a social relationship. This limit is likely to be linked back to the clan sizes of our hunter and gatherer ancestors. Research evidence shows that it is hard, if not impossible, for us humans to share an identity with more than about 150 people.[24] Experience has shown that this number is a good benchmark for the cascade of value creation maps, in terms of content rather than structure.

The best way to cascade a value creation map is to use an internal or external facilitator; preferably someone who has been involved in the creation of the organization's overall (or master) value creation map. The process is the same as the one describing the construction of a value creation map above. However, the external analysis will be reduced to a minimum as it only consists of identifying the key stakeholders and their needs. This can often be derived from the existing organizational value creation map. If this is not the case, then some of the external analysis tools can be used to determine how the business or business unit helps to deliver the overall value proposition. Once the value proposition is clarified, the internal analysis will provide the data to create a cascade of the value creation map.

Value creation maps and narratives in practice

The approaches outlined above have been implemented by many organizations around the globe. They have proven successful for a very diverse group of organizations from leading international blue-chip corporations to very small and medium-sized companies, as well as many public sector and not-for-profit organizations, including central and local government institutions, schools and charities. It is important to highlight, however, that every organization takes its own journey, with its own interpretations of the tools and techniques. Below I have outlined some illustrative case studies that demonstrate how leading organizations have translated these concepts into reality and applied the tools in practice. They serve the purpose of being real-life examples that I hope might provide some guidance, but they will never provide templates you can simply copy to reduce the efforts that you have to go into creating your own value creation maps and narratives. Every context and every strategy is different, and value creation maps are unique descriptions of your organization at one point in time.

Case study: DHL[25]

DHL is the global market leader in international express, air and ocean freight, overland transport and logistics. With annual revenues of nearly €24.5 billion in 2004, DHL offers innovative and customized solutions from a single source. DHL has more than 170 000 full-time employees in about 4400 offices and 450 hubs, warehouses and terminals around the globe. DHL ships more than 1 billion shipments each year for its 4.2 million customers. It has global expertise in express, air and ocean freight, overland transport and logistics solutions; DHL combines worldwide coverage with an in-depth understanding of local markets.

The development of the value creation map formed part of a wider initiative to establish a more sophisticated Performance Management system by understanding its value proposition and the required performance drivers. The example in this case study was developed for DHL Greece. In the Greek market, DHL is the dominant player and clear market leader. However, with other competitors entering this market, DHL's goal is to maintain its high market share through delivering superior customer service.

In order to establish the value proposition, the required core competencies, and key resources, two surveys and a set of in-depth interviews and workshop sessions were conducted. An internal survey of all DHL employees in Greece explored their views on the key output deliverables, competencies, and key resources. At the same time a survey of 300 key customers was conducted to ascertain their perceptions of the value DHL is delivering to them. The insights from these two surveys were then explored further in a set of interviews with the senior management team as well as a selection of middle managers and front-line employees. This gave DHL a comprehensive understanding of its value proposition and the value drivers that enable DHL to deliver its value proposition.

DHL identified high quality shipments together with superior customer service as the key output deliverable in order to deliver sustainable financial performance and shareholder value. In order to deliver these, DHL needs core competencies in the harmonization of their processes and networks, as well as an ongoing competence in understanding changing customer needs. For this, relationship resources and structural resources were most critical, followed by human and physical resources. Figure 4.7 shows the bundled value creation map with the key components of DHL's strategy, namely its value proposition, core competencies, and resource architecture.

Once the bundled map had been created, a set of in-depths interviews and workshop sessions were used to identify the key interdependencies between the different resources. Figure 4.8 shows the map with its interdependencies. The map shows how the key resources interact to demonstrate the most important interdependencies. At the bottom of the map are the DHL values and the leadership style as well as the strong brand reputation that DHL has in this market. DHL is seen as a clear market leader with the strongest brand and a multinational reputation, which in turn allows DHL to recruit the best people and build stronger customer trust. The leadership style and values are what shapes the organizational culture in DHL, which is open and entrepreneurial. Values include

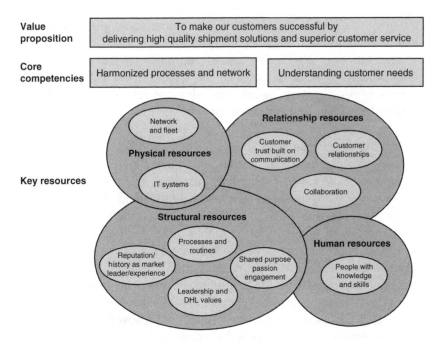

Figure 4.7   Bundled value creation map for DHL

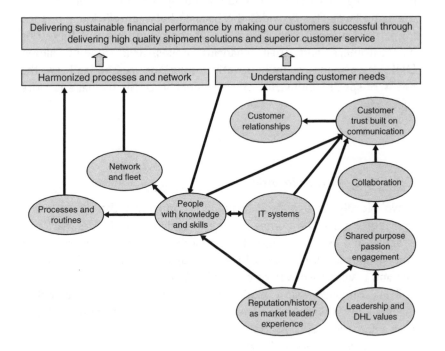

Figure 4.8   DHL's value creation map with interdependencies

integrity (internally and externally), accepting social responsibilities, and a continuous drive for excellence.

The flat hierarchy, which passes responsibility on to front-line employees, is seen as different to the typical Greek culture. This in turn changes the way people feel about their job. It provides a shared purpose and engages people. In the interviews many employees and managers talked about 'being part of the family' and 'going the extra mile'. The shared purpose and passion for the job is a key enabler for collaboration within and between the different departments, which in turn builds customer trust based on communication. Consequently, customers understand and feel good about working with DHL as there is openness, and DHL provides customers with honest information. In order for this to work well it is also important to have the relevant IT systems in place and have employees with the rights skills and knowledge. Together, they provide the foundation for customer relationships, the key driver for understanding customer needs. On the left-hand side of the map it is the people with their skills and know-how that allow DHL to refine its processes and routines and build the appropriate network and fleet that allows DHL to harmonize its processes.

For DHL it is important that the two core competencies of harmonizing processes and understanding customer needs are on the same level. This provides the balance between efficiency needed for a multinational corporation but at the same time not forgetting its customers and their changing needs. This balance allows DHL to provide many innovative solutions customized to the needs of specific industries or customers, in order to make it more successful.

Case study: Novo Nordisk[26]

Novo Nordisk is a focused healthcare company and a world leader in diabetes care. The company has its headquarters in Denmark and is active in 179 countries, with production facilities in six countries and affiliates in 78 countries. Novo Nordisk has over 21 000 employees and a sales turnover of over €3900 million.[27]

The company vision explicitly states its aspiration: to defeat diabetes by finding better methods of diabetes prevention, detection and treatment. To do so, Novo Nordisk actively promotes collaboration between all parties in the healthcare system in order to achieve common goals. Another objective is to offer products and services in other areas where the company can make a difference. Here, the company is focused on biopharmaceuticals – haemostasis management, growth disorders and hormone replacement therapy – areas in which the company has gained a leading position.

Further, the company believes that its focus is its strength, which will enable it to achieve competitive business results. A job in Novo Nordisk is never just a job. The company is committed to being there for its customers whenever they need it, and to be innovative and effective in everything it does. This also implies attracting and retaining the best people by making the company a challenging place to work. The company values are expressed in everyone's actions. 'Decency is what counts,' it says in the company vision. 'Every day we strive to find the right balance between compassion and competitiveness, the short and the long term, self and commitment to colleagues and society, work and family life.'

The project to develop a value creation map was part of a wider knowledge strategy initiative in Novo Nordisk to identify and prioritize a set of strategic value drivers that can be influenced in order to increase future value creation. The internal analysis consisted of 16 interviews with managers/specialists as well as internal observations and reviews of internal documents. These lasted between 1 and 2 hours. Together they delivered the contextual information which was used to create an initial value creation map and a value creation narrative of the business context in Novo Nordisk. In a facilitated workshop the map was finalized and subsequently a value creation narrative was produced to accompany the map. Both the narrative and the map are outlined below.

Novo Nordisk's value creation narrative

Overall, Novo Nordisk's promise is to be 'leading the fight against diabetes. Defeating diabetes is our passion and our business'. To be able to deliver on this promise it must continuously develop innovative products, processes and services. The key knowledge-based elements to achieve this are good collaboration and creativity facilitated by the best skilled, committed and motivated people that are able to leverage external relationships.

People in Novo Nordisk are a cornerstone of its performance and Novo Nordisk's people strategy aims to improve their ability to address business challenges across borders. A key driver of performance is having the best skilled and most knowledgeable people with the capabilities needed to perform their job. This includes both recruiting the best people as well as developing high performers internally.

In order to collaborate and be creative, people have to be committed and motivated. A key driver for commitment and motivation in Novo Nordisk is if people feel passionate about what they do and are engaged and feel pride in their job. Engagement and pride derive from sharing a meaningful purpose with the organization. This is further supported by the fact that Novo Nordisk has a strong brand reputation and history, which also makes people feel good about their job.

The values and commitments of Novo Nordisk are a key foundation for its performance. The key values are 'accountable', 'ambitious', 'responsible', 'engaged with stakeholders', 'open and honest', and 'ready for change'. The company is committed to pursuing its objectives in a way that considers the Triple Bottom Line – a business principle that requires balancing social, environmental and financial responsibility in every decision and action. This business principle influences Novo Nordisk's reputation, enables Novo Nordisk to build and maintain external relationships, fosters a shared sense of purpose and creates a culture in which employees are valued and empowered to develop and try new things. This in turn motivates people.

Its market position as a leading player in a niche market, as well as its values and its open and honest communication, helps to create the brand needed to facilitate the development of external relationships and also helps to attract the best people. These people are then able to flourish and deliver the innovations needed for a sustainable future performance.

Novo Nordisk's value creation map

Figure 4.9 visualizes the above outlined narrative in a value creation map. The bubble at the top represents the overall objectives and the output deliverables, namely a strong R&D pipeline as well as innovative products, processes, and services. The key competencies are 'commercialization', 'collaboration', and 'creativity'. The bubbles underneath the competencies indicate the different resources that were identified in Novo Nordisk and how they interact to deliver core competencies and output deliverables.

Today, the value creation map is at the heart of a new prototype Performance Management report called 'Foresight' (see Figure 4.10). The aim of this new report will be to provide senior management

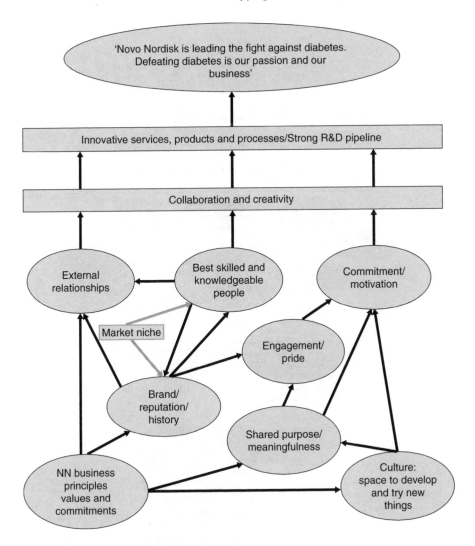

Figure 4.9   Value creation map for Novo Nordisk

with an overview of the key drivers of performance. The objectives are to offer: (1) strategic guidance and performance monitoring; (2) qualitative assessment and data analysis/interpretation; (3) indicators that are then available for external reporting and benchmarking. Once fully implemented, the report will not only describe the value creation and identify the performance drivers but also provide performance assessments and indicators for each of the performance drivers.

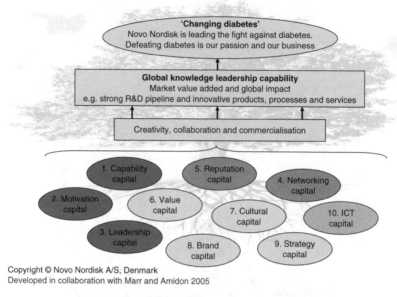

Copyright © Novo Nordisk A/S, Denmark
Developed in collaboration with Marr and Amidon 2005

Figure 4.10 Value creation reporting in Novo Nordisk

Case study: TT Club[28]

The TT Club is a leading provider of insurance and related risk management services for the international transport and logistics industry.
The company has its global headquarters in the City of London, the
central hub for insurance firms, but has 20 office locations around the
world. Its customers range from the world's largest shipping lines,
busiest ports, global freight forwarders and cargo handling terminals,
to smaller companies operating in niche markets. Since its inception,
the TT Club has grown steadily in terms of premium income, at
an average rate of 10% per annum for the last 20 years. Customer
loyalty has been an essential factor in this growth. Indeed, 90% of its
customers renew their policies with the TT Club each year.

The project to develop a value creation map was part of the strategic planning cycle. The TT Club wanted to better understand their
strategic value drivers, with an emphasis on the non-financial and intangible drivers of performance. The development of the map involved a
set of interviews with members of the senior management team, the
CEO, as well as board members. In a facilitated one-day planning workshop with the senior management team, the map was finalized. The
value creation map for the TT Club is outlined in Figure 4.11.

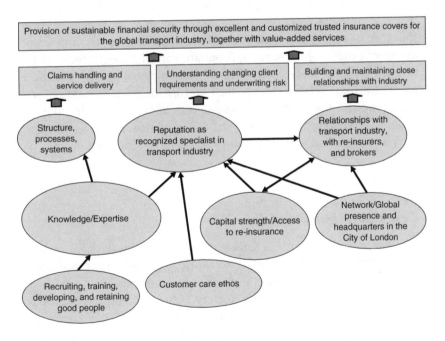

Figure 4.11   Value creation map for TT Club

BLACKBURN COLLEGE LIBRARY

The TT Club decided that their value proposition was to provide sustainable financial security for the global transport industry by offering excellent and customized insurance covers and value-added services that people trust. They identified three key competencies: (1) the claims handling and delivery of services such as risk assessments and advice; (2) the deep understanding of the industry and changing client demands and underwriting requirements; (3) the ability to build and maintain close relationships with the industry, which gives the TT Club the status of an independent body of the industry.

These competencies are delivered through the structures, processes and systems in place, together with the reputation and recognition of the TT Club as a specialist and member of the transport industry. These competencies are also delivered through relationships not just with the transport industry, but also with re-insurers and brokers. At the foundation of the value creation map is the ability to recruit, train, develop, and retain good people who help to create the knowledge and expertise needed. This knowledge, together with the strong customer care ethos, helps to shape the TT Club's reputation in the industry. Knowledge also shapes the development of processes, structures, and systems.

At the centre of the map is capital strength and access to re-insurance, one of the strongest resources in the TT Club. There is a dynamic relationship between the relationships with re-insurers and the access to re-insurance. Capital strength is also an important driver of reputation; without appropriate capital strength the reputation would suffer very quickly. The TT Club's global presence helps it to create local relationships, which in turn help its reputation and recognition in the field. The headquarters in London enable the TT Club to develop the crucial relationships with brokers who sell their products and with re-insurers to make re-insurance deals.

Case study: UK Home Office[29]

The purpose of the Home Office, a key central government institution in the United Kingdom, is to work with individuals and communities to build a safe, just and tolerant society, enhancing opportunities for all. In such a society rights and responsibilities go hand in hand, and the protection and security of the public are maintained and enhanced. This involves reducing crime and the fear of crime, including combating terrorism and other threats to national security; ensuring the effective delivery of justice; regulating entry to and settlement in the United Kingdom effectively in the interests of sustainable growth and social inclusion; facilitating travel by UK citizens; and supporting strong and active communities in which people of all races and backgrounds are valued and participate on equal terms. The latter being achieved by developing social policy to build a fair, prosperous and cohesive society in which everyone has a stake.

This case study is based on the work of the Immigration and Nationality Directorate (IND), one of the Home Office departments which, together with the Department for Constitutional Affairs (DCA) and UK visas, will deliver the Government's asylum and immigration strategy. The project was part of a wider initiative of the Government to improve Performance Management.

IND's value creation narrative

The high-level objective as set out in the published Home Office Strategic Plan and the vision statement in the DCA five-year strategy, is that migration is managed to the benefit of the UK, while preventing abuse of the immigration laws and of the asylum system.

The key output deliverables IND needs to deliver in order to achieve the high-level objective are effective control, the support of legal migration, value for money, and community cohesion. This involves continuing to encourage legal migration, which supports the UK economy, while remaining firm against abuse, and increasing value for money with demonstrable year-on-year efficiency gains across the organization. Value for money here is a combination of: (i) doing the same for less, i.e. reducing costs; (ii) increasing the amount it achieves with the same money; and (iii) using money more effectively. It also involves building strong, cohesive communities and for this it is important that long-term migrant workers and genuine refugees are swiftly integrated into society through settlement and citizenship. Effective integration will empower migrants to achieve their full potential as members of British society and thus help to build cohesive communities.

Key competencies that help IND to deliver its output deliverables are continuous process improvement and effective stakeholder management. Stakeholder management focuses on international collaborations, effective delivery partnerships, responsiveness to customers, and public confidence. Process improvement focuses on improved quality and productivity, simplified and joined-up processes, and effective resource management.

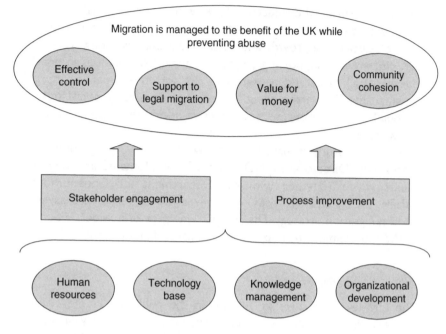

Figure 4.12 IND value creation map

To achieve the above, IND needs to develop as an organization and build the right resources for the future. Achieving its core competencies and output deliverables is based on the right human resources, the right technology base, the right knowledge management processes, as well as continuous organizational development.

IND's value creation map

Figure 4.12 visualizes the strategy of IND in a value creation map format. The overall output deliverables together with the high-level objective are at the top. Below are the two competencies IND needs to excel at in order to deliver its proposed value proposition. At the bottom of the map are the key drivers that IND needs to manage in order to be successful.[30]

These actual case examples, from a very diverse set of organizations, illustrate the type of outputs that can be expected from the vital process of creating a value creation map and accompanying value creation narrative.

References and endnotes

1 Sun Tzu. (1981). *The Art of War*. Hodder & Stoughton: London.

2 This analogy is borrowed from Kaplan, R. S. and Norton, D. P. (2000b). Having Trouble With Your Strategy? Then Map It. *Harvard Business Review*, Sept–Oct, pp. 167–76.

3 Deutsch, G. and Springer, S. P. (1998). *Left brain, right brain*. W. H. Freeman: New York; and Gardner, H. (1996). *Leading Minds – An Anatomy of Leadership*. BasicBooks: New York.

4 Gardner, H. (1996). *Leading Minds – An Anatomy of Leadership*. BasicBooks: New York.

5 Bukh, P. N., Larsen, H. T. and Mouritsen, J. (2001). Intellectual Capital and the 'Capable Firm': Narrating, Visualising and Numbering for Managing Knowledge. *Accounting, Organizations and Society*, Vol. 26, No. 7–8, pp. 735–62.

6 For a good overview of how mapping is used in strategic management see: Huff, A. S. and Jenkins, M. (2002). *Mapping Strategic Knowledge*. Sage: London.

7 See for example: Ibid, Kaplan, R. S. and Norton, D. P. (2000b) (see note 2 above); or Kaplan, R. S. and Norton, D. P. (2004a). *Strategy Maps – Converting Intangible Assets into Tangible Outcomes*. Harvard Business School Press: Boston, MA; or Kaplan, R. S. and Norton, D. P. (2000a). *The Strategy Focused Organization: How Balanced Scorecard Companies Thrive in the New Business Environment*. Harvard Business School Press: Boston.

8 Ibid, Kaplan, R. S. and Norton, D. P. (2000b) (see note 2 above); Kaplan, R. S. and Norton, D. P. (2004b). Measuring the Strategic Readiness of Intangible Assets. *Harvard Business Review*, Vol. 82, No. 2, Feb, pp. 52–63.

9 Marr, B. and Adams, C. (2004). The Balanced Scorecard and Intangible Assets: Similar Ideas, Unaligned Concepts. *Measuring Business Excellence*, Vol. 8, No. 3, pp. 18–27.

10 Irwin, D. (2002). Strategy Mapping in the Public Sector. *Long Range Planning*, Vol. 35, No. 6, pp. 637–47.

11 See for example: Atkinson, A. A., Waterhouse, J. H. and Well, R. B. (1997). A Stakeholder Approach to Strategic Performance Measurement. *Sloan Management Review*, Spring, pp. 25–37; or Maltz, A. C., Reilly, R. R. and Shenhar, A. J. (2003). Beyond the Balanced Scorecard: Refining the Search for Organizational Success Measures. *Long Range Planning*, Vol. 36, No. 2, pp. 187–204; or Ahn, H. (2001). Applying the Balanced Scorecard Concept: An Experience Report. *Long Range Planning*, Vol. 34, No. 4, pp. 441–61; Ibid, Marr, B. and Adams, C. (2004) (see note 9 above).

12 Ibid (see note 9 above), Marr, B. and Adams, C. (2004).

13 Ibid, Neely, A., Adams, C. and Kennerley, M. (2002). *The Performance Prism: The Scorecard for Measuring and Managing Business Success*. FT Prentice Hall: London. For more information on the Performance Prism concept also visit www.cranfield.ac.uk/som/cbp.

14 The definition of a value creation map was facilitated by the definition of a map, provided by Huff, A. S. and Jenkins, M. (2002). Mapping Strategic Knowledge. Sage: London, pp. 2–15.

15 One of the earliest uses of influence diagrams was by J. Forrester to represent a causal loop in a feedback system. Later, Professor Ronald Howard from Stanford University and his colleague, Dr James Matheson, refined and popularised influence diagrams. See: Howard, R. A. and Matheson, J. E. (1990). *Principles and Applications of Decision Analysis*, Volume I. Strategic Decisions Group: Menlo Park, California; and Howard, R. A. and Matheson, J. E. (1990). *Principles and Applications of Decision Analysis*, Volume II. Strategic Decisions Group: Menlo Park, California; and Howard, R. A. (1965) Dynamic Inference, *Journal of the Operations Research Society of America*, Vol. 13, No. 5, Sept–Oct, pp. 712–33.

16 Initial strategy maps showed linkages between individual objectives (see Kaplan, R. S. and Norton, D. P. (1996b). Linking the Balanced Scorecard to Strategy. *California Management Review*, Vol. 39, No. 1, pp. 53–79), whereas later templates only visualize relationships between the perspectives (see Ibid, Kaplan, R.S. and Norton, D.P. (2004a) – see note 6 above).

17 For examples of influence diagrams see: Gupta, O. and Roos, G. (2001). Mergers and Acquisitions Through an Intellectual Capital Perspective. *Journal of Intellectual Capital*, Vol. 2, No. 3, pp. 297–309; or Marr, B., Pike, S. and Roos, G. (2005). Strategic Management of Intangible Assets and Value Drivers in R&D Organizations. *R&D Management*, Vol. 35, No. 2, pp. 111–24.

18 See for example the work by John Sterman at the Systems Dynamics Research Group at MIT; or Sterman, J. (2000). *Business Dynamics: Systems Thinking and Modelling for a Complex World*. McGraw-Hill.

19 If the organization wants to involve more than 15 people in the workshop, it is suggested that a number of workshops should be conducted. Experience has shown that smaller groups seem to work better.

20 Professor Jan Mouritsen of Copenhagen Business School, with other colleagues from Denmark, proposed the use of narratives for providing contextual information for intellectual capital statements. See for example: (DATI) Danish Agency of Trade and Industry (2000).

A Guideline for Intellectual Capital Statements – A Key to Knowledge Management. Ministry of Trade and Industry: Copenhagen.

21 Scott recommends the adoption of the language used in a serious conversation, meaning using only as many words as necessary. See: Scott, R. (1989). *Secrets of successful writing*. Reference Software International: San Francisco.

22 For more details see: www.shell.com

23 See for example: Becker, B. E., Huselid, M. A. and Ulrich, D. (2001). *The HR Scorecard: Linking People, Strategy, and Performance*. Harvard Business School Press: Boston, MA; or Keyes, J. (2005). *Implementing the IT Balanced Scorecard: Aligning It With Corporate Strategy*. Auerbach Publishers: Philadelphia; or Graeser, V., Pisanias, N. and Willcocks, L. P. (1998). *Developing the IT Scorecard: A Detailed Route Map to IT Evaluation and Performance Measurement Through the Investment Cycle*. Business Intelligence: London.

24 See for example: Nicholson, N. (1997). Evolutionary Psychology: Toward a New View of Human Nature and Organizational Society. *Human Relations*, Vol. 50, No. 9, pp. 1053–78.

25 This case study was jointly produced with Gary Crates, Head of Commercial, DHL, South-East Europe and North Africa.

26 This case study was jointly produced with Hanne Schou-Rode, Vice President Corporate Stakeholder Relations at Novo Nordisk and Charlotte Winther, Project Manager, Corporate Stakeholder Relations at Novo Nordisk.

27 These figures are as per 2005, based on the 2004 Annual Report.

28 This case study was jointly produced with Paul Neagle, CEO of the TT Club and Nick Baker, Business Planning Director at the TT Club.

29 This case study was jointly produced with Emma de-la-Haye, Carol Jones and Mark Rigby from the Performance Management and Governance Team.

30 Please note that the relative importance and relationships between the resources has been taken out to protect confidentiality and competitive information.

Part II

Managing performance in an enabled learning environment

Introduction to Part II: from command-and-control to learning

For any Strategic Performance Management initiative to become successful, we need to create the appropriate environment and routines in our organizations. What we have to move away from is the command-and-control mentality, in which backward-looking, pseudo-relevant metrics are being used to reward or punish people. In the command-and-control model, measures are used to assess people's performance and then make a judgement on whether they have achieved their targets or not. In an enabled learning environment, indicators are instead used to learn, challenge, and improve future performance.[1] This part of the book will outline how we can create an enabled learning environment, in which relevant performance indicators are collected and used as management information – management information that is then used by a broad spectrum of the organization's staff to assess and challenge its defined strategy and, in general, to help staff make better management decisions.

A parallel from educational assessments

There is an interesting parallel that we can find in the education world, where different forms of assessing students yield different outcomes. Traditionally, we tend to use *summative assessments* in schools. Summative assessment is an assessment, typically an exam or test, that determines the learning outcome of an academic programme, let's say a language course, at the end of the programme or at the end of a particular phase of the programme. Such assessments are judgements about the student's learning, mostly in the form of a grade, which is given compared to some standard or to the performance of others. These assessments often have high stakes attached to them, e.g. a qualification, access to university, etc. Most exams and standardized tests today are summative in nature. They are seen to provide reliable and comparative data, and the assumption is that such tests produce improvements in student learning. However, this assumption is questioned by many since these assessments are not designed to provide contextualized feedback that is useful for helping students and teachers during the course of a programme to improve learning.

By contrast, *formative assessment* is a feedback process into an ongoing programme in order to improve the learning. It occurs when teachers feed performance information back to students in ways that enable the student to learn and fine-tune or modify what they have been doing, or when students can engage in a similar, self-reflective process.

Whereas in summative assessments the result (e.g. grade) is at the centre of attention, in formative assessments the improvement of learning is the key objective. The former is backward-looking, whereas the latter is about positively impacting on the future. Formative assessment is more about detecting learning shortcomings early enough and doing something about them. It also engages the students and provides them with useful information about their progress and any learning gaps, which they can then use to make decisions about how to improve future learning.

Research in this area provides strong evidence that formative assessment is a powerful means to improve student learning, whereas summative assessments such as standardized exams can, in fact, have a harmful effect.[2] An article on the topic highlights the fact that most classroom testing encourages rote and superficial learning.[3] Professors Paul Black and Dylan William found that teachers often emphasize quantity of work over high quality. Actual assessment practices show that marking and grading are overemphasized, while giving useful advice is underemphasized. Overall, summative assessments tend to have a negative effect on student learning.

This problem is made worse by the fact that in many countries schools or universities are now being assessed on the outcome of such standardized summative assessments. The laudable aim is to make schools accountable for their teaching quality and the progress in learning achieved by the students. The numerical outcomes of these assessments are then used to create, for example, school league tables which are published in order to inform parents and students about the performance of different schools.[4]

The problem is that what is being measured is a proxy measure for learning that only measures the numerical outcome of the exams and not whether any real learning has taken place. This focus on proxy outcome measures leaves the system open to cheating and therefore can create dysfunctional behaviour. Teachers might only teach what is important to pass the exams with little actual learning, and students might try to do as little as they can get away with to meet the minimum requirement. Suddenly, the emphasis is not on learning, but on playing the numbers game.

The reasons for this dysfunctional system are two-fold. First, the wrong approach towards Performance Management is taken. Summative assessments focus on the past performance and provide little or no guidance on what could be done differently in future learning. Students who receive a grade at the end of a course can't do anything differently to improve it. At the same time, schools that are being assessed with a league table score receive no constructive feedback on how teaching quality could be improved. Second, the measures that are being used are proxy measures that are open to cheating. If we can't see any value in the measures we collect and don't agree with the way these measures are used, we get frustrated. This in turn has the effect that many people believe they might as well 'cheat the system' with the outcome that there is only superficial learning and a greater emphasis on quantity over high quality. In short, there is a massive loss of real learning potential.

Once we've been 'educated', we get a job (hopefully). In organizations we then tend to get much the same dysfunctional behaviour and gaming of numbers. If we don't collect and apply the most relevant indicators (instead of opting for the ones that are easy to measure or provide a view only of historic performance) and if we don't create an environment in which indicators are used to inform our decision-making and learning, then we are heading down the very same shallow track.

Managing performance in an enabled learning environment

In Part I of this book I focused on the strategic context of the organization and the process of describing and mapping the organizational strategy. This provides us with a business model, which is the starting point for Strategic Performance Management. In order to create an enabled learning environment we must now collect the relevant performance indicators and use them to analyse, review, and challenge

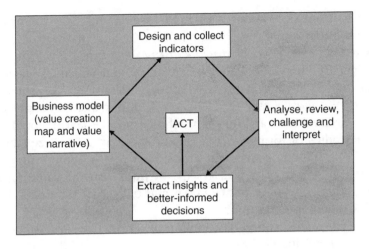

Managing performance in an enabled learning environment

our business model. We then need to interpret the indicators in order to extract management insights and make better-informed decisions. This in turn allows us to either review our business model or to act on the insights (see diagram above).[5]

Chapter 5 discusses how to develop relevant indicators and not just measure what is easy to measure. I will also discuss the limitations of measuring performance in a social context and the managerial consequences of this limitation. This will lead us to Chapter 6, in which I discuss how to create an enabled learning environment and how to redesign your performance review meetings. In Chapter 7 I will address how to analyse and interpret the performance data in order to challenge the business model, how to assess potential risks, and how to evaluate potential mergers and acquisitions.

References and endnotes

1   The importance of learning as opposed to controlling or reporting has recently been emphasized by various experts. For example, Professor Andy Neely highlighted the important role of learning from measurement data in his opening address at the 2004 PMA conference in Edinburgh and Karl-Erik Sveiby did the same in his opening address at the 2004 IC Congress in Helsinki. See also: Sveiby, K.-E. (2004). When Measurement Fails – Try Learning! *International Journal of Learning and Intellectual Capital*, Vol. 1, No. 3, pp. 370–76.

2 For a discussion about formative assessments, see for example: Black, P., Dylan, W., Harrison, C., Lee, C., and Marshall, B. (2003). *Assessment for Learning: Putting It into Practice*. Open University Press: Maidenhead; or Black, P. and William, D. Inside the Black Box: Raising Standards Through Classroom Assessment. *Phi Delta Kappan*, October 1998. Black and William recognize that standardized tests are very limited measures of learning and report that studies of formative assessment show an effect size (the ratio of the average improvement in test scores in the innovation to the range of scores of typical groups of pupils on the same tests) on standardized tests of between 0.4 and 0.7, larger than most known educational interventions.

3 See: www.fairtest.org, The Value of Formative Assessment, *The Examiner*, Winter 1999.

4 For UK school league table results see: www.dfes.gov.uk/performancetables

5 The thinking presented here is an evolution based on extensive experience and research conducted at the Centre for Business Performance at Cranfield School of Management Performance, where the Planning Value Chain was developed. The basic idea of it is that organizations need to start by developing a business model that reflects their basic hypothesis about their business; only then should they start collecting data and analysing and interpreting that data to extract insights. We then need to communicate these insights in order to make decisions and take actions.

5

Performance indicators

This chapter focuses on how to design appropriate performance indicators. It explores the role of measurement in organizations and why we need indicators. A key challenge is that many of the things we would like to measure are inherently difficult, if not impossible, to measure. I therefore take a look at the limitations of measurement and its implications for the usage of performance indicators. This chapter then outlines how to design meaningful indicators and collect the relevant data that allows organizations to assess and challenge their strategy. Questions addressed in this chapter include:

- Why do we need performance measures?
- What can we really measure, and where are the limitations of measurement?
- What implications do the limitations have on the usage of measures?
- What is the difference between measurement and assessment, and between a measure and an indicator?
- How can we design meaningful performance indicators?
- How can we collect and report relevant performance data?

Why do we need performance indicators?

Measurement has a central role in our society. Take this quote:

> . . . when you can measure what you are talking about and express it in numbers you know something about it; but when you cannot measure it, when you cannot express it in numbers, your knowledge is of a meagre and unsatisfactory kind.

This passing comment by Sir William Thomson (later Lord Kelvin) in a lecture to the Institution of Civil Engineers in 1883, is one of the most frequently cited quotes in measurement circles. The sentiment of this statement can be traced back to the philosopher Philolaus, in the fifth century B.C., who said that 'without numbers, we can understand nothing and know nothing'.[1] In 'business-speak', these statements are often reduced to simple homilies, such as 'you can't manage anything unless you measure it' or Tom Peters' well-known 'what gets measured gets done'. In his book about business Performance Measurement, my colleague Professor Andy Neely provides a more considered view and provides four key reasons why organizations measure performance. These are to: check position; communicate position; confirm priorities; and compel progress.[2]

- *Check position*: measures are used to establish where we are as an organization. It is hard to define strategies or plan improvement initiatives if we don't know our starting point. Measurement also enables us to compare ourselves with other companies to understand where we are in comparison to others. Once the position is established, measures allow us to monitor our progress. Here the flying of an airplane is often used as an analogy. For a plane you need to know where you are – your point of departure (A) – and then you need to know where you want to go – your destination (B). This allows the crew to map out how to get from A to B. Once on their way, measures provided by the various instruments on the dashboard enable the crew to monitor their progress.
- *Communicate position*: measures give you a means of communicating performance. These can be voluntary or legislative communications. Legislative requirements, for example taxation and accounting purposes, force organizations to produce things like annual reports. In many industries regulators require organizations to communicate performance. And increasingly organizations voluntarily produce reports on issues such as customer service, environmental performance and whether they are meeting their social responsibilities.
- *Confirm priorities*: once measures are in place they allow organizations to highlight what matters the most. Measures enable us to improve organizational control, i.e. control of costs and management control.
- *Compel progress*: measures influence people's behaviour and attitudes. Here the homily 'you get what you measure' is often used to demonstrate the point. If organizations measure aspects of performance, it sends a signal that this is what is important. 'Show me what you will measure and I will show you what I will do. Confuse

Figure 5.1   Reasons for measuring performance

me as to what you will measure and even I do not know what I will do.'[3] This is especially true if measures are linked to reward systems.

Others have identified seven purposes of performance measures in firms, namely look back, look ahead, compensate, motivate, roll up, cascade down, and compare.[4] There are many other categorizations of reasons why we are measuring performance in organizations; however, I think they can all be summarized into the following three main categories (see also Figure 5.1):

1 *Reporting and compliance* – measures are used to communicate with the organization's stakeholders, be it either voluntarily or compulsorily for compliance reasons.
2 *Controlling people's behaviour* – measures are used to motivate people and change their behaviour. Measures are used to quantify the value of compensation for compliance with objectively verifiable standards of work.[5]
3 *Strategic decision-making and organizational learning* – measures are used to inform management decisions, to challenge strategic assumptions and to continuously learn and improve.

It is this last reason, measuring for strategic decision-making and learning, that is the focus of this book. As outlined in Part I, Strategic Performance Management is about gaining strategic insights that allow people to challenge strategic assumptions, refine strategic thinking, and inform strategic decision-making and learning. And measurement should support this process. But let me first define what is meant by measurement, and explore the measurement limitations in today's organizations.

What we can and can't 'measure'

Measurement has been defined as the assignment of numerals to represent properties.[6] It is seen as the assignment of particular mathematical characteristics to conceptual entities in such as way as to permit an unambiguous mathematical description of every situation involving the entity and the arrangements of all occurrences of it in a quasi-serial order.[7] Whereas these technical definitions have been especially useful in disciplines such as physics, in management we talk about organizational performance measures. These have been defined as parameters used to quantify the efficiency and/or effectiveness of past action.[8]

> An *effectiveness* measure of performance reveals how many units of the purpose were accomplished. It is a response to the question: 'Are we doing the right things?' On the other hand, an *efficiency* measure of performance reveals how many units of the purpose were accomplished per unit of resources consumed. It is a response to the question: 'Are we doing the things in the right way?'[9]

Often the emphasis in measurement is on quantifications and numbers, with the intention to provide us with an *objective*, *uniform* and *rigorous* picture of reality. However, this seems to work in some areas better than in others. We find it easy to quantify things like profits, return on assets, or cycle times and we can count incoming orders, service visits, or rejected deliveries. Some things though are not easily counted or quantified. Things like organizational culture, our know-how, the strengths of customer relationships or the reputation of our brand are all inherently difficult if not impossible to measure. At the same time, as we have seen from Chapter 3, it is often these less tangible resources that drive our future performance.

Albert Einstein, one of the great thinkers of the twentieth century, emphasized that 'Not everything that can be counted counts, and not everything that counts can be counted'. The problem arises when we use numbers to measure things that can never be measured in a 'measurement' sense. The author David Boyle, in his book on counting and numbers, writes that

> 'We admit that numbers can't reveal everything, but we try to force them to anyway. We tend to solve the problem by measuring ever-more ephemeral aspects of life, constantly bumping up against the central paradox of the whole problem, which is that

the most important things are just not measurable. The difficulty comes because they can *almost* be counted. And often we believe we have to try just so that we can get a handle on the problem. And so it is that politicians can't measure poverty, so they measure the number of people on welfare. Or they can't measure intelligence, so they measure exam results or IQ. Doctors measure blood cells rather than health, and people all over the world measure money rather than success. They might some-times imply almost the same thing, but often they have little more than a habitual connection with one another. They tend to go together, that's all.[10]

When it comes to the more intangible aspects of our organizations we must rely on proxies or indirect measures.[11] And these often only capture a fraction of what we want to measure. Figure 5.2 depicts the example discussed earlier, where we want to measure intelligence but what we actually measure is IQ, which measures only limited dimen-sions of intelligence. Organizations are often prepared to sacrifice rich realities in order to achieve alleged rigour and clarity through meas-ures. The American social theorist Daniel Yankelovich said that:

> The first step is to measure whatever can be easily measured. This is OK as far as it goes. The second step is to disregard that which can't be measured or give it an arbitrary quantitative value. This is artificial and misleading. The third step is to pre-sume that what can't be measured easily isn't very important. This is blindness. The fourth step is to say that what can't easily be measured doesn't really exist. This is suicide.[12]

The implications of these measurement limits are discussed below.

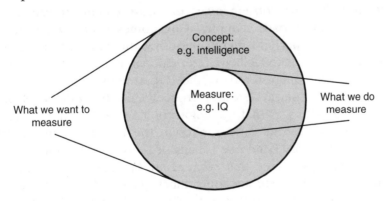

Figure 5.2 Limitations of measuring intangibles

Implications for the usage of measures

The mechanical objectivity that we often aim for in organizational measurement serves as an alternative to personal trust.[13] Measures provide a moral distance and make knowledge impersonal in a quest for objectivity. Objectivity is required for the first two measurement reasons outlined above:

1 Reporting and compliance requires objectivity and in many cases even external auditing. Organizations use external auditors to provide an objective verification of the numbers they put in their annual reports. Some companies such as Shell, for example, go even further and also use external auditors to audit their numbers on environmental and social performance.
2 Using measures as a means of controlling people's behaviour necessitates objectivity, especially if measures are linked to reward and compensation.

In both scenarios personal trust is replaced with what are believed to be objective numbers. There is, in fact, a complex relationship between trust and quantification. For example, when farmers and merchants didn't trust each other to provide the right amount of wheat, they could use the standard barrel stuck to the wall of the town hall, which would measure the agreed local bushel.[14] It has been demonstrated that throughout history we were often able to win greater trust for claims by giving them quantitative expressions.[15] Nevertheless, it is dangerous to replace trust with measures, since the big assumption is that we can measure everything that matters. The fact is that what matters the most in modern-day organizations is difficult to measure and often impossible to express in meaningful numbers.

The dysfunctional consequences of measurements replacing trust can be seen in myriad examples. One comes from food standards. Similar to the farmer and merchants using the standard barrel, today we rely on standards to facilitate international trade. The US food standards, which are administered by the Department of Agriculture, specify that, for example, a 'US Fancy broccoli stalk' has a diameter of not less then 2½ inches, or that the colour of a Grade A canned tomato is at least 90% red.[16] The same applies to the European Union, which specifies the standard bend of a banana or the size and shape of apples. We presumably all agree that what really matters are the intangible factors such as the taste and nutritional quality of this produce, but these are again difficult to measure. The standards are almost entirely based on the easy-to-measure physical appearance of the produce.

And, in fact, studies have found that this has encouraged farmers to use dangerous pesticides, not to increase yields, but for the sole purpose of maintaining cosmetic appearance to meet such standards.[17]

Problems with measurement and their implications for reporting and compliance

Measurement for external reporting and compliance can be compared to summative assessments, as discussed above. Here, measures provide objective assessments about the overall effectiveness, impact, and/or outcomes of organizational performance.[18] Reports to regulators or financial reports fall into this category of stakeholder reporting and compliance. According to the Financial Accounting Standards Board, the role of financial reporting is to provide useful information about the performance of an organization. However, with an ever-increasing gap between the book value and market value of companies, accountants are trying to get a handle on objectively measuring intangibles. The problem is that currently there are no meaningful standards to report on intangible resources, such as relationships, know-how, or culture.

Thomas Johnson and Robert Kaplan wrote in their influential book, *Relevance Lost*, that the decreasing relevance of accounting is partly due to the increasingly mechanical use of management accounting by uninspired executives trained to manage by numbers.[19] While accountants are working hard to regain relevance, many organizations are exploring alternative routes of providing more relevant information in the form of voluntary reports. One example is the global investment bank and financial services firm UBS. They realized that their annual financial report was insufficient in communicating the value of the intangible drivers of their business. UBS therefore spent 14 pages of their annual review explaining their value drivers and how they are measured. In the introduction to that section, USB writes:

> To the outside world, our strength is often perceived as being derived from the financial success of our business. Yet, at the same time, we also believe our strength is projected through other more intangible factors – factors such as the values we share, our culture, our client relationships and our brands. We have distilled these factors into the five key elements of Client Focus, Innovation and Learning, Talent and Culture, Brand and Identity, and Financial Intelligence. They are the value drivers of our business.[20]

There is a clear requirement for summative Performance Measurement to enable organizations to report to external stakeholders or comply with regulations and laws. This is not a problem as long as organizations understand that these measures are designed for that purpose only. Much care should be taken before any of those measures are used for any of the other measurement purposes.

Problems with measurement and their implications for controlling people's behaviour

Measures can be used to influence what people do. The theoretical model behind this is called 'Agency Theory'.[21] Its argument goes that employees (agents) don't have the same objectives as the owner or instigator of a business (principal). This is why the principal puts measures in place that will guide the behaviour of the agent, and therefore align their objectives. However, this model can only work if the principal can measure all critical dimensions of performance. If the principal misses some aspects of performance it leaves a gap. And as we have seen from the discussion above, this gap between what we want to measure and what we can measure is endemic.

Marshall Meyer, professor at the Wharton School of the University of Pennsylvania, argues in his book on Performance Measurement, that

> people will exploit the gap between what we want to measure and what we can measure by delivering exactly what is measured rather than the performance that is sought but cannot be measured.[22]

This causes dysfunctional behaviour and sub-optimal performance. Let's take the example of a sales manager, whose main objective it is to visit customers in order to introduce a set of new products, which these customers will hopefully want to buy. Figure 5.3 shows that optimal performance is comprised of some easy-to-measure dimensions, e.g. number of sales visits and amount of time spent with customers, as well as some difficult-to-measure dimensions of performance, e.g. quality of the sales visits and preparation for the visit.[23]

What usually happens is that only the easy-to-measure dimensions of performance are measured and then linked to a reward system. It is therefore not surprising that, in many firms, the number of sales visits sharply rises towards the end of the month just before the numbers are collected. The fact that these visits are of low quality and with little preparation is not taken into account. UK government targets on

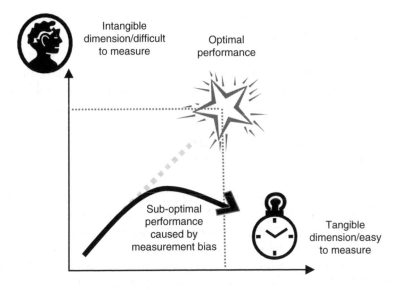

Figure 5.3   Biased measurement systems[24]

waiting times to see your doctor are another good example. Since doctors are assessed on meeting a 48-hour target from making an appointment to seeing the patient, most surgeries have now intro-duced a rule that patients can only book appointments up to two days in advance (even if they don't want one until next week). Therefore, every doctor meets his or her targets.

The creation of an environment in which trust is replaced with numbers to increase control causes social stratification. It is argued that by imposing control measures on people, it will invariably acti-vate the self-centred drives of organization members and as a result, rank, territoriality, possessiveness, fear, and anger will dominate social relationships. Furthermore, it has long been argued that no measure-ment system can be designed to preclude dysfunctional behaviours.[25] Meyer says:

> Compensating people for performance on multiple measures is extremely difficult. Paying people on a single measure creates enough dysfunctions. Paying them on many measures creates even more. The problem is combining dissimilar measures into an overall evaluation of performance and hence compensation. If measures are combined formulaically, people will game the for-mula. If measures are combined subjectively, people will not understand the connection between measured performance and their compensation.[26]

The above arguments therefore seriously question the usage of measures for influencing behaviour in a command-and-control fashion.

> Controlling machines makes sense; however, trying to control the behaviour of people creates negative and unpredictable consequences. For instance, showing a child how to cross the street by holding his or her hand for the first few times makes a lot of sense. Holding the child's hand for the rest of his or her life makes no sense at all, and interferes with growth.[27]

In his book on measuring and managing performance, Robert Austin, Professor at Harvard Business School, makes a very strong case that measurement for controlling people's behaviour does not work in today's organizations. Instead, we should focus our efforts on what he calls 'informational measurement' used for learning and strategic decision-making.[28] In the next section we will take a closer look at what measurement for strategic decision-making and learning means.

Measurement for strategic decision-making and learning

This book focuses on measurement for decision-making and learning. For this, the meaning of measurement is extended to not only focus on the narrow sense of measurement used in physics or mathematics. Here the words 'performance assessment' are used, rather then 'measurement'. It is, therefore, not only about quantification and the assignment of numerals. Performance assessment is about the systematic collection of information to enable comparison of a given situation or status relative to known objectives or goals; it enables organizations to evaluate performance. Inherent in it is the notion of value. Performance assessment can, therefore, not only take the form of numerals but also the form of written descriptions, symbols, or colour codes.

As we all know, the perceived value of something is in the eye of the beholder. For some of us, a Rolex or Patek Philippe wristwatch is valuable and we are willing to pay several thousand dollars or euros to own one. We might see the value in its mechanical perfections, in the craftsmanship, in the design, or we might value it as a prestige symbol. If we only want a device to tell us the time, a simple Timex or Swatch would do the job perfectly. This means, in order to assess the value of something, we need to understand the value system and, in this case, how the watch fits into this value system.

The same is true for organizational resources and competencies. The know-how of building engines is essential for Honda but of little value to a financial services firm. This is why we have to start with the value creation map. It provides us with the necessary strategic information of how value is created and what resources and competencies matter; it therefore supplies the starting point for an evaluation. It also allows us to take into account the context-specific value and interdependencies between resources. For example, it is impossible to value a brand name without taking into account all the other important factors, such as reputation, people, processes, etc. Cases such as Enron have shown how a brand name can disappear overnight if the supporting resources fall away.

Management writer Charles Handy said 'Measuring more is easy, measuring better is hard', and Professor Marshall Meyer adds that 'measuring performance is difficult and the choice of performance measures is often arbitrary, since it is difficult to prove that any one measure is better than others'.[29] Too many organizations brainstorm what they could possibly measure and therefore end up with a shockingly long list of everything that is easy to measure. Instead, we need to start with the value creation map. The value creation map tells us the most important components of our strategy and it will therefore guide us to measure what really matters.

We have learnt that in any social context it is hard, if not impossible, to capture the whole truth in one measure. I prefer therefore to use the word 'indicator', rather than 'measure'. An indicator 'indicates' a level of performance, but it does not claim to 'measure' it. If, for example, we introduce a new indicator to assess customer satisfaction levels, this indicator will give us an indication of how customers feel; however, it will never 'measure' customer satisfaction in its totality.

In Strategic Performance Management, we therefore talk about performance assessment, rather than Performance Measurement, and about performance indicators, rather than performance measures (see Figure 5.4). The value creation map guides the assessment and the

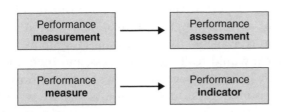

Figure 5.4 Towards assessment and indicators

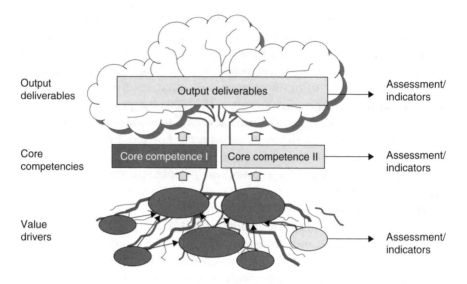

Output deliverables

Core competencies

Value drivers

Assessment/ indicators

Assessment/ indicators

Assessment/ indicators

Figure 5.5 Assessment and indicators for strategic elements

development of performance indicators for each of the elements on the map (see Figure 5.5).

Assessing performance and selecting indicators

Dee Hook, founder of the Visa network, said that:

> in years ahead, we must get beyond numbers and the language of mathematics to understand, evaluate and account for such intangibles as learning, intellectual capital, community, beliefs and principles, or the stories we tell of our tribe's values and prosperity will be increasingly false.[30]

Many books on Performance Measurement often assume that all relevant performance data is either already available or can be easily collected. Unfortunately, this is mostly not the case. Even though we might have a lot of performance data in our organizations, it is often not the relevant and meaningful information we need. Instead of relying on data that is available in our existing IT systems, we should first identify what we would really like to assess, and then compare it with what we already have in place. This allows us to see how close we can get with our existing indicators to what it is that we want to assess.

In many cases, the information we want is not at all, or only insufficiently, available. This means we have to collect more data. One way to get a good idea about how to assess performance in a particular area is to ask the people who are most closely involved in that area. Far too often we impose measures on people. Assessing performance for strategic learning means that people have to believe in the indicators and use them to inform their decision-making. Therefore, involving people (both internal and external) is critically important.

Not only should we involve people in the selection of possible indicators, but also in the assessment of performance and the collection of data. Many studies have shown that perceptional assessment is as reliable, if not more reliable, than archival data.[31] It can provide richer insights into the real level of performance because our brain is able to comprehend performance more holistically. The way we involve people is to ask them to, for example, rank competitors, evaluate the service delivery, assess the level of relationships with different suppliers, etc. These assessments can take the form of numerals, or grades; however, they can also take the form of a written assessment. Written assessments are able to capture much more information and allow us to more naturally communicate assessment outcomes. If numerals are used, these should be supplemented with at least a comments field to provide some explanatory narrative assessment in addition to a number.

Traditionally, organizations have used archival data or larger-scale surveys to access performance. Below, different data collection methods are outlined to provide some alternative ways of collecting performance information and perception data:

- *Surveys and questionnaires* provide a relatively inexpensive tool to collect data from a large pool of people who can be at different locations.[32] This can be done via mail, e-mail, or internet. One big problem with this is that there has been a huge influx of surveys over the past few years as more and more organizations require data for their non-financial indicators. The consequence of this is that it is getting harder to make people complete a survey. It is always a good idea to reduce the amount of time and effort required to collect performance data, not only for your organization, but also for your customers, employees, suppliers, etc.

  It has been argued that surveys and questionnaires are one of the most difficult data collection methods to do well, as it takes a significant time to construct clearly worded questions that will result in useful and valid data. Surveys should always be pilot tested on a number of people before being used. This allows mistakes to be eliminated and clarifying questions to be added before the surveys are sent out.

- *Observations* allow us to collect information by observing situations or activities with little or no manipulation of the environment. The observer can either take the role of a passive onlooker/outsider, or can become involved in activities and, therefore, take the role of partial or full participant observer.

> The power of using observation methods is that it engages all of our senses not just our sight. It enables us to talk in and make sense of the entire experience through our nose (smell), eyes (sight), ears (hearing), mouth (taste), and body (touch). Unlike other data collection methods, observation data can provide us with a more holistic understanding of the phenomenon we're studying.[33]

Observation data has the purpose of describing, which can take the format of score sheets, checklists, narrative reports, video taping or audio taping, depending on the level of detailed contextual information required.

- *In-depth interviews* are guided conversations with people, rather than structured queries. They involve putting forward open-ended (how, why, what) questions in a conversationally friendly and non-threatening manner.[34] Interviews can be conducted face-to-face or via telephone or video-conference. Interviews enable us to interact directly with respondents and may result in new insights about performance and provide examples, stories, and critical incidents that are helpful in order to understand performance more holistically.[35]
- *Focus groups* are facilitated group discussions in which participants can express and share their ideas, opinions and experiences. They provide a unique and interactive way to gather information and allow the collection of rich, qualitative information. Typically, a focus group will comprise between 5 and 20 pre-selected people who are willing to participate.
- *Mystery shopping* is the assessment of a service by a 'secret shopper' posing as a client or customer. Some companies have in-house programmes, whereby the company hires its own mystery shoppers; other firms hire external suppliers to provide this service.
- *Peer-to-peer assessment* is the assessment of performance in which participants vote or assess each other's performance. This can either be done openly or anonymously. This enables people to learn from each other and to consider their own performance from other people's perspective.

Organizations have become much more creative about the way they are assessing performance. Call centres now regularly audiotape phone conversations between service agents and customers. You might recall an automated message before you are connected to a service agent notifying you that the call might be recorded for training purposes. Many call centres now use a coach to listen to conversations and then sit down with service agents to see how they could improve the qualitative aspects of their calls.

One organization introduced two types of carpets with sensors in the entrance hall, one red and one green. Whenever employees entered or left the building they could choose to step on either the green carpet, indicating they were happy, or on the red, indicating they were unhappy. Another organization automated their phone system to play a message once a conversation had ended, asking customers to rate their experience by pressing a button on their phone. Many service providers, such as hotels or banks, use focus groups to identify what really matters to customers and then employ mystery shoppers to assess service levels according to the identified criteria. There are many more fascinating ways of collecting qualitative performance data - for more information see, for example, the *Handbook of Qualitative Research*.[36]

It is a good idea to collect performance data using different techniques and methodologies. This allows organizations to contrast and compare the information gathered from the different methods. This is called 'triangulation'. The rationale behind it is that the more information we have from as many sources as possible - which all have advantages, disadvantages, and different biases - the greater the likelihood that the information is reliable.

Organizations are often unaware of biases in their data. A frequently cited anecdote is the Wald story.[37] Abraham Wald was a statistician during World War II who helped the air force to assess where airplanes were most vulnerable to enemy fire. The plan was to subsequently reinforce the most vulnerable parts of the plane. Each airplane was examined for bullet holes and the areas that were disproportionately more often hit than others were identified. The air force naturally concluded that the areas with the most bullet holes should be reinforced. However, Wald made them aware of the bias in the sample. Only airplanes that returned to the base were examined and included in the analysis! This, therefore, shows that the areas with the many bullet holes have proven able to sustain enemy fire and so these planes returned safely, whereas the areas with no bullet holes might be the best to reinforce since planes hit in these areas did not return.

Triangulation, on the other hand, means that organizations collect data from different data sources (e.g. interviews with board members, middle managers, and front-line workers), use different methodologies (e.g. survey 70% and interview 30% of your suppliers), or use different people to conduct the data collection. This can reduce bias and increase reliability.

Designing a performance indicator[38]

This section presents a template for designing performance indicators. Completing this template ensures that organizations develop a sound and comprehensive understanding of each of their performance indicators. This is important because it ensures that the data is consistently collected and interpreted. It eradicates the ambiguity, ambivalence, and inconsistency that we see far too often with performance indicators. If indicators are to become the basis for decision-making and learning, it is essential that everyone understands what these indicators mean, how reliable they are, where the data comes from, etc. The template presented here can be used to develop completely new indicators or to develop a more comprehensive picture of existing performance indicators. Each aspect of the performance indicator design template is explained below and summarized in Figure 5.6 (see opposite).

- *Name* – any performance indicator needs a name which should clearly explain what the indicator is about.
- *Strategic element being assessed* – the value creation map has identified the different strategic elements (resources, core competencies, and output deliverables). Which of these elements the indicator is helping to assess is clarified here.
- *Purpose* – what is the main purpose of and reason for assessing performance of this element? Why is this indicator being introduced? Do we really need it? Is there any particular issue that is being observed and requires indicators? Is it to establish where we are at this point in time with any of our resources or competencies? Is it to establish a base line for our output deliverables? Is it to monitor progress and the delivery of our strategy? Or is it to test our assumptions of cause and effect relationships between specific strategic elements?
- *Data collection method* – this describes the method by which the construct will be assessed and how the data will be collected. Here it is important to keep the purpose of the indicator in mind. Far

Name	Clear indicator name
Strategic element being assessed	*Identification of what strategic element is being assessed (e.g. a specific resource, a core competence, one of the output deliverables)*
Purpose	*Description of the key purpose*
Data collection method	*Short description of how the data is collected*
• Formula and/or scale	*Identification of the scale used to assess performance*
• Source of data	*Identification of where the data comes from*
• Frequency	*How often is the indicator measured?*
• Data entry	*Who is collecting and updating the data?*
Ownership	*Identification of the person(s) or function(s) responsible for the measured element*
Targets and performance thresholds	*Identification of targets, benchmarks, and thresholds for traffic lighting*
Reporting/notifications	
• Audience/access	*Identifies the audience, outlets, and access rights*
• Reporting frequency	*Identifies how often the indicator is reported*
• Reporting formats	*Identifies how the performance is presented (numerical, graphical, narrative formats)*
• Notifications/workflows	*Identifies proactive notifications and workflows*
Expiry/revision date	*Identifies an expiration or revision date*
Cost estimate	*Estimation of the costs incurred by introducing and maintaining this indicator*
Confidence level	*Evaluation: e.g. good ☺ fair ☺ imperfect ☹*
	Written comment

Figure 5.6 Template for designing performance indicators

too often the data collection method is an automatic response or a selection of traditional methods that might not be able to provide the necessary insights. Instead, it is important to consider the strengths, weaknesses, or appropriateness of different data collection methods.[39] Here, the designer of an indicator should include a brief description of the data collection method, specify the source of the data, how often the data is collected, what scale will be used to measure it, and who is in charge of collecting and updating the data.

☐ *Formula and measurement scale* – here the designer of the indicators identifies how the data will be captured. Is it possible to create a formula? Is it an aggregated indicator that is composed of other indicators? Here the designer also specifies if one of the following scales is used: nominal (numbering of categories, e.g. football players); ordinal (determination of greater or less, e.g. street numbers); interval (determination of intervals, e.g. temperature in Fahrenheit or Celsius); and ratio (determination of equality and ratio in a continuum with a real zero, e.g. length, time, temperature in Kelvin); or whether the indicator is not expressed in any numerical form.

☐ *Source of the data* identifies where the data comes from. This ensures that the designer of an indicator thinks about the access to data. Is the data readily available? Is it feasible to collect the data? Will the data collection method, for example interviews with senior managers, provide honest information? Maybe different data collection methods could be combined?

☐ *Frequency of data collection* identifies how often the data for that indicator should be collected. Some indicators are collected continuously, others hourly, daily, monthly, or even annually. Here it is important to think about what frequency provides sufficient data for that indicator and how often is it feasible to measure. Organizations might want to continuously track indicators for website usage since some of them might be readily available from the server reports. Indicators for employee satisfaction might only be feasible once or twice a year and need to be linked to the employee survey. However, some firms are experimenting with random daily satisfaction surveys to a subset of employees.

☐ *Data entry* identifies the person, function, or external agency responsible for the data collection and data updates. This could be an internal person or function, or an external agency, since many organizations outsource the collection of specific indicators. This is especially common for indicators such as customer satisfaction, reputation, brand awareness, and employee satisfaction.

■ *Ownership* – identifies the person(s) or function(s) responsible for the management of the strategic element that is being assessed. This can be an individual employee or it can be a department.

■ *Targets and performance thresholds* – identify the desired level of performance in a specified timeframe (e.g. 5% increase of market share by the end of March next year) as well as the performance direction. Performance directions indicate at a glance whether it is better to exceed the planned target, hit the target value exactly, or whether it is better to stay beneath the planned value. Financial results or employee satisfaction are usually indicators where the 'bigger is better' performance direction applies (the bigger the number of performance achieved in this area the better). On the other hand customer complaints or harmful emissions are indicators where 'smaller is better' (the fewer customer complaints a company receives or the less a company pollutes the environment the better).

An example for 'balance' or 'target is best' would be quality indicators with SPC (Statistical Process Control) charts where there are upper as well as lower limits that should not be exceeded and it is best to hit the targeted tolerance range. Many firms use 'traffic lighting' to illustrate the levels of performance. Here, the designer of an indicator would therefore specify the thresholds for red/underperformance, amber/medium performance, green/good performance, and sometimes blue/over performance. Here, it is also worth thinking about internal or external benchmarks; these can be derived from past performance, from other similar organizations or departments, or from forecasts.

- *Reporting* – Here, the designer of an indicator identifies the way the performance indicator is reported. It identifies the audience, access restrictions, the reporting frequency, reporting formats and possible notifications and workflows.
  - *Audience and access* identifies who will receive the reports on this performance indicator, possible outlets or reports, as well as possible access restrictions. Indicators can have different audiences. It might therefore be a good idea to identify primary, secondary, and tertiary audiences. The primary audience will be the people directly involved in the management and decision-making related to the strategic element that is being assessed. The secondary audience could be other parts of the organization which would benefit from seeing the data. A possible tertiary audience could be external stakeholders.

    This part of the design process would also look at possible reports (existing or new) in which this indicator would be included. The designer of an indicator should also consider access restrictions to this indicator. There might be reasons why the access to certain indicators is restricted to individuals, groups of people, departments, or outsiders.

☐ *Reporting frequency* identifies how often this indicator is reported. If the indicator is to serve a decision-making purpose within the organization, then the indicator needs to provide timely information. The reporting frequency can be different from the measurement frequency. An indicator might be collected hourly, but then reported as part of a quarterly performance meeting.

☐ *Reporting formats* identify how the data is best presented. They should clarify whether the indicator is reported as, for example, a number, a narrative, a table, a graph or a chart. The best results are usually achieved if performance is reported in a mix of numerical, graphical and narrative formats (see also section on Reporting Performance Indicators). Considerations here also include the presentation of a data series and past performance. A graph containing past performance might be very useful in order to analyse trends over time and this could also include targets and benchmarks. Increasingly too, organizations use traffic lights or speedometer dials to present performance data.

☐ *Notifications/workflows* identify proactive notifications and possible workflows. Workflows are predefined and automated business processes in which documents, information or tasks are passed from one person or group of persons to others. Notifications are predefined and automated messages and involve the proactive push of performance data, messages or alarm notifications to predefined individuals or groups. For example, e-mail notifications or workflows could be automatically triggered if an indicator is updated or moves over a predefined threshold.

■ *Expiry/revision date* – indicators are sometimes introduced for a specific period of time only (e.g. for the duration of major projects or to keep on eye on restructuring efforts). The common practice is that a significant number of indicators are introduced once and collected for ever because no one ever goes back and identifies the indicators that are not needed any more. Other obviously temporary indicators are introduced without giving them an expiration date; however, for those indicators a revision date should be set that allows the designers to review the template and check whether it is still valid.

■ *Estimated costs* – another aspect that should be considered is the costs of introducing and maintaining a performance indicator. There is often an implicit assumption by many managers and measurement experts that creating and maintaining measurement systems does not incur significant costs.[40] However, on the contrary, measurement is expensive, especially if the indicators are supposed to be relevant and meaningful to aid decision-making and learning.[41] Costs can include the administrative and/or outsourcing costs of collecting the data, as well as the efforts needed to analyse and report on the performance.

- *Confidence level* – once the above aspects of an indicator have been addressed, it is time to think about the validity of the indicators. To what extent do the indicators enable us to assess the given strategic element? For financial performance, the confidence level would normally be high, since established tools are available to measure it. However, when we try to measure our intangibles, such as organizational culture, the confidence level would necessarily go down a peg or two. The assessment of the confidence level is subjective but forces anyone who designs an indicator to think about how well an indicator is actually 'measuring' what it was that it set out to 'measure'. Organizations have different preferences of how to express confidence levels; some use percentages (0–100%), others use grades (1–5; or low, medium, high), colour codes (e.g. red, amber, green), or symbols (such as smiley faces). In addition, it is suggested that a brief written comment is included to clarify the level of confidence.

Reporting performance indicators

Performance indicators are rarely reported in a manner that gives people sufficient information about the indicator. Any ambiguity leads to doubts which in turn hamper decision-making and learning. It is therefore important to provide a comprehensive picture of an indicator. The design template outlined in Figure 5.6, provides much of the information needed to improve the way performance is reported. In order to report performance comprehensively, the following information should be included:

- *Name of the indicator* (see section above)
- *Strategic element being assessed* – what strategic element is being assessed (see section above). Often the best way to do this is to provide a picture of the value creation map and highlight the element that is being assessed.
- *Purpose* – why is the indicator being used (see section above)?
- *Confidence level* – how confident are we that this is a 'good' or valid indicator (see section above)?

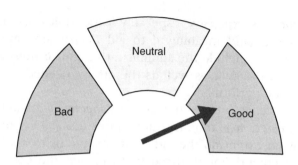

Figure 5.7 Speedometer display

- *Data collection method* – it is important to clarify where the data comes from and how performance was assessed (see section above).
- *Narrative assessment of performance* – any report of a performance indicator should have a short written assessment of the performance that highlights what the data is telling us. This allows organizations to capture the performance in natural language, which makes it easier for people to interpret.
- *Traffic light assessment* – provides at-a-glance assessment of the performance. Colour coding and traffic lighting is very intuitive and useful for most people. However, beware that there are a lot of people who have difficulties distinguishing colours (especially the difference between red and green), which is better known as colour blindness. It is estimated that about 8% of males and 1% of females have difficulties with colour vision impairments and, therefore, it may be appropriate to complement or even replace colour-coding with symbols or icons (like thumb up or down, smiley face, etc.) in order to indicate performance.[42] Some organizations prefer speedometer style displays that indicate current performance in comparison to the targets or expectations (see Figure 5.7).
- *Numerical presentation* (if applicable) – this provides a number of the indicator status. However, in order to be meaningful, this number has to be put into context of expectations, targets, or benchmarks. A number on its own is completely meaningless unless we understand the scale and the relative performance. This can be provided in tabular format or in a graph (see next point).
- *Graphical representation* – performance representations should be made easily understandable. One way to do this is in graphical representations. Generally speaking, line graphs or bar charts seem to work well. They allow organizations to show past performance levels and allow inclusion of target lines and benchmark information (see Figure 5.8).

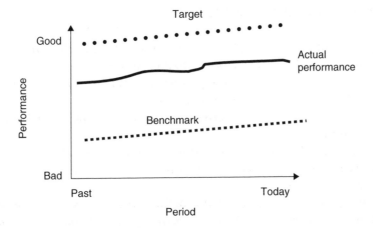

Figure 5.8 Line graph display

- *Comment by owner* – the person(s) or function(s) responsible for the management of the strategic element that is being assessed should provide a comment on what this performance level means and whether there are any actions or initiatives being taken. This engages people in the active review of indicators and provides a starting point for a discussion or dialogue about improvement.

There are other elements and information that could also be included. To identify the necessary components, it is best to think about the audience and their requirements. In Strategic Performance Management, data is primarily reported to facilitate learning and strategic decision-making. And so the more *useful* the information that is provided the better, since it consequently ensures people understand the indicator and what it means better.

Air force pilots are trained to trust the measures that they get from their instruments. They learn not to look out of the window but just to concentrate on the instruments. In a fighter jet, it is possible to reliably measure all critical dimensions of performance and, therefore, enable the pilot to base his or her decisions and actions on the measures available. In the socio-cultural environment of modern day organizations, it is impossible to reliably 'measure' all critical dimensions of performance. Measures become indicators, with all their limitations, and have to be treated as such. Indicators become the decision-support instruments in a learning organization. However, for this to work, organizations need to align their processes and routines with the principles of a learning organization. They have to create what I call an enabled learning environment; how to create such an environment will the subject of the next chapters.

References and endnotes

1 Quoted in Boyle, D. (2001). *The Sum of Our Discontent: Why Numbers Make Us Irrational.* Texere: New York.

2 Neely, A. (1998). *Measuring Business Performance: Why, What and How.* Economist Books: London.

3 Stein, R. E. (1997). *The Theory of Constraints.* Marcel Dekker Inc.: New York.

4 Meyer, M. W. (2002). *Rethinking Performance Measurement – Beyond the Balanced Scorecard.* Cambridge University Press: Cambridge, p. 31.

5 This definition is based on the definition of motivational measurement by: Austin, R. D. (1996). *Measuring and Managing Performance in Organizations.* Dorset House Publishing: New York, p. 193.

6 Campbell, N. R. (1928). *An Account of the Principles of Measurement and Calculation.* Longmans: London, p. 1.

7 Caws, P. (1959). Definition and Measurement in Physics. In *Measurement: Definition and Theories* (C. W. Churchman and P. Ratoosh, eds), pp. 3–17, John Wiley & Sons: New York.

8 Adams, C., Kennerley, M. and Neely, A. (2002). *The Performance Prism: The Scorecard for Measuring and Managing Business Success.* FT Prentice Hall: London.

9 Mason, R. O. and Swanson, E. B. (1981). Measurement for Management Decision: A Perspective. In *Measurement for Management Decision* (R. O. Mason, Swanson, E. B.), Addison-Wesley: Reading, MA, pp. 10–25.

10 Ibid, Boyle, D. (2001), p. 30. (See note 1 above.)

11 Blair, M. M. and Wallman, S. M. H. (2001). *Unseen Wealth.* Brookings Institution Press: Boston, p. 15.

12 From an interview with Daniel Yankelovich quoted in Adam Smith [pseudonym of George J. W. Goodman] (1973). *Supermoney.* Michael Joseph: London, p. 286.

13 Porter, T. M. (1995). *Trust in Numbers: The Pursuit of Objectivity in Science and Public Life.* Princeton University Press: Princeton.

14 Ibid, Boyle, D. (2001), p. 38. (See note 1 above.)

15 See for example: Gooday, G. J. N. (2004). *The Morals of Measurement: Accuracy, Irony, and Trust in Late Victorian Electrical Practice.* Cambridge University Press: Cambridge; and Porter, T. M. (1995). *Trust in Numbers: The Pursuit of Objectivity in Science and Public Life.* Princeton University Press: Princeton.

16 See: Austin, R. D. (1996). *Measuring and Managing Performance in Organizations*. Dorset House Publishing: New York, p. 13.

17 Sugarman, C. (1990). US Produce Standards Focus More on Appearance Than Quality, *The Pittsburgh Press*, August 5, p. E1.

18 See Torres, R. T., Preskill, H. S. and Piontek, M. E. (1996). *Evaluation Strategies for Communicating and Reporting: Enhancing Learning in Organizations*. Sage: Thousand Oaks, p. 2.

19 Johnson, T. H. and Kaplan, R. S. (1987). *Relevance Lost: The Rise And The Fall Of Management Accounting*. Harvard Business School Press: Boston, MA.

20 UBS *Annual Review* 2002, www.ubs.com (p. 25).

21 For more information on the Agency Model see for example: Ross, S. A. (1973). The Economic Theory of Agency: The Principal's Problem. *The American Economic Review*, Vol. 63, No. 2, pp. 134-9; and Holström, B. (1977). *On Incentives and Control in Organizations* (unpublished Ph.D. thesis), Stanford University, Stanford.

22 Meyer, M. W. (2002). *Rethinking Performance Measurement – Beyond the Balanced Scorecard*. Cambridge University Press: Cambridge (page xxi).

23 The classic example is referral interview in a government agency, here the number of interviews is measured whereas the quality of referrals is not. See: Blau, P. M. (1963). *The Dynamics of Bureaucracy: A Study of Interpersonal Relations in Two Government Agencies*. University of Chicago Press: Chicago.

24 This figure was inspired by the cases and diagrams used by Austin, R. D. (1996), Ibid (see note 5 above).

25 Ridgway, V. F. (1956). Dysfunctional Consequences of Performance Measurements. *Administrative Science Quarterly*, Vol. 1, No. 2, pp. 240-7.

26 Meyer, M. W. (2002). *Rethinking Performance Measurement – Beyond the Balanced Scorecard*. Cambridge University Press: Cambridge, p. 8.

27 Ehin, C. (2000). *Unleashing Intellectual Capital*. Butterworth Heinemann: Boston, p. 138.

28 Ibid, Austin, R. D. (1996). (See note 5 above).

29 Meyer, M. W. (2002). *Rethinking Performance Measurement – Beyond the Balanced Scorecard*. Cambridge University Press: Cambridge, p. 2.

30 Quoted in Boyle, D. (2001), Ibid, p. 29. (See note 1 above.)

31 See for example: Ketokivi, M. A. and Schroeder, R. G. (2004). Perceptional Measures of Performance: Fact or Fiction? *Journal of*

Operations Management, Vol. 22, No. 3, pp. 247–64; or Boyd, B. K., Dess, G. G. and Rasheed, A. M. A. (1993). Divergence Between Archival and Perceptional Measures of the Environment: Causes and Consequences. *Academy of Management Review*, Vol. 18, No. 2, pp. 204–26; or Ramanujam, V. and Venkatraman, N. (1987). Measurement of Business Economic Performance: An Examination of Method Convergence. *Journal of Management*, Vol. 13, No. 1, pp. 109–12.

32 For more information see for example: Dillman, D. A. (1999). *Mail and Internet Surveys: The Tailored Design Method*. Wiley: New York.

33 Preskill, H. and Russ-Eft, D. (2001). *Evaluation in Organization – A Systematic Approach to Enhancing Learning, Performance, and Change*. Perseus: Cambridge, MA, p. 200.

34 See for example: Yin, K. (2003). *Case Study Research. Design and Methods (Applied Social Research Methods Series, Vol. 5)*. Sage: Newbury Park, CA.

35 Preskill, H. and Russ-Eft, D. (2001). *Evaluation in Organization – A Systematic Approach to Enhancing Learning, Performance, and Change*. Perseus: Cambridge, MA.

36 Denzin, N. K. and Lincoln, Y. S. (eds) (2005). *The Sage Handbook of Qualitative Research*, 3rd edition. Sage: Thousand Oaks.

37 See for example: Mangel, M. and Samaniego, F. J. (1984). Abraham Wald's Work on Aircraft Survivability. *Journal of American Statistical Association*, June, pp. 259–67.

38 The majority of the thinking behind this section is credited to the work conducted by my colleagues at Cranfield School of Management and Cambridge University. For more details see: Bourne, M., Neely, A., Mills, J., Platts, K. and Richards, H. (2002). *Getting the Measures of Your Business*. Cambridge University Press: Cambridge, p. 69; or Adams, C., Kennerley, M. and Neely, A. (2002). *The Performance Prism: The Scorecard for Measuring and Managing Business Success*. FT Prentice Hall: London, p. 34; or Bourne, M. C. S., Mills, J. F, Neely, A.D., Platts, K. W. W. and Richards, H. (1997). Designing Performance Measures: a Structured Approach. *International Journal of Operations & Production Management*, Vol. 17, No. 11–12, p. 1131.

39 Preskill, H. and Russ-Eft, D. (2001). *Evaluation in Organization – A Systematic Approach to Enhancing Learning, Performance, and Change*. Perseus: Cambridge, MA, p. 178.

40 Ibid, Austin, R. D. (1996), p. 66. (See note 5 above.)

41 Gray, D. J. (2005). *A Multi-Method Investigation into the Costs and into the Benefits of Measuring Intellectual Capital Assets* (unpublished Ph.D. thesis). Cranfield School of Management: Cranfield.

42 For more information see Prevent Blindness America: http//www. preventblindness.org

6

Creating an enabled learning environment

In today's fast-moving global environment, organizations are forced to continuously innovate their products, services and processes to meet constantly changing external demands. In order to innovate, improve and refine, organizations need to learn. Organizational learning occurs when individuals inquire on the organization's behalf.[1] Creating an enabled learning environment forms the 'space' or 'social context' in which all individuals gain strategic insights, which in turn allows them to challenge strategic assumptions, refine strategic thinking, make better decisions and learn. This chapter focuses on how to create an enabled learning environment. Questions addressed in this chapter include:

- What is an enabled learning environment?
- How can we create an enabled learning environment?
- How can we create the right social context for successful Strategic Performance Management?
- How can we align the performance review processes?
- How have organizations created an enabled learning environment in practice?

The previous chapters outlined how organizations can define and articulate their strategy in value creation maps and value creation narratives, and how this strategic understanding can then be used to guide the development of meaningful performance indicators. The chapters have therefore addressed how organizations can avoid the 'strategy trap' and 'measurement trap' (as discussed in the introduction to this book). Here, I will look at ways of creating an environment in which everyone in the organization uses their strategic understanding and the corresponding performance indicators in order to improve and learn. An enabled learning environment is essential if organizations want to avoid the 'management trap'.

What is an enabled learning environment?

Most theorists agree that organizational learning takes place when individuals and teams engage in dialogue, reflection, asking questions, and identifying and challenging values, beliefs, and assumptions.[2] An enabled learning environment is an organizational environment in which all employees are actively seeking new strategic insights, which are based on their understanding of strategy and the performance indicators collected, to allow them to challenge strategic assumptions, refine strategic thinking, to make better decisions and to learn. The word 'enabled' stresses the fact that employees are also enabled or empowered to use strategic insights. Having insights about how to improve things without the authority to do something about it, is often a source of employee frustration. In an enabled learning environment, the value creation map and the performance indicators become the means for providing information for learning, decision-making and action.

Chris Argyris, professor at Harvard Business School, defines learning as occurring under two conditions. First, when an organization achieves what it intended to achieve and there is a match between the intention and outcome. Second, when an organization identifies a mismatch between the intention and outcome and this mismatch is corrected, so that a mismatch is turned into a match.[3] In order to learn, organizations therefore require an understanding of their intentions and a way to test the match or mismatch between their intended and actual performance. The value creation map and the value creation narrative make the organizational intentions explicit. They represent the assumed business model of how the organization is intending to create value. The performance indicators enable organizations to then test these assumptions. This allows individuals in the organization to reflect on the assumptions, learn from the insights, and improve their decision-making.

It is possible to distinguish between two types of organizational learning: single-loop learning and double-loop learning.[4] Single-loop learning takes place when, for example, an assumed business model is tested, and then insights, decisions, and actions are derived from it. Double-loop learning takes place when, for example, an assumed business model is tested and the insights lead to questioning of the underlying

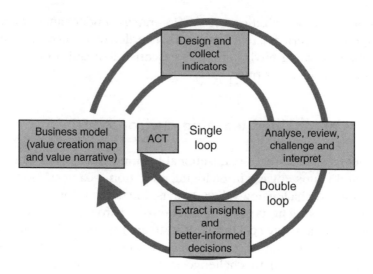

Figure 6.1   Single-loop and double-loop learning

assumptions and possible revision of the business model. A thermostat is often described as a single-loop learner. A thermostat is programmed to detect states of 'too cold' or 'too warm', and then corrects the situation by turning the heat on or off. If a thermostat were able to ask itself such questions as why the thermostat was set to, for example, 68 degrees, or why it was programmed as it was, then it would be a double-loop learner.[5]

The difference between single-loop and double-loop learning is depicted in Figure 6.1, using the Performance Management framework introduced earlier. The inner circle describes single-loop learning. Here the business model is taken as a given. Indicators are collected, analysed, and interpreted in order to take actions. Single-loop learning takes place when organizations review their performance against targets or intentions. The outer circle indicates double-loop learning. Here, the same logic is followed, but instead of only testing performance against intentions, the business model and its underlying assumptions are challenged. In order to learn, it is important that our assumptions, which often manifest themselves in the taken-for-granted behaviour and opinions, are continually questioned, tested and validated.[6]

In their book on the Balanced Scorecard, Kaplan and Norton write that:

> Of course, managers need feedback about whether their planned strategy is being executed according to plan – the single-loop learning process. But even more important, they need feedback

about whether the planned strategy remains a viable and successful strategy – the double-loop learning process.[7]

I go even further than that and say that it is not just the managers who need to question the underlying assumptions, it is everyone in the organization.

In order for any learning to take place, organizations need to create the right social context. What I call an 'enabled learning environment' is diametrically opposed to the traditional command-and-control environment. In the previous chapter, I have outlined the limitations of measurement as a reason why the command-and-control environment will create dysfunctional behaviour. There is another important reason why the command-and-control environment is no longer appropriate in today's business environment: because it inhibits learning. I will now take you through a closer look at some of the barriers to an enabled learning environment.

Barriers to an enabled learning environment

Our organizational structures are one of the key barriers to an enabled learning environment. Too many firms still operate the command-and-control model in which a blame culture exists which brings out the worst in people. A hierarchical command-and-control culture creates fear, distrust, self-centredness, and protectionism. In such an environment, no one is willing to openly and voluntarily share their insights and knowledge. There is no incentive for collaboratively exploring performance improvement and, therefore, real innovations are rare.

Another structural barrier is the way most performance review meetings are conducted. As the name 'performance *review* meeting' suggests, most of these are focused on past performance; often with a heavy bias towards financial indicators, they tend to be centred on budgets. One of the key questions is whether the budget was achieved in the last quarter or not. Even worse, much time is wasted presenting excuses about why the performance targets weren't met, often shifting blame from one individual or department to the other. Little time is spent thinking about the future and how the performance drivers have to be managed to improve performance in the next quarter.

The way in which most organizations communicate and report performance is not conducive to learning. Organizations today seem to have a tendency to produce cryptic spreadsheets containing performance data, which are then distributed as e-mail attachments. The fact that most people will only have one quick glance at the data, and then quickly decide that they can't really make sense of it, is rarely taken into account. If organizations are unable to engage people in a dialogue and make them reflect on performance, no learning will ever take place.

Another barrier is more personal and related to our human nature. In their professional environment, people are not very good at admitting failure and are, therefore, intrinsically unable to learn from their mistakes. We seem to have universal human tendencies to avoid embarrassment or threat, and we don't like feeling vulnerable or incompetent. In his Harvard Business Review article, entitled '*Teaching Smart People How To Learn*', Chris Argyris explains that failure produces defensive reasoning which can block learning, even if people's commitment to learning is high. He says:

> Put simply, because many professionals are almost always successful at what they do, they rarely experience failure. And because they have rarely failed, they have never learned how to learn from failure. So whenever their single-loop learning strategies go wrong, they become defensive, screen out criticism, and put the 'blame' on anyone and everyone but themselves. In short, their ability to learn shuts down precisely at the moment they need it the most.[8]

Next I will discuss how organizations can create an enabled learning environment and address some of the barriers outlined here.

Creating an enabled learning environment

In a subsequent HBR article, Argyris says 'Most executives understand that tougher competition will require more effective learning, broader empowerment, and greater commitment from everyone in the company.'[9] In order to make learning more effective, organizations need to create an enabled learning environment. However, there is no easy step-by-step process that can be followed to create an enabled learning environment. And it takes time too. Creating the right social context, communicating performance more effectively, and aligning organizational processes and routines are all major components. Where to start is a little bit of a 'chicken and egg' question – it's hard to say which must come first. Changing the social context helps to change the routines and practices, and changing the way we do things has an impact on the social context. I will now go on to discuss first how organizations can create the right social context before I suggest ways to align performance review meetings.

Creating the right social context

True Strategic Performance Management does not simply emerge; it requires a supportive organizational or social context. This social context needs to emphasize self-directed learning, personal commitment to performance, mutual support, and trust. Different names and descriptions have been given to this social context: Janine Nahapiet from Oxford University and the late Sumantra Ghoshal from London Business School talk about 'social capital',[10] whereas Ikujiro Nonaka and Noboru Konno use the Japanese word 'Ba'[11] to describe the physical, virtual, or mental space in which learning takes place.

Research shows that there is a big human and social element that determines whether Performance Management will be successful or not.[12] Charles Ehin, of the Gore School of Business, presents four interwoven tenets for fostering positive social connections, voluntary collaboration and learning; and these seem to be a good starting point for the creation of what I call the 'right social context'.[13] Here I outline my interpretations of these tenets:

- *Line-of-sight relationships* – they allow us to create trust and to share tacit understanding. Trust is one of the key components of the right social context. Humans are physiologically designed to be social creatures.

  'Thus, an organization where people are unable to have periodic face-to-face contact soon becomes dysfunctional because its members cannot develop a trusting relationship.'[14]

  Tacit knowledge and routines, as opposed to explicit knowledge, are things we find hard to write down or explain in descriptions. Examples of tacit knowledge include the ability to ride a bike or how to swim – as well as aspects of organizational culture and 'the way we do things here'. It is difficult, if not impossible, to sit down and write a manual of how to ride a bike and then give it to someone and expect them to go off and be able to ride a bike. Tacit knowledge is best shared by observation, imitation and supervised practice, for which line-of-sight relationships are required.[15]

- *Sense of community* – a community is a social entity that serves both its members individually and the community as a whole. Underpinned by effective line-of-sight relationships, it creates a base for a group of people with shared interests, where compassion, empathy, and trust pervade.[16] It gives individuals a sense of belonging, which fosters commitment, collaboration, and mutual respect.

- *Common purpose* – this is about meaning and an implicit agreement about direction. Can individuals associate themselves with the aspirations and perspectives of the organization or the team? Common purpose can often be linked to the boundary conditions of an organization (see Chapter 1). Genuine commitment to the performance of an organization simply does not happen unless individuals feel that they are empowered and respected partners on a joint journey.

■ *Visualizing wholes* – this is about our capabilities to picture the whole and engage in 'systems thinking'. Instead of seeing individual parts of an organization, separate silos and departments with often opposing interests, individuals in organizations are able to see the relationships between the different parts and how they integrate to create value as a whole.

Creating the right social context is not about esoteric communities in which everyone happily does whatever they want. It is about creating a performance-driven culture where trust, self-directed learning, mutual respect and support lead to personal commitment to continuous performance improvement. The acts of developing a value creation map and a value creation narrative (see Chapter 4) and then, where appropriate, cascading it throughout the organization to make it relevant to local operating centres, help to visualize the whole and contribute to the development of a common purpose and a sense of community. This is especially so if organizations begin by engaging everyone in the development process. However, the softer dimensions around human relationships and trust cannot simply be implemented by using a set of tools. They will have to be cultivated over time. One way to do this is to change the way performance is reviewed in organizations, which I will address in the following section.

Aligning performance review meetings

In my experience, the way performance is reviewed in organizations can be one of the most powerful barriers to Strategic Performance Management. Below I outline three different scenarios of meetings used to review organizational performance (see also Figure 6.2). Which one most resembles the process used in your organization?

■ *'On trial' reviews*: this resembles a court of law, whereby individuals are required to present their 'numbers' and explain to 'the boss' and the other individuals present why some are good and, particularly, why some are bad. It is a tense atmosphere of 'trial by presentation'. If any executive cannot deliver a glossy PowerPoint presentation and, most importantly, answer penetrating questions about their

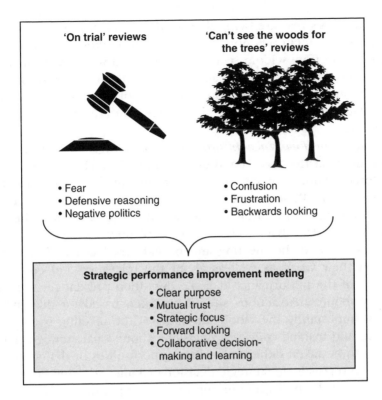

Figure 6.2 Different performance review meetings

department's performance satisfactorily, then he or she is likely to be humiliated and chastised by the boss, remanded in custody pending an appeal at the next meeting or added to the list for execution. The whole activity is similar to prosecutors and defendants arguing about who is to blame for the 'bad news'. However, here there this no jury, just a judge.

■ *'Can't see the wood for the trees' review*: this is more like a random walk in the park – the discussion could go anywhere. Individuals present their 'numbers', but there is such a plethora of them that a somewhat random debate then occurs about the causes of particular good and bad 'numbers', especially the potential causes of specific unusual 'spikes'. This results in these meetings tending to go into too much detail. The outcome of the debate tends to be to cut the discussion short (because the agenda is long and its planned timings have already over-run) and move on without making any strategic decisions because too much time has been expended on deliberating the minutiae.

The issues that are being discussed are not put into the context of strategic intentions. Some strategic considerations might get discussed, but they seldom seem to get resolved with practical actions that are agreed. One manager compared this kind of meeting to driving a car where you have lots of data and information from the dashboard, but no idea where you are or where you are heading.

- *'Strategic performance improvement' meeting*: participants know exactly what the agenda and discussion will be about and how the different elements being discussed fit into the strategic plan of the organization. Performance data (quantitative and qualitative) has been circulated in advance and individuals present only the story behind the data that is relevant to the planned discussion. Business analysts attend the meeting and provide feedback and comments about their work, as well as about the relevance and confidence levels of the performance data. Leaders then present recommendations about what actions should be taken based on this analysis. Most importantly, the whole emphasis of the meeting is about dialogue and making *collective* decisions about what strategic actions need to be taken either to explore opportunities or deflect threats. The emphasis is on strategic decision-making and using both single- and double-loop learning to improve future performance.

Obviously there is territory in between these three extremes, but I am certain that many employees in many organizations will recognize some of the symptoms of the 'on trial' and 'can't see the wood for the trees' review meetings. If so, I believe they should reconsider the way they approach this vital process and, therefore, suggest that they need to have a debate among themselves about how they could move towards Strategic Performance Improvement Meetings. For a start, the name 'review' meeting automatically focuses the attention on past performance. Whereas it is important to look at past trends and see how this might give us insights into future performance, many performance 'review' meetings only look at the past and are too concerned about finding excuses and shifting blame instead of concentrating on future performance and decision-making.

I have been a witness to several meetings that typify 'on trial' reviews and each time I have been appalled by the tensions and dysfunctional behaviour that this type of review invokes. Clearly, there is no spirit of co-operation between individuals simply because this is a struggle for survival – each person or department pitted against the others. This way of conducting performance reviews is very closely linked to the aim of 'controlling people's behaviour', discussed in the previous chapter. 'On trial' reviews destroy any social context that is conducive to collaboration and learning, and instead bring out an array of self-centred characteristics, negative politics, and a focus on compliance.

My colleagues at the Centre of Business Performance – Andy Neely, Chris Adams and Mike Kennerley – describe in their book[17], *The Performance Prism*, an excellent actual example of a (predominantly 'can't see the wood for the trees') dysfunctional Strategic Performance Review meeting that I believe illustrates very clearly a process that is not uncommon in boardrooms today. It is reproduced in an edited version below.

Example of a dysfunctional Strategic Performance Review process

The executive team of a leading logistics company would meet on a monthly basis to review performance. They would examine performance in terms of its ability to achieve 'notional result', the company's internal measure of profitability. They would also review the operational performance. One of the problems with the latter was that the amount of data and number of definitions of operational performance were vast. For this company, operations could be reviewed in terms of shipments (either by weight or number), shipments delivered (on time, to the right destination, in one piece), shipments collected (before a specified time or from a specified location), packages lost (or re-routed), and so on. The volume and variety of data meant that the executive team could easily get engrossed in incredibly detailed reviews of specific areas of performance. While interesting in themselves, such detailed reviews of specific performance areas are not useful if the strategic context of these areas is forgotten.

The executive team clearly recognized this issue and began to question whether the structure and focus of their performance reviews were appropriate for their business. They began to ask themselves: how should we structure and coordinate performance reviews in a business of the company's size and complexity in the twenty-first century? Far too often organizations seem to allow performance reviews to evolve haphazardly. Because specific measures are available, they are put on the agenda. When a particular problem occurs, a new performance indicator is developed, implemented and added to the agenda. Fifteen years later that indicator is still on the agenda, even though the original problem is lost in the mists of time and the root causes of it have long ago been eliminated. A director in another organization explained to me why it was good for him to have a lot of indicators. He said 'By having so many key performance indicators, I can always find at least one that is moving in the right direction!'.

In this logistics company all of these factors added up. The performance reviews had begun to lose their strategic focus, structure and purpose. They provoked interesting discussions amongst the executive team, but often the same discussion took place month after month after month. Parodying this, one director commented how the performance review process would encourage him and his colleagues to bring massive spreadsheets to the meetings. These would be copied onto acetates and then, in the meeting, they would pick specific cells on the spreadsheet more or less at random to talk about during their respective presentations. Often their opening statements would be prefaced with comments such as, 'Oh, look at this. This is interesting. It is down 15% from last month'. The executive team would then spend 15 minutes debating why the number in cell C72 was down by 15%, before the director concerned would spot another interesting number in another interesting cell on the spreadsheet and so provoke another highly therapeutic, but ultimately futile discussion. Another director described this as 'numerical crosswords'.

The point was that the performance reviews had lost any strategic purpose and any clarity was destroyed by the random data that was reviewed. The executive team was getting so dragged into the minutiae of the data that they were losing sight of the big picture. Why so? It was not the fault of the people, as such. It was actually the fault of the process. The aims and objectives of the performance review process were not clearly articulated or widely understood. Without clear structure and purpose, the performance review had drifted and evolved into a process that simply encouraged the executive team to debate the minutiae.

Creating Productive Strategic Performance Improvement Meetings

Below I outline how organizations can get away from performance reviews that create dysfunctional behaviours and frustrations, and how they can create what I call a 'Productive Strategic Performance Improvement Meeting'.

I have created a list of what I believe are the ten most important aspects of successful Strategic Performance Improvement Meetings. I have divided this list into two parts: 'Before the meeting' and 'At the meeting' (see Figure 6.3).

Strategic performance improvement meeting

Before the meeting:

1. Name the meeting appropriately
2. Use the value creation map to guide the meeting structure and meeting agenda
3. Cruise at the right 'flight altitude'
4. Use questions to guide and focus the discussions
5. Use performance indicators to facilitate finding answers
6. Circulate possible answers and supporting performance indicator data in advance
7. Have a process in place for double-loop learning

At the meeting:

8. Create an atmosphere of purpose, trust, and respect
9. Ensure that performance and alternative options are presented as a story, supported by performance indicator data
10. Ensure that collaborative decision-making and learning takes place

Figure 6.3   Ten aspects of a successful Strategic Performance Improvement Meeting

Let me try to put some 'meat on these bones' for you:

Before the meeting:

- *Name the meeting appropriately*: take the word 'review' out of the name of the meeting. The main purpose of the meeting is to improve future performance. Insight from the past can help us with decision-making about the future, but it can't be the main focus of the meeting. Therefore, call them Strategic Performance Improvement Meetings or something along this line, so that the title reflects the purpose of the meeting.
- *Use the value creation map to guide the meeting structure and agenda*: the value creation map is used to guide the meeting and provides a structure or agenda for the Strategic Performance Improvement Meeting. A good way to do this is to take the individual elements from the map and make them agenda items. A few organizations

I have worked with have taken the key elements of their value creation map and divided their Strategic Performance Improvement Meeting into a set of sub-meetings, each of which then addresses the different elements of their value creation map. They might spend the morning discussing the output deliverables, e.g. the latest financial performance and customer satisfaction. Then a subsequent meeting might focus on, for example, 'building better relationships with key customers', another key element on their value creation map. In this way, organizations ensure that all strategic elements are covered.

- *Cruise at the right 'flight altitude'*: for these meetings it is important that they take place at the right 'flight altitude';[18]. By this I mean that the elements, and especially the information and data discussed, must be relevant and appropriate for the individuals in the meeting. The executive board should take the corporate or overall value creation map to guide their meetings, departments would use their cascaded value creation map, and so on (see also the section 'Cascading value creation maps in Chapter 4). In order to be actionable, the content and information discussed has to be relevant and meaningful to the purpose of each meeting and its participants. It simply wouldn't be right if executive board members were to review performance at a detailed operational level (unless some key aspect had been referred up to them by an operational team meeting for a decision that it was not able to make itself). Neither would it make sense for operational teams to review the strategic elements of the corporation (unless they had some exceptional reason to do so, which can occasionally occur).
- *Use questions to guide and focus the discussions*: design a set of questions you want to answer during the meeting. Asking questions in an inquiring way develops a spirit of curiosity that serves as a catalyst for learning.[19] If one of the elements on the value creation map and agenda is, for example, 'reputation' or 'external relationships', then the questions could for instance be: 'Is our reputation increasing?'; 'Are we moving towards the reputation we want?'; 'Are we building the right relationships?'; 'Are our relationships as strong as we want them to be?'. The questions can then become the agenda items or even headings for sub-meetings.
- *Use performance indicators to facilitate finding answers*: the individuals, or group of individuals, responsible for the different strategic elements take responsibility for analysing the performance data prior to the meeting with the aim of answering the posed question(s). The indicators that were developed for the different elements of the value creation map are used to develop answers to the questions posed for the different strategic elements. Data analysts

work closely with leaders who are seeking answers to their performance questions. The job of the analysts is to produce relevant analysis of the available data so that these leaders can present the results supported by the information derived from the performance indicators. Analysts also help with the presentation of the data, finding the most appropriate way of visualizing indicator data and performance. In many cases it might be impossible to come up with a clear answer based on the data; in those cases a selected set of alternative options should be produced.

- *Circulate answers and supporting performance indicator data in advance*: the answers or a set of alternative options, together with the essential indicators and performance data are circulated in advance of the meeting. The latter should be the minimum standard; submission of some alternative options can be helpful to directing pre-meeting thought processes for discussion, but some of the answers might have to wait until the meeting (where there can be a relevant and proper debate about them). This allows people to reflect on performance. Reflection, which is an important component of learning, often takes place in between meetings when we have a minute to ourselves, or when we go for a walk, stare out of the window, or wash the dishes.[20]

- *Have a process in place for double-loop learning*: to avoid the trap of discussing the existing elements of the value creation map without ever questioning the underlying map itself, a strategic review meeting is scheduled. How frequently these strategic reviews take place depends on the speed of change in the industry (see the section 'How to construct a value creation map' in Chapter 4); in my view they should be scheduled at least once annually.

At the meeting:

- *Create an atmosphere of purpose, trust, and respect*: the atmosphere in these meetings is purposeful but relaxed and friendly. Mutual trust, respect and support lead to personal commitment, joint decision-making, and learning. Instead of a blame culture, the focus is on future performance, dialogue, decision-making, and actions. A chairman ensures that the agenda items are fully discussed and that any dialogue is constructive and aimed at improving future performance. Dialogue is an enabler for learning.

Through dialogue, individuals seek to inquire, share meanings, understand complex issues, and uncover assumptions. In other words, dialogue is what facilitates evaluative inquiry learning processes of reflection, asking questions, and identifying and clarifying values, beliefs, assumptions, and knowledge.[21]

Dialogue, as opposed to discussion, has the goal of understanding, not competition.[22] Dialogue requires the suspension of defensive reasoning and is about learning for change. It empowers everyone to share their thoughts and be heard, in order to reach joint conclusions.

- *Ensure that performance and alternative options are presented in a story, supported by performance indicator data*: the meeting starts with a look at the value creation map and it is highlighted where the strategic element that is being discussed fits into the strategy of the organization. Presenters come to the Strategic Performance Improvement Meeting with possible answers to the questions on the agenda and (a set of alternative) proposals for acting, based on the indicator data they have collected and analysed. Performance is presented as a cohesive 'story' and data from the performance indicators is used to support these 'stories'. Performance indicator data will usually be presented in graphical form and the analysts who helped to analyse the data attend the review meetings.

  Each 'story' tells participants about where the organization is succeeding and where it is failing in its endeavours to achieve its strategic goals. It is accepted and *expected* that presenters report on issues where the organization has underperformed and highlight possible shortcomings and problems. The chairperson for the meeting ensures that any story will contain a mix of good and bad news, since the point of the meeting is to decide on the implications and to make decisions about future actions. In order to do this it is important to assess performance in the context of the value creation map.

- *Ensure that collaborative decision-making and learning takes place*: the implications of the stories and proposals are openly discussed and the performance indicator data is used to evaluate different alternatives. For this it is important that the validity and confidence level of the various indicators is understood (see also the section 'Designing a performance indicator' in Chapter 5). Here the role of the performance analyst is critical, as he or she can answer questions about data collection methods, data analysis, possible bias, and overall validity of the data. The indicator data is therefore assessed and put into the strategic context of the organization. This facilitates a better-informed debate and enables collaborative decision-making and mutual agreement on next steps and actions. In this kind of environment it is acceptable to say 'I don't know the answer', instead of finding any answer for the sake of it. Sometimes it is best to have an open discussion about possible answers or to decide to collect more data. Actions are agreed on, captured in the minutes, and then followed up at the next meeting.

The ten steps outlined here provide the ingredients for successful Performance Improvement Meetings in an enabled learning environment. It will, however, take time and efforts by everyone involved to make them work. Next I will share how Fujitsu was able to create an enabled learning environment as part of its Strategic Performance Management initiative.

An enabled learning environment in practice: the case of Fujitsu Services[23]

Fujitsu Services is one of the leading IT services companies in Europe, the Middle East and Africa. It has an annual turnover of £1.74 billion, employs 14 500 people and operates in over 20 countries. It designs, builds and operates IT systems and services for customers in the financial services, telecommunications, retail, utilities and government markets. Its core strength is the delivery of IT infrastructure management and outsourcing across desktop, networking and data centre environments, together with a full range of related services, from infrastructure consulting through to integration and deployment.

In Fujitsu Services, the helpdesks provide a critical function. These helpdesk call centres represent an integral part of service delivery and the primary point of contact for customers. If you are a customer that has outsourced their IT infrastructure management to Fujitsu Services, the helpdesk would be your point of contact if anything goes wrong or if you experience any problems with your computer hard- or software. Helpdesk agents can then either solve the problem or pass the work on, e.g. to an engineer who then comes out and fixes the problem. It is often argued how call centres are changing the way companies communicate with customers and that they are a strategic asset in delivering exceptional service quality. Many organizations believe they are using their call centres to differentiate their product or service offering, to build and maintain customer relationships, and drive customer satisfaction.

The reality, however, is often very different. I am sure most of you can relate to the aggravation that is often caused when customers try to contact call centres or helpdesks. It often starts with a finger ballet to communicate with the interactive voice response (IVR) system, then endless queuing listening to the same irritating piece of music, and when we finally speak to someone they can sometimes be abrupt and unhelpful. Instead of treating call centres as service providers, they are often treated as unnecessary cost centres that have to be squeezed for efficiency. In many cases this is due to outsourcing service level agreements, which specify performance targets of everything that is easy to measure such as queuing time, the number of calls taken, or average call duration.

In 1999, there was a growing realization at Fujitsu that the traditional approach to Performance Management was failing customers. Operating in the IT outsourcing sector, Fujitsu found it almost impossible to differentiate itself in a very aggressive marketplace. A functional focus resulted in a lack of cohesion and fragmentation. Not dissimilar to other call centres, many client accounts were operating at contractual obligation levels and no higher, while 15% were at critical levels of dissatisfaction and were unlikely to be renewed. Furthermore, the turnover of front-line call centre staff was 42%.

The message was stark for Fujitsu – it had to rethink its Strategic Performance Management approach if it wanted to stand out from the crowd. What Fujitsu found was that the traditional way of measuring and managing performance stood in the way of a new strategic approach towards Performance Management. Fujitsu changed both the way that it approached Performance Measurement and Performance Management. In addition, Fujitsu saw this as an opportunity not only to redesign the organization but also to change the way Fujitsu worked with its customers. It was clear that customer satisfaction had to be a given. However, what Fujitsu wanted to change was its relationship with its customers – from service level contracts to a partnership model where customer success became a new goal. For this, it was critical to understand what was creating value for customers and what was not.

Fujitsu recognized that information about what was creating value for its customers had to come from its front-line agents, since they are the ones speaking to customers all day long. However, the way performance was measured – with a strong focus on efficiency measures – prevented call centre agents from spending time 'listening' to customers. All focus was on speed and numbers.

The first step Fujitsu took was to remove these measures from front-line employees to avoid the 'measurement trap' and prevent dysfunctional behaviour. Call duration and number of calls are still important indicators for managers to ensure the correct levels of resourcing, but they are the wrong measures to influence the behaviour of front-line agents. Fujitsu realized that if front-line agents are measured and rewarded on overall service delivery, they are the ones who can help to improve exactly this. They can provide critical information about service shortcomings, possible bottlenecks, and future innovation. For that reason, Fujitsu changed its approach and started to treat call centre agents as knowledge workers and began to leverage their knowledge for process and product innovation.

In order to create the context for knowledge work, the second step was to establish what I call an enabled learning environment. Fujitsu redesigned its management approach with a new emphasis on people, the problem-solving process and value creation. This involved a change in management style with leadership principles based on intrinsic motivation and the creation of possibilities for others to succeed in a way that provides choice, not ultimatums. It involved the identification of training needs, the deployment of new skills, and the reorganization of roles and responsibilities. The hierarchy within Fujitsu was essentially turned upside down. The role of managers was changed from one of authority to one of support. The central responsibility for them became the provision of the necessary knowledge and tools to allow front-line staff to handle the needs of the customer and assume responsibility for the end-to-end service, even if that service left the confines of the helpdesk at Fujitsu and was transferred to other client suppliers.

Today, dedicated front-line teams take on the role of establishing how they add value to their clients. They address questions such as 'what do our customers want to achieve?' and 'what is Fujitsu's role in this?' Its new Strategic Performance Management approach enabled Fujitsu to move from a make-and-sell mentality toward a sense-and-respond mentality.[24] To understand how Fujitsu is creating value for their customers, front-line agents create a value creation map – a visual representation of the value proposition to their customers and the key competencies and performance drivers required from Fujitsu to help deliver the value proposition. In a so-called 'intervention process', front-line agents analyse the customer requirements and map out how they can help to deliver these. This often involves a visit to the customer sites to better understand their environment, working conditions, and value proposition. Subsequently, the front-line agents design appropriate performance indicators which they own, review, and act upon.

One of Fujitsu's customers is, for example, an airline company that has outsourced its IT management to Fujitsu. Airline employees would ring the helpdesk if they experienced any problems with their IT equipment (e.g. printer doesn't work or servers are down). The success measures for the helpdesk team which handles the airline calls will be the overall service rating from the airline, i.e. has the IT infrastructure been managed satisfactorily by Fujitsu, instead of 'have the calls been handled within 2 minutes'. Front-line employees in Fujitsu now analyse and classify incoming calls in order to understand whether they are 'creating value' or 'restoring value'. The latter might be preventable by improving processes as part of Fujitsu's service delivery, e.g. an engineer didn't turn up soon enough to fix an essential ticket printer at the airport and the customers are chasing up.

Front-line agents now look at what kind of calls they are getting and see what they tell them about their overall end-to-end service delivery. They might get calls because other parts of the business are not delivering and therefore customers are chasing their products. Trying to knock off a few seconds to optimize such calls would clearly be the wrong thing to do; instead, this information needs to be passed on in order to improve performance along the entire value chain. Cross-functional performance improvement meetings are used to explore how overall service delivery can be improved, and the input from front-line agents is of critical importance. Here new processes are established to ensure, for example, that either the engineer turns up more quickly, the printers are replaced with more reliable printers, or maybe clients are trained to fix essential equipment by themselves.

Sometimes, sub-optimal processes in the customer organization are responsible for problems with the IT systems and are, therefore, preventable calls. In such cases the information is fed back to the clients so that they can improve their own internal processes. In one case, Fujitsu discovered that many employees were ringing to reset passwords at night, when no helpdesk was available for that client. This meant that they sometimes had to wait hours until the helpdesk agents were available again in the morning to reset a backlog of passwords. Instead of arranging 24-hour helpdesk service, the solution was for the client company to change their processes and give some of their employees the ability to reset passwords when the helpdesk was not available. Under the old regime there would have been no incentive for anyone in Fujitsu to suggest this approach. For the airline company, helpdesk intelligence has managed to reduce queues at ticket offices, check-ins and boarding gates. Calls into the helpdesk have fallen by 30%, system availability has increased, and client IT operating costs have decreased.

This new approach created completely new relationships between Fujitsu and their clients. Instead of operating at only contractual obligation level according to efficiency measures specified in service level agreements, Fujitsu now operates on a partner level that allows mutual performance improvements. Commercial contracts between Fujitsu Services and its clients had to be restructured to realize mutual benefit from call reduction and mutual value maximization. The results of this change in the way performance is managed in Fujitsu Services are impressive. Today, Fujitsu achieves 20% higher customer satisfaction, and was further able to increase its employee satisfaction by 40%. Its staff attrition decreased from 42% to 8%, operating costs decreased by 20%, and contract renewal and service upgrades amounted to £200 m. Since implementation of its new Strategic Performance Management approach, Fujitsu won the National Business for the Best Customer Service Strategy and was awarded the European Call Centre of the Year award for the best people development programme.

Today, Fujitsu is continuously redesigning its capabilities and offerings, not based on market intelligence but on customer-knowledge and Strategic Performance data. Fujitsu recognized the potential of a new Strategic Management approach and applied it in a wider context. In addition to the helpdesk environment, these principles have now been applied to many other parts of the organization.

I believe that this case study demonstrates the power of an enabled learning environment and how it can help to make Strategic Performance Management a reality. It enables organizations to continuously learn and innovate, and therefore ensures long-term success. The time is right for more organizations to think about their Strategic Performance Management processes and how to create an enabled learning environment. In the next chapter I will discuss how the value creation maps and associated indicators can be used to validate assumed causal models, to assess risks, and to evaluate potential mergers and acquisitions.

References and endnotes

1 See for example: Argyris, C. and Schön, D. A. (1978). *Organizational Learning: A Theory of Action Perspective*. Addison-Wesley.

2 See for example: Preskill, H. and Torres, R. T. (1999). *Evaluative Inquiry of Learning in Organizations*. Sage, Thousand Oaks; and Senge, P. M. (1990). *The Fifth Discipline: The Art and Practice of the Learning Organization*. Doubleday Currency: New York.

3 See for example: Argyris, C. (1999). *On Organizational Learning*, 2nd edition. Blackwell: Malden.

4 Argyris, C. (1978). Double Loop Learning in Organizations. *Harvard Business Review*, Sept–Oct, pp. 115–25.

5 Argyris, C. (1999). *On Organizational Learning*, 2nd edition. Blackwell: Malden.

6 Ibid, Preskill, H. and Torres, R. T. (1999), p. 66. (See note 2 above.)

7 Kaplan, R. S. and Norton, D. P. (1996a). *The Balanced Scorecard – Translating Strategy into Action*. Harvard Business School Press: Boston, MA, p. 17.

8 Argyris, C. (1991). Teaching Smart People to Learn. *Harvard Business Review*, May/June, pp. 99–109.

9 Argyris, C. (1994). Good Communication Blocks Learning. *Harvard Business Review*, July/August, pp. 77–85.

10 Ghoshal, S. and Nahapiet, J. (1998). Social Capital, Intellectual Capital, and the Organizational Advantage. *Academy of Management Review*, Vol. 23, No. 2, Apr, pp. 242.

11 See for example: Konno, N. and Nonaka, I. (1998). The Concept of 'Ba': Building a Foundation for Knowledge Creation. *California Management Review*, Vol. 40, No. 3, pp. 40–54; or Konno, N., Nonaka, I. and Toyama, R. (2000). SECI, Ba and Leadership: A Unified Model of Dynamic Knowledge Creation. *Long Range Planning*, Vol. 33, No. 1, Feb, p. 5.

12 See for example: de Waal, A. A. (2002). *Quest for Balance: The Human Element in Performance Management Systems*. Wiley: New York; or de Waal, A. A. (2001). *Power of Performance Measurement: How Leading Companies Create Sustained Value*. Wiley: New York.

13 See for example: Ehin, C. (1998). Fostering Both Sides of Human Nature – the Foundation for Collaborative Relationships. *Business Horizons*, May–June, pp. 15–25; and Ehin, C. (2000). *Unleashing Intellectual Capital*. Butterworth Heinemann: Boston, MA.

14 Ehin, C. (2000). *Unleashing Intellectual Capital*. Butterworth Heinemann: Boston, p. 106.

15 For more information on tacit knowledge see: Polanyi, M. (1958). *Personal Knowledge: Towards a Post-Critical Philosophy*. University of Chicago Press: Chicago, Il.

16 Ehin, C. (2000). *Unleashing Intellectual Capital*. Butterworth Heinemann: Boston, p. 110.

17 Neely, A., Kennerley, M. and Adams, C. (2002). *The Performance Prism – The Scorecard for Measuring and Managing Business Success*. FT Prentice Hall, Chapter 11, pp. 345–6.

18 I borrowed this phrase from Heinz Ahn, who uses it for a similar purpose in his article Ahn, H. (2001). Applying the Balanced Scorecard Concept: An Experience Report. *Long Range Planning*, Vol. 34, No. 4, pp. 441–61.

19 Ibid, Preskill, H. and Torres, R. T (1999), p. 65. (See note 2 above.)

20 Ibid, Preskill, H. and Torres, R. T. (1999), p. 60. (See note 2 above.)

21 Ibid, Preskill, H. and Torres, R. T. (1999), pp. 53–4. (See note 2 above.)

22 See for example: Bohm, D. and Nichol, L. (eds) (1996). *On Dialogue*. Routledge: London.

23 This case study is based on my work with Fujitsu Services. For more information see also: Marr, B. (2005). *Strategic Performance Management: Lessons From Call Centres*. Cranfield School of Management: UK; or Marr, B. and Parry, S. (2004). Performance Management In Call Centers: Lessons, Pitfalls and Achievements in Fujitsu Services. *Measuring Business Excellence*, Vol. 8, No. 4, pp. 55–62.

24 See for example: Barlow, S., Parry, S. and Faulkner, M. (2005). *Sense and Respond: The Journey to Customer Purpose*. Palgrave, Basingstoke; Haeckel, S. (1999). *Adaptive Enterprise: Creating and Leading Sense-and-Respond Organizations*. Harvard Business School Press: Boston, MA.

7

Extracting more management insights

Most decisions made by managers either destroy long-term value or don't create any. . . . To be fair, most managers today don't have a fighting chance to create value. They are often forced to plan, decide, and act without clear, coherent, or comprehensive roadmaps.

I very much agree with this statement made by James Heskett, Earl Sasser, and Leonard Schlesinger in their book on the value profit chain.[1] Successful organizations in today's global knowledge economy will be those that create clear and comprehensible strategy roadmaps, and use performance data in order to extract management insights for learning and decision-making. In the previous chapter, I have discussed how, in an enabled learning environment and through performance improvement meetings, the value creation map can be used to foster learning and improve everyday decision-making. This is the most powerful way to engage everyone in strategic thinking and learning. However, the value creation map can be used for other types of analyses that allow you to 'validate' your business model, to assess your risks, and to evaluate possible diversifications, acquisitions, and mergers. In this chapter, I will look at these aspects and address the following questions:

- In what ways can we use the value creation map to analyse our organization?
- How can Strategic Performance Management facilitate dynamic capabilities?
- How can we test our business model and our assumptions?

- How can we assess the risks our organization is facing?
- How can the value creation map help us to assess mergers and acquisitions?

Using Strategic Management to support dynamic capabilities

One of the latest concepts in Strategic Management is dynamic capabilities. Whereas ordinary capabilities represent the abilities of an organization to do something with its existing resources (see Chapter 3), dynamic capabilities represent the ability to integrate, build, and reconfigure the resources of an organization in order to create new capabilities.[2] Dynamic capabilities thus reflect an organization's ability to achieve new and innovative forms of competitive advantage and value creation. For this, organizations need to understand their resource architecture as well as changes in the external and internal environment that might require reconfigurations of resources and capabilities.

As outlined before, there is an increasing need for organizations to rely on continuous 'morphing' (i.e. metamorphosing), which helps them to regenerate their competitive position and value propositions.[3] For me, dynamic capabilities are closely linked to double-loop learning, which I discussed in the previous chapter. Figure 7.1 illustrates how Strategic Performance Management can create dynamic capabilities.

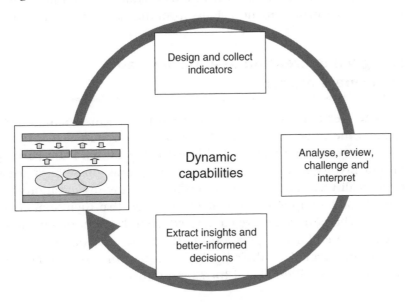

Figure 7.1 Strategic Performance Management and dynamic capabilities

By understanding and visualizing the business model in a value creation map, you can collect the appropriate indicators that you can then use to analyse, review and challenge the business model, and therefore extract insights that allow you to make decisions about any necessary reconfiguration of organizational resources and capabilities.

In Fujitsu, dynamic capabilities are not just a theory any more.[4] Fujitsu has embraced the concept and realized that unless everyone continuously compares the created strategy roadmap with the emerging reality, a mismatch can quickly be created between what the organization does and what the customers require. In its helpdesk environment (as discussed previously in Chapter 6), Fujitsu has put processes in place that enable front-line agents to understand how they are creating better value for their clients.

However, in the same way that the external business environment is changing, so are the demands and requirements of each client. By talking to the clients day in and day out, front-line agents are now skilled to listen to what the customers are saying in order to detect any changes in demands. This is reviewed on a regular basis and compared with the existing value creation assumptions. If any mismatches are identified, required actions are explored and implemented.

Testing the value creation assumptions and assessing potential risks to the current business model are other forms of analysis that help organizations to see possible areas where they need to reconfigure their current resource base. Below, I will explore how those can be used to extract management insights from the value creation map.

Testing value creation assumptions and the business model

The value creation assumptions expressed in the causal value creation maps and the value creation narratives are usually just that – assumptions. However, if the map is developed correctly, with the participation and involvement of as many key people as possible, it usually reflects reality extremely well. Nevertheless, many organizations want to 'test' their assumptions and collect 'evidence' that their assumptions hold true. The performance data derived from the performance indicators can be used for that purpose and the value creation map, or parts of it, can be verified. In their book *Evaluative Inquiry for Learning in Organizations*, Preskill and Torres write that:

> no longer can senior management rely solely on gut feelings and information from their inner circle to make decisions.

Organizations that survive will be those that have cultures that support asking the hard questions and have developed methods, processes, and systems to answer those questions.[5]

Chris Ittner and David Larcker from the Wharton School in Pennsylvania found in their survey of leading companies that just over 20% of them consistently laid out the cause-and-effect relationships between chosen drivers of strategic success and outcomes, and even fewer actually verified these causal models. Yet, those companies who did, had on average an almost 3% higher return on assets, and over 5% higher return on equity, than companies that didn't use causal models.[6]

Chris Argyris from Harvard Business School argues that:

> Any sophisticated strategic analysis, for example, depends on collecting valid data, analyzing it carefully, and constantly testing the inferences drawn from the data. The toughest tests are reserved for the conclusions. Good strategists make sure that their conclusions can withstand all kinds of critical reasoning.[7]

In their book *The Value Profit Chain*[8] James Heskett, Earl Sasser, and Leonard Schlesinger talk about fact-based analysis. They argue that in most companies there are only a few 'bundles' of business drivers; identifying those and then verifying them using fact-based analysis will allow management to establish the credibility necessary to 'sell' them to all parts of the organization. This kind of verification of your strategic assumptions can be conducted to varying levels of sophistication. What approach is picked also depends on the confidence organizations have in their value creation maps. The more confident they are that the map reflects reality, the less complex the validation techniques need to be. This does not mean that organizations that are confident about their map can't perform sophisticated verifications of their map; it just means that this often involves significant efforts which might not add any significant value. Instead, they just confirm what everyone knew in the first place. Testing entire maps often entails complicated modelling and statistical analyses, and it might be better to start with testing individual parts of the map in areas where organizations might be most unsure.

Organizations can identify sub-sets of their causal value creation map or individual linkages between elements of the map, and then 'test' those (see Figure 7.2). Various companies have been successful in testing relationships between elements of their strategy. One example comes from Sears, Roebuck and Co., a leading retailer that offers a wide range of home merchandise, apparel and automotive products and services through more than 2400 stores in the USA and Canada.

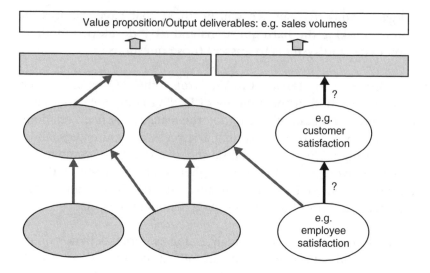

Figure 7.2   Testing sub-sets of the value creation map

Sears wanted to validate the relationship between employee satisfaction, customer satisfaction, and sales volumes – a key output measure.

Arthur Martinez, CEO of Sears at the time, initiated this effort to understand and test the drivers of performance. Sears collected data to test the assumed relationships between sales volume, customer satisfaction, and employee satisfaction. Analysing their data, Sears was able to validate its assumptions and establish that a 5-point increase in employee satisfaction led directly to a 1.3-point increase in customer satisfaction and a 0.5% higher sales volume over a 9-month timeline.[9] The leading financial management and advisory company Merrill Lynch also conducted an analysis of its value drivers. It was able to show that there was a direct link between client satisfaction and the number of times that particular clients had contact with their broker throughout the year.[10]

I was personally involved in the design and validation of a sub-set of a value creation map for a company called Calia Salotti.[11] Calia Salotti is a large Italian furniture manufacturer that designs, produces, and sells residential upholstered furniture, with leading market shares in North America and Europe. About 90% of its production is designed for the export market in Europe and the USA. Calia Salotti produce about 250 different models each year. New Product Development (NPD) is, therefore, a core competence with strategic importance. NPD, and especially the conformity of any new prototypes with the product design principles, were key elements in Calia Salotti's overall strategy. However, the process itself was not well understood as it is characterized by

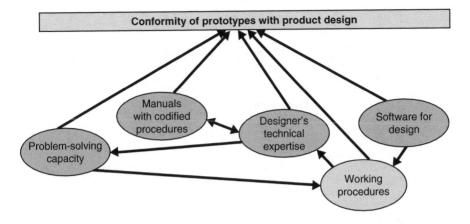

Figure 7.3 Sub-set of Calia Salotti's value creation map

non-formalized processes that are based on know-how and knowledge with a tacit dimension, creative intuition, and the exceptional craftsmanship of some key individuals operating in different phases of the process.

Calia Salotti created a value creation map for the NPD process and went on to collect data to test a sub-set of their assumptions. In a process similar to the one described in Chapter 4, Calia Salotti identified the key drivers and drew the causal map of direct and indirect dependencies (see Figure 7.3). The improvement of conformity of prototypes with the product design relied on the technical expertise of the designer, the codification of procedures, the correct working practices, as well as having the right software in place and the prototype designers possessing sufficient problem-solving capabilities.[12]

Once the map was created, performance indicators were collected to test the causal relationships. Over a period of six months, a lot of data was gathered and fed into a mathematical model to test the relationships between these elements. The data confirmed that most of the assumptions were right. With this assured confidence and a slightly amended map, Calia Salotti initiated various projects and training programmes to improve their NPD process.

As mentioned above, not only sub-sets of the value creation map can be tested, but also entire maps and causal logics. This type of analysis can be performed to shed more light on the dynamics between all the different elements of a strategy (see Figure 7.4).

A company I have worked with very closely over the past six years is Royal Dutch Shell, and one of the projects I managed for Shell was the testing of the dynamic interactions of their strategy elements.

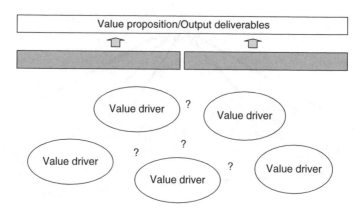

Figure 7.4 Testing the dynamic relationships in value creation map

Without giving away too much sensitive information, Shell's overall model included the following four areas:[13]

- *Efficiency and financial*: a key output deliverable is generating shareholder value, measured against Shell's major competitors, as well as creating relatively high levels of return on (average) capital employed as an efficiency measure.
- *Brand and reputation*: Shell's brand image across the world as well as the reputation Shell has among governments and other key stakeholders.
- *Sustainable development and HSE*: Shell's ethical and social commitments as well as its performance in the area of Health, Safety and Environment (HSE).
- *Human resources*: Shell employees – here Shell measures performance against its 'People Strategy'. This included, for example, leadership, diversity, people skills and talent as well as employee attitudes and satisfaction.

Shell, like most multinationals, has a considerable number of performance indicators. The plan was to collect relevant data for each of the areas identified and then use sophisticated statistical tools to identify and test all relationships in the model.[14]

The first big hurdle was that the data was held in separate databases across different businesses as well as individual countries or even continents. This is a common problem in many organizations and represents a key barrier for analyses of this kind. This is even more true for measuring relationships across a value creation map, which usually requires data from different functions and business units. Common scenarios are that companies collect HR information in HR departments and financial data in finance departments; unfortunately this data is also often kept in separate and non-integrated databases. Adding to this problem is the fact that large organizations regularly outsource particular aspects of their Performance Measurement, most commonly employee surveys and customer or brand surveys. In many cases this means that organizations do not own the full data-set that was collected and therefore are unable to include it in their analysis.

At Shell, we collected financial data over two years from over 120 countries. We used data from over 48 000 brand and customer interviews, and from over 50 000 staff surveys, as well as HSE and social data from all countries. Using this systematic approach allowed us to create a more complete picture of performance and to understand the interrelationship between the different performance areas. The analysis provided some interesting insights that were then investigated further. However, most importantly, it facilitated discussions and debate about strategy and inter-relationships. Even with the massive amount of data in Shell, which gave us fantastic statistical reliability, we didn't take the outcomes of the analysis as truth that can't be challenged. We all agreed that it is impossible to isolate all variables and 'measure' them reliably (as discussed in Chapter 5).

Whereas the exercise was valuable and triggered many worthwhile discussions as a 'one-off' project in order to gain a better understanding of current strategy, I would question the value of such exercises on a more regular basis. They require massive efforts and are quite expensive to execute. Furthermore, I would question whether there are many organizations around that have sufficient valid performance data to perform such an analysis. Having said that, evolutions in Performance Management software applications mean that increasingly this kind of analysis can now be performed routinely with the latest software tools (more on this in Part III).

Understanding and assessing risks[15]

Organizations (both corporations and not-for-profit) face many potential areas where they are vulnerable to significant risks and it is important that these risk factors are actively managed. Risk management as a management tool started to emerge in the 1990s (although the problem has of course been around for much longer than that!). However, the main emphasis has been on financial risks and external risks. Financial risks are concerned only with financial uncertainties, whereas external risks are often identified in the external strategic analysis (see Chapter 2). More recently, organizations have started to look at risks more holistically in order to identify possible threats to their business model and value creation.

Research carried out in 2004[16] found that half of 950 small and medium-sized companies (with revenues between €30 and 360 m) in eleven European countries do not know how to manage the most significant risks they perceive to their businesses. Most senior executives surveyed admitted that that they did not have processes in place to effectively manage strategic and operational risks. The three most significant perceived risks, and those that businesses feel least able to manage, were: increased competition; adverse changes in customer demand; and reduced productivity due to staff absenteeism and turnover. While more than 75% of the companies surveyed claimed that increased competition was their most significant business risk, only half said that they had a robust mitigation plan to counter this risk.

One of the key problems has been for organizations to identify the areas where they face risks and are vulnerable. Since organizations still find it difficult to identify everything that matters, they often revert to the traditional areas of risk: financial and external. However, the value creation map is a visual representation of your business model and all the components required to deliver your value proposition. It can, therefore, guide the risk assessment and it allows organizations to identify potential focus areas for their risk mitigation strategies much more comprehensively (see Figure 7.5).

Your organization's unique value creation map can be used to assess the risks in the value proposition as well as the risks concerning the resources identified to deliver the value proposition. In this way organizations can cover all areas they believe are important for their business and are able to weigh up the potential significance of the risks that they face. Below, I will highlight some common risk areas in the external environment together with examples for each of the resource categories identified in Chapter 3.

External risks

Many of the external risks will usually be identified and addressed in the external strategic analysis (see Chapter 2), when organizations look at the political, economic, social, technological, environmental or legal conditions in their potential markets. Also, the five forces framework will identify threats from competitors, suppliers, etc. Here, I will briefly look at two common external risks – competition and market risks.

■ *Competition risk*. Risks in this category can range from the emergence of a new supplier to the market (from a low labour cost

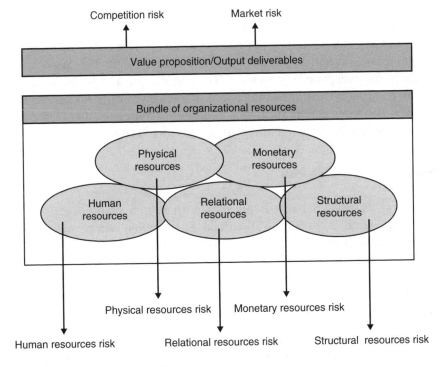

Figure 7.5 Organizational risks

country that is able to significantly undercut on price) to the threat of a competitor company developing a superior product, service or process that is difficult to replicate, and which allows it to capture market share from other incumbent suppliers to that industry.

For example, Xerox never believed that a manufacturer of personal desk-top copiers, Canon, could ever displace its dominant position as the world's most prolific copier manufacturer – they were wrong. James Dyson tried for years to sell his invention of a stylish, bag-less vacuum cleaner that used cyclone technology to the major players in the industry. None of them were interested, so he started manufacturing and marketing it himself. When this venture eventually took off in the UK, he then expanded it into an international operation – the rest, as they say, is history.

- *Market Risk*. This is simple Darwinian theory of adaptability to environment changes. If customers stop buying (or reduce their consumption of) products or services due to economic or other environmental factors, then this will generally affect all players in that marketplace. However, those who accurately identify the trend and react fastest to changes in market demand will normally be in the best position to survive a market downturn and prosper in the future, while others will be less fortunate.

As Gary Hamel and C. K. Prahalad observe: 'The cues, weak signals, and trend lines that suggest how the future might be different are there for everyone to observe.'[17] Getting caught in a position of having too much debt at the time of a market downturn is likely to lead to a Dickensian 'Mr Micawber moment' – witness all the dot-com companies that crashed and burned as soon as the bubble burst.

Monetary resource risk

Monetary or financial risk is an area with which many organizations are quite familiar; especially financial institutions, where money is a real resource that needs to be actively managed. Insurance companies or banks have to make sure that their monetary resources are sufficient and that the risk levels are adequate (or at least they should be, but there have been some notable exceptions). Here I will briefly look at cash flow or capital risk as well as price risk.

- *Cash flow and capital risk.* For financial risk management, organizations deploy practices to optimize the manner in which they take financial risk. This involves upholding relevant policies and procedures, such as monitoring the risk that the cash flow of an organization will be adequate to meet its financial obligations. Many companies use hedging as a technique to reduce or eliminate financial risk by, for example, taking two investment positions that will offset each other if prices change.

  A prominent example of when financial risk management strategies go wrong can be seen in the case of Barings Bank. One of its young traders, the now infamous Nick Leeson, went to Singapore and was trading a very low risk strategy of just betting on the same futures contracts in two different markets in Asia and basically just buying low and selling high. At first he was phenomenally successful and was regarded as a hero by Barings, who gave him more money to trade. Subsequently, when Nick lost a little bit of this money, he managed to cover up those losses by hiding them in a separate account. However, when trying to make back those losses, he began to take much bigger risks with much larger sums of money. This produced further losses when the markets went against his expectations, so that he needed to hide these too and, as we all know, this resulted in the collapse of the entire bank.

- *Price risk.* Companies have long been used to mitigating risks associated with fluctuations in critical financial elements of their business.

Currency exchange rates and the price of certain commodities, such as oil or metals, have long been the bane of predictable earnings and the fluctuating costs of these are commonly 'hedged'. There are other approaches to managing this kind of risk though.

For example, customers of Johnson Matthey, the UK-based international producer of precious metal products, are obliged to purchase their precious metals (mainly gold, platinum and palladium) separately and ahead of the products that the company supplies. This is so that JM minimizes the inherent risks of price fluctuations in its metal stocks while it manufactures the end products, such as automotive and industrial catalysts. Consumers and small businesses, however, have no means of off-setting price risk other than stocking up ahead of price rises; this can have significant short-term economic effects.

Physical resource risk

There seems to be an increasing risk to our physical resources due to more frequent natural and man-made disasters. A series of natural disasters and increased levels of international terrorist activities have both contributed to a heightened awareness of these risks. However, these are not the only types of physical resource risks – some are much more mundane. Here, I will examine disaster risk and bottleneck risks.

- *Disaster risk.* Customers and investors alike need the comfort of assurance that in the event of a major catastrophe, such as a devastating fire, bomb attack, airplane crash or a natural disaster at one of their vital premises, a close to normal service can be provided by the company very rapidly after the event. For example, following the 9/11 attacks several financial services companies who used the World Trade Center and other nearby buildings were able to resume customer service activities within just a few hours from back-up facilities they had set up for such a catastrophic event (though few would have predicted the severity of it). The same is true of London-based companies following the damage caused to the Baltic Exchange by IRA bombs in 1992.
- *Bottleneck risk.* If Eliyahu Goldratt taught manufacturing companies anything in his groundbreaking 1984 novel *The Goal*[18], it was the simple fact that a breakdown, failure or delay within a key constraint part of an organization (in this context, a particular machine tool or production section on the factory floor) creates a problem for the *whole* plant. There are areas of vulnerability in almost all

organizations where, if glitches occur, the resulting impact will be far greater than if there is a failure elsewhere, which can relatively easily be recovered.

Note to all call centre operators: make sure your telephone lines are always available and, in emergencies, offer a call-back facility that works – the enormity of the harm that bad call centres can do has become legendary, but so real too in terms of retaining customer loyalty. Internal capacity constraints need to be recognized and managed – they are 'arteries' that must be kept open at all costs. Although this has been classified here as a physical resource risk, and it generally is, the problem it defines can also be about key people in the organization too (see below) – particularly critical decision-makers and authorizers.

Human resource risk

A key risk that is regularly overlooked in organizations is risk related to its staff and to the knowledge they possess. Organizations are often unaware that there might be some individuals with critical knowledge and expertise who could walk out any day. In Chapter 3, I discussed how the cost of losing experienced staff can be several times the costs of hiring and training a replacement. Another associated risk is the fact that knowledge is an important but also very vulnerable resource – it tends to deplete over time if it is not nurtured. Furthermore, unfortunately, a small percentage of employees may not necessarily be as trustworthy as we would like them to be. Here I will look at knowledge risk, staffing risk, and employee theft risk.

- *Knowledge risk.* Like tangible assets, knowledge has to be maintained to retain its value. Knowledge that is not kept up to date can quickly lose its value or even disappear. Our civilization seems to have lost the knowledge of how the Egyptian pyramids were built; even with modern calculation techniques it cannot be explained how these structures remain standing. Knowledge, like all resources, is context specific. Changes in the external environment can make knowledge and skills redundant, as many craftsmen experienced during the industrialization process that took place in the nineteenth and twentieth centuries. For example, companies that held a lot of knowledge and expertise about how to build a typewriter experienced how quickly this knowledge can become redundant with the arrival of the computer.

  Today, knowledge can be very short lived. Computer programs may be standard one day, but can be replaced by new innovative programs the next day. It is critical therefore for organizations to understand the value of their knowledge and ensure that continuous training keeps knowledge up to date.

■ *Staffing risk.* The impact on productivity of disaffected staff not being engaged with their organization's objectives can be substantial (see also Chapter 6). While strikes and increased levels of absenteeism provide evidence of extreme levels of employee dissatisfaction, more subtle disaffection is achieved by slowing down, not answering the telephone, being rude to customers, gaming imposed performance measures, and so on. A number of studies have verified the positive link between satisfied employees and happy customers, particularly in retailing (e.g. the well-known Sears, Roebuck case illustrates this[19]).

It doesn't work on a 'standalone' basis though because the merchandising element has to be good too, but it is a vital success factor nevertheless. Organizations need to carefully monitor the pulse of employee perceptions about the firm and their relationship with it. In addition to employee morale, firms need to be aware of their staffing needs both in terms of numbers of employees and the skillsets with which they need to be provided. The availability of authorized staff to make particular decisions is an important facet of this equation too.

■ *Employee theft risk.* This is the principal reason that most large companies have an internal audit department. It is also the reason why many organizations appear to have elaborate control procedures that seem to exhibit a lack of trust in their staff. Some staff are dishonest, albeit a small percentage, and there are many examples of employees (often in collaboration with others) who have ripped their employers off for considerable sums of money. For example, in the United States, theft by staff in retail stores alone is estimated to have reached a level of $14.9bn in 2000[20]; employee theft is responsible for more than 46% of what the retail industry calls 'shrinkage' – far more than theft by shoplifters.

Another study by KPMG of 5000 businesses, agencies and nonprofit organizations in 1998, revealed that losses *averaged* $624000 from cheque fraud by employees, including forgeries and mailroom theft; looting of company bank accounts by employees came in at an average of $300000 per organization; theft and misuse of company credit cards amounted to an average of more than $1.1 million; and the average loss from expense account abuse was $141000.

When the Association of Certified Fraud Examiners, based in Austin, Texas, conducted one of the USA's first comprehensive studies of employee fraud in 1996, it reported that companies typically lost 6% of their annual revenues to such theft.[21] There is research that suggests organizations may be able to reduce the risk of theft by creating what I call an enabled learning environment (see Chapter 6).

Structural resource risks

Risks to structural resources include threats to organizational processes and routines, especially those posed by losing database contents and software because of hackers and viruses. There is also an increasingly common risk of intellectual property theft, as well as the danger to business success created by more powerful regulatory regimes that are rightly intolerant of 'old school' exploitation practices. Below, I will observe and illustrate each of these risks.

■ *IT systems risk.* Hackers, viruses, worms and the like have created a whole new industry in computer protection. Many large companies' and governmental organizations' computer systems have been paralysed in the last few years by malignant individuals with high levels of knowledge about information technology protocols who are intent on exposing the vulnerabilities of IT systems and their contents. Apart from the damage they create, which has to be repaired, viruses cause lost data, lost work time and lost revenues (customers go elsewhere). While the internet has many upsides, it does have a downside too.
■ *Intellectual property rights theft risk.* Luxury goods and technology companies are particularly, but by no means exclusively, prone to this type of risk. As I have noted earlier (in Chapter 3), intellectual property rights can take many forms, from branded goods, trademarks, logos and characteristic styling to more mundane industrial patents and media copyrights. We have all seen shady traders in almost every major city and resort in the world that sell copies of Rolex watches, Gucci or Prada handbags, Louis Vuitton luggage, DKNY or Calvin Klein jeans and various fanware, such as New York Yankees caps or Manchester United shirts. And sometimes they are remarkably good copies. But, while you may think that this is relatively harmless since these traders are selling to a largely different set of consumers than the original brand owners do, the damage to the exclusivity of the brand is being done.

   However, arguably, it all gets a bit more alarming when copy aerospace parts start being found at the spares stockists and maintenance hangars of commercial airlines. But it is perhaps the music, film and software industries that have been hardest hit by IPR theft. For years, audio and video cassettes and, more recently, CDs and DVDs have been illegally copied by so-called pirates and sold internationally in very large quantities.

Then along comes Shaun Fanning, the founder of Napster, who developed a brilliant way of keeping lawyers very busy indeed by using the internet to share music files among its community of users so that anyone, anywhere in the world, could download music tracks completely free of charge. Millions did. Musicians weren't too happy about it either since it deprived them of royalties from their songs. Evil pirate or 'Robin Hood'? Despite losing a US Supreme Court case with the Recording Industry Association of America, Fanning's legacy can still be found on the internet today. Overall, in our global economy, it has become increasingly difficult to protect our intellectual property.

■ *Regulatory risk.* The reason I have included regulatory risk within the structural resource category, rather than in external risks or stakeholder relationship risks – although glitches in this area tend to have an adverse effect on the latter too – is that the root cause is often a failure in the framing, communication or policing of internal policies. As the power of regulators has escalated in recent years, the risks of deliberate cheating and sloppy management are escalating too. Compliance issues are fundamental to doing business. For example, Transco, a UK gas utility company, was fined a record £15 m in 2005 for breaching health and safety laws after a leaking gas main led to an explosion that killed four people.

Today, companies need to be sure that the whole of their organization is operating within regulatory rules and guidelines. The litany of major companies who have been exposed and fined considerable sums for being involved in illegal activities expands almost daily in the financial press. For example, in 2005 alone, regulatory bodies in the United States and Europe have meted out substantial fines for: accounting fraud; price fixing cartels; bid rigging; bribery; market abuse; mis-selling of financial services; mishandling of complaints; misleading advertising; failing to inform investors; and sales of abusive tax avoidance schemes. In addition, several senior executives have been jailed for terms ranging from 5 to 25 years. Firms need to examine where they are at risk from regulatory investigation and clean up their ethical acts.

Relational resources risks

In today's networked economy, relationships are crucial ingredients for all organizations in both the private and public sectors. Their reputation hangs on these vital relationships and often the risk needs to be cascaded through the supply chain that helps to deliver the products and/or services that the organization sells or provides. Here I will, therefore, examine reputation risk and supply chain risk.

- *Reputation risk.* This is probably the most under-rated and least understood category of risk in this list. If a company fails to live up to its declared (or expected) values and is then consequently exposed to adverse media attention, then the consequences can be catastrophic. This has the potential to instantly disenfranchise all of a company's branding efforts. Naturally, this category not only includes both product quality failures (such as recalls and warranty claims) and customer service quality failures but also negative media publicity. For example, Arthur Andersen, one of the 'Big 5' worldwide accountancy firms, imploded in just a period of weeks after a few of its partners were involved in several high profile financial scandals that hit the worldwide media – its clients walked away in droves.
- Since 1992, Nike has been the focus of international scrutiny of how huge western companies treat their suppliers in some of the poorest parts of the world. It has frequently been accused of promoting the use of 'sweatshops' in Indonesia, Vietnam, China and South America, where labour abuses, forced overtime and unsanitary conditions abound. About 500 000 workers in over 350 factories across the globe make Nike footwear and apparel. Activist groups, such as Global Exchange, first bombarded the media alleging abuses. By 1997–98, an anti-Nike campaign led by human rights activists culminated in several 'Protest Nike' days in the USA.

  Nike's initial response was sluggish, but quickly gathered momentum when it realized the damage that could be done to its brand and also to its college campus sales. It, therefore, introduced a code of conduct for its suppliers, created a remediation plan and implemented independent monitoring of its suppliers' factories. It even published the location of many of these factories, which it had previously refused to do on competitive grounds. Lost reputation cannot only disenfranchise customers, but also current and potential employees. The best people will move to the organizations with the best reputation.
- *Supply chain risk.* Suppliers are a critical component of an organization's ability to deliver products and services to its customers, especially in the age of outsourcing 'non-core' activities. If a supplier defaults for reasons of capacity shortages, quality failures, a strike, or a fire at their premises, then such disruptions are likely to have a major impact on customer service. Since the advent of 'Just-in-Time'

delivery systems, which eliminate buffer stocks in the production system, the impact of such events can have a very rapid impact.

For example, when Ford's supplier of door and boot latches defaulted (not components that most people would associate with production criticality issues), plants in Dagenham and Cologne came to a halt. Consequently, output of nearly 3000 cars a day was lost and more than 10 000 workers were either sent home or diverted to plant maintenance.

In 2005, British Airways' sole supplier of in-flight meals at London's Heathrow airport, Gate Gourmet, sacked over 650 unionized workers when a festering industrial dispute erupted into an illegal strike. (Gate Gourmet is part of a US private equity-owned company that was once part of British Airways before BA decided that catering was not one of its core competencies.) The situation rapidly escalated when 1000 British Airways workers at Heathrow, many of whom had relatives affected by the Gate Gourmet strike, started their own unofficial sympathy strike. This action forced the cancellation of flights and more than 100 000 passengers were stranded, mostly at Heathrow, one of the busiest airports in the world, causing scenes of anger and chaos at the height of the August holiday season.

As a corollary to this drama, it was revealed that British Airways had squeezed its supplier so hard in pricing negotiations that Gate Gourmet had no alternative but to reduce its mainly Asian-origin workforce substantially, since the contract had become financially unviable (although, arguably, it could have examined other ways of parting company with them – to avoid insolvency of its UK operations).

This is a classic example of a clash of interests and cultures within the supply chain that affected all the key stakeholders adversely. The customer (BA), the supplier, the customer's passengers, both the supplier's and customer's employees, and the shareholders of both BA and Gate Gourmet were all losers. The trade unions involved may yet, at the time of writing, also suffer recriminations.

In recent years, during which high profile cases of corporate wrongdoing have caught the attention of the media and NGO (Non-Governmental Organization) activists have become more vocal in attacking corporate behaviour, reputation management has climbed the ladder of boardroom priorities. Reputations take years to develop, but can be destroyed very rapidly indeed. Because of the internet, the speed with which a reputation can be attacked by a broad range of different stakeholders – customers, employees, former employees, former suppliers, labour and human rights activists, and so on – on a global scale has been reduced to a matter of hours. Shareholders and financial analysts increasingly notice these factors too. It is not surprising, therefore, that this element of risk now has the full attention of major companies' boards worldwide.

A 2003 survey[22] found that 60% of the world's CEOs view corporate reputation as a 'much more important' aspect of business than five years ago. The study also found that maintaining a good reputation has become so important that 65% of the world's CEOs have taken full responsibility for managing this aspect of performance. This figure rises to 80% in the USA, whereas in Europe it stood at just 44% (possibly due to closer relations between CEO and the board). CEOs acknowledge customers as the external force with greatest effect on reputation, followed by print media, financial analysts and shareholders.

Risk assessment then is a highly significant factor for managing in today's business environment. So, executives need to get to grips with the various risks that their organization faces. Given that there are many potential risks, it is advisable to begin accumulating data that gives organizations useful information about where they are most exposed. In the next section I will discuss how the value creation map can be used to analyse and evaluate potential risks.

Analysing risk

The first step in assessing risk, therefore, must be to identify possible areas of risk. The best way to do this is to take the value creation map and go through all its elements, identifying potential risks (see Figure 7.6). These risks can then be captured in what I call a 'risk log'. This is a table that can be used to capture, describe, assess and quantify potential risks (see Table 7.1). This often requires obtaining factual information about these risks and then prioritizing their relative importance. Organizations need to assess the potential risk areas for the component parts of their organization, categorize them, and then assess which are most important to manage.

Completing a risk log

In a risk log, organizations can capture their key risks. It can become a working document that is part of the Performance Management system. Below, I outline the various steps involved in creating such a risk log.

1 For each element on the value creation map, potential risks are identified. This element-by-element approach ensures that all potential

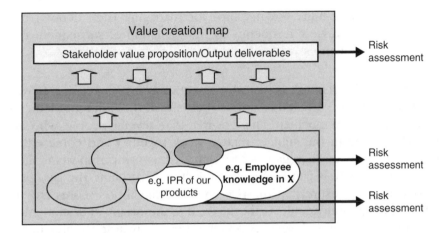

Figure 7.6 Identifying potential risk areas

risk areas are discussed – both external and internal. Moreover, using the value creation map also helps organizations to identify how potential risk areas might impact each other. However, it is unlikely that all potential risks for each element are identified and prioritized straightaway. The risk log will usually grow over time as more potential risk areas are identified, but the relevance of some will also tend to fall away as they are either mitigated or become less relevant over time (see below).

2 Describe the essence of the particular potential risks for each element. Here, it is possible to give the risk a name, but more importantly to create a short narrative *description* of the type of risk.

3 Define the *risk level*. Here the likely consequences and potential impact of this risk are evaluated, were the risk to occur.

4 Define the *likelihood level*. Here, the likelihood that this risk might turn into a reality is evaluated. In addition, the likelihood is compared to the likelihood of the last review cycle. This indicates whether the likelihood is increasing, staying the same, or decreasing.[23]

5 Ascribe an appropriate scoring system according to: a) the *risk level* (potential severity) of each risk (e.g. 1–5), the criteria for which may not necessarily be all financial ones, and b) the *likelihood level* (probability of occurrence) of the risk (e.g. 1–5). These two scores can then be added up to create the risk score. The rationale for this scoring system is not only to help identify management priorities but also to assess whether the likely severity of each risk has moved over time and whether the firm's potential exposure to it has increased or diminished since the last review.

6 Assign responsibility (ownership) for managing each defined risk and define a review frequency for re-evaluation of subsequent risk mitigation activities.

Completing the risk log is best done within a project team. Different sub-teams can be assigned to assess the risks of the different elements of the value creation map. This ensures that several people who are knowledgeable in the subject matter work together and come either to a unanimous or aggregate score. Here, teamwork is important since this type of analysis can be highly subjective. That being the case, it is a good idea to ensure that the risk level and likelihood scores are not left to a single individual. Furthermore, it is important to document as much information and logic as possible for the awarded scores in the risk log so that these can be revisited at the next review.

For each area, additional data can be collected and referenced in the risk log. However, there is a real danger here too of making this an overly bureaucratic process, and that is why I advocate a relatively simplistic approach. The Pareto principle applies: 80+ % of the risk can be identified and assessed with 20% of the potential effort required to do it.

Having identified the highest priority risks (with high risk level and high likelihood level), management actions can be taken to modify their consequences and potential impacts on the firm. Typical actions resulting from a risk analysis include:

- Buying insurance against occurrence
- Development of mitigation plans (especially for emergencies/crises – scenario planning techniques can assist this process)
- Renegotiation of supplier contracts
- Introduction of (internal/external) compliance audits
- Introduction of new performance indicators to monitor emerging trends.

This does not mean that lower severity/likelihood risks can be ignored altogether; it is just that management is unlikely to be able to set in motion the corrective actions for large numbers of risks simultaneously. However, if this is treated as part of a company-wide programme, then actions on lower priority risks might – with appropriate guidance – be delegated to lower ranking managers. Otherwise, they will have to wait until the senior executives have first dealt with the highest priority risk category and that might mean that the firm is still exposed to some pretty substantial risks with which it is unready to cope.

Table 7.1 Risk log

Key elements (from the value creation map)	Description of risk	Risk level: potential consequences/impact	Likelihood level/changing probability: probability that this risk will occur, changes in likelihood	Risk score: risk level + likelihood level	Accountability/Review frequency: who is accountable, how often is this risk reviewed?
Employee knowledge	Our knowledge in Y software might become redundant if X becomes new standard	About a third of our leading programmers could become redundant	Not very high, most research shows that Y will stay the main standard Constant likelihood	3 + 1 = **4**	Amanda Simon – quarterly
IPR	Our patented software is copied in India and China	Could lead to significant revenue losses and loss of reputation	Very high – first reports indicate that this is happening Increasing likelihood	4 + 5 = **9**	Peter Smith – monthly
IT Infrastructure	...	...	...	...	...
Reputation	...	...	...	...	...
Etc...	...	...	...	...	...

Although organizations have certainly been at risk for many centuries (how else would the insurance industry have become so wealthy?), arguably they have never been *so* at risk. Today, it is becoming increasingly common and necessary for organizations to appoint a senior risk manager. This is a post that often reports to a non-executive director but where the incumbent needs to work closely with operational executives in far-flung parts of the organization. In international companies senior risk managers need to work closely with operational executives in far-flung parts of the globe, as only they know where their part of the firm is most vulnerable. Introducing an evaluation methodology that everyone can relate to and then conducting a fair assessment of the potential risks is the first step towards mitigating the likely impacts that those risks could have on the firm.

Assessing mergers and acquisitions

M&A mania peaked around the turn of the last century. At that time, it was virtually impossible to pick up a business publication that did not contain a story about an M&A deal. In 1999 alone, over 26 000 M&A deals were registered worldwide valued at $2.3 trillion and announcements of cross-border deals amounted to $1100 billion. Then, soon after, stock markets began to plummet in the wake of the dot-com crash and the number and value of M&A deals dried up too. The events of '9/11' and fears about the Iraq war also exacerbated low levels of business confidence. However, since the recovery of stock markets across the globe began after the first quarter of 2003, activity has picked up once again. M&A is back on the corporate agenda.

So why are mergers and acquisitions so popular in good times? The short answer to this is that they offer a short-cut to growth that simply cannot be attained by organic growth within the same timescales. Growth is what investors want companies to deliver – sales growth but, more importantly, profit and cash flow growth too – so that share prices and dividend yields grow in parallel. There are other strategic reasons too, such as:

- to eliminate a competitor by buying the company and so reduce the number of players in the industry sector
- to broaden geographic spread
- to add additional products or services to the company's portfolio of offerings in order to increase penetration into lucrative existing markets
- to enter attractive new market segments

- to add new strategic resources or fully-fledged capabilities to the organization by buying things such as a facility, customer lists, brands or technology, together with the people skill-sets and practices that come with it. (The reason for buying resources can be that they are cheaper to buy than to make, or, more commonly, that it is faster than developing them internally.)

Clearly, there are several ways of pursuing the M&A approach. Some companies prefer the 'bolt-on' acquisition route, whereby a series of relatively small companies are added to the parent company over time. Others opt for more ambitious strategies with takeovers of much larger companies, which may either complement their existing business or create a completely new arm to it. Greater extremes can be created by merging with another company of approximately equal size, or even – if sufficient financing can be found – buying one that is even bigger (known as a reverse takeover).

Occasionally too, it may be preferable to 'put a toe in the water' before deciding to fully invest in a new direction and so it may be a valid strategic option to create an alliance or joint venture before committing large amounts of capital to a full acquisition. There can be economies of scale benefits too by opting for a joint venture investment where an acquisition or merger may not be a practical option (a common practice in the automotive and pharmaceutical industries). The various types of business combinations and alliances are summarized in Figure 7.7.

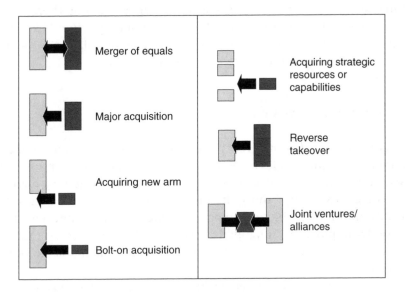

Figure 7.7   Types of business combinations and alliances[24]

However, there are well-documented problems with this M&A approach to growth. The biggest is that study after study has shown that only around *half* of M&A transactions enjoy a successful outcome (with, perhaps surprisingly, domestic acquisitions perceived as only slightly more successful in achieving their aims than cross-border ones). The worse news is that the figure for joint ventures is even lower. So that means, given the $2.3 trillion invested in M&A deals in 1999, about $1.15 trillion or so was a wasted investment.[25] That's one hell of a lot of money and, even at somewhat lower levels of activity today, anything that can be done to alleviate that level of waste has got to be worthwhile.

There are of course many reasons why mergers go 'pear-shaped': different leadership styles leading to personality problems at the top; cultural differences; incompatible information systems; breakdowns in critical stakeholder relationships, and so on. But without doubt the most common culprit is the failure, in one way or another, to successfully integrate the two entities. After the ink dries when the companies complete the deal, unity proves elusive, and instead of coming together things fly apart.

'A whole consulting industry thrives by advising companies on post-merger integration, a salvage operation to recover something from the wreckage of impossible promises and ill-considered goals,' said The Economist,[26] prescriptively adding that 'companies that agree on a clear strategy and management structure before they tie the knot stand a better chance of living happily ever after.'

Integrating two firms requires advance planning. But there is the rub. Intelligent planning seems to be in short supply when M&A deals are done. The sheer thrill of the 'mega-deal' can stimulate poor assessments of suitability and complementarities.

Pre-merger assessment

Mergers and acquisitions represent an exchange of both tangible resources and intangible resources, requiring these resources to be assessed and valued. The takeover prices paid for targets in many of these deals, especially those in knowledge-intensive industries like telecom, multimedia, biotechnology, etc. include very large payments for goodwill and other intangible resources. Goodwill is essentially a 'kitchen-sink' measure of an organization's many intangible resources that cannot be easily identified.

Value creation in these acquisitions, therefore, depends critically upon the acquirer's ability to leverage the resources that it has acquired.

In acquisitions, the acquirer needs to combine at least some of its own resources with those of the acquired firm to a greater or lesser degree, depending on the nature of the acquisition and the acquiring company's independence/integration philosophy towards its strategic development. This requires an understanding of the nature of the tangible and especially the intangible resources of the two firms, how they complement one another and how they can be leveraged to improve future performance. Effective leveraging of intangible assets in acquisitions requires the ability to:

- Identify
- Assess
- Redeploy, and
- Integrate the acquired resources.

Identifying, assessing, redeploying and integrating tangible resources is so much easier than doing the same for the intangible resources. Since many of the intangible resources are deeply embedded in the organizational architecture, routines and cultures, this process poses a formidable challenge. Adding to the problem is the fact that access to the target firm's intangibles in an acquisition context can be limited. Recent reports of massive post-acquisition goodwill write-offs and restructuring charges, amounting to billions of dollars, by Vodafone, Vivendi, Marconi, AOL-Time Warner, and so on emphasize the challenge of this process.

At the same time, assessing intangible resources is often characterized by poor audits at the pre-acquisition stage and poor post-acquisition integration planning.[27] Without correct identification and assessment, the acquirers may overvalue the intangible resources thus causing value destruction for the acquiring organization's shareholders and other stakeholders. Or the acquirer might initially misjudge the suitability and complementarities of those resources, which will then cause problems at the post-acquisition integration phase.[28] Furthermore, the inability to properly identify and assess the resource architecture of organizations might mean that acquirers overlook potential acquisition targets because they do not understand the value of the intangible resources the potential target company might possess.

The best way to complete a pre-merger assessment is to create a value creation map for the target organization and then compare it with the value creation map of the acquiring organization. Sometimes this might be a problem because of access restrictions to the target organization in the pre-merger or pre-acquisition phase. However, where the takeover is a friendly (rather than hostile) one, in most

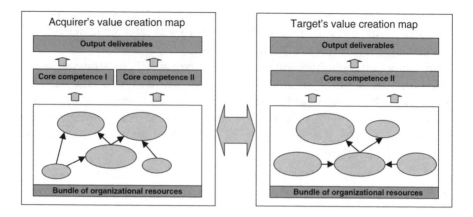

Figure 7.8 Assessing suitability and complementarities

cases it may even be appreciated by the target organization, since this action can help to identify possible conflicts and clashes which can then be addressed.[29] What's more, the insights can be used to shape the post-merger integration strategy.

Pre-merger assessment case study

I was involved in an assessment of a possible merger between two seemingly identical pharmaceutical organizations. For the purpose of this case study, I will call them PharmaScience and PharmaLab.[30] Initial pre-merger investigations allowed us to analyse the resource architecture of both organizations. This analysis showed that the two firms had an almost identical resource structure with complementary products for similar markets. The initial conclusion was that by merging them, both could be brought together and therefore enjoy better economies of scale and economies of scope; $1 + 1 = 3$.

And so causal value creation maps were created for both organizations in order to kick off the pre-merger planning. However, what this revealed was that, even though the resource structure was almost identical, the value creation logic wasn't. Figure 7.9 shows both value creation maps in a slightly different format than I have shown before. The output deliverable 'financial success' is integrated into the map (bottom right-hand side) and no core competencies are included in this version. Both maps show different causal logics and different emphases illustrated by the widths of the arrows (see also Chapter 4). Please note too that, for this case study only, broad categories are used and illustrated in the value creation maps to protect confidentiality.

Resource interactions – Organization I (PharmaScience)

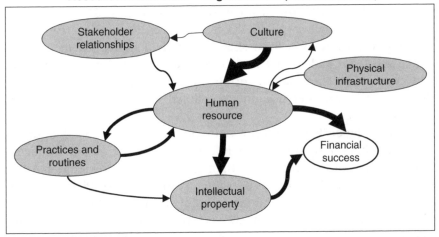

Resource interactions – Organisation II (PharmaLab)

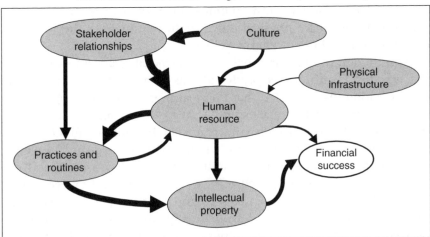

Figure 7.9 Value creation maps for PharmaScience and PharmaLab

Creating the two value creation maps revealed that in PharmaScience each team had one or two 'stars' – highly creative team leaders who generated much of the R&D output themselves. These individuals were able to bring ideas together by being open-minded, but also had a very strong ability to consolidate ideas into outputs. They were backed by a culture of support from their teams who worked towards the ideas of one leader. Knowledge was only shared within teams and there was little knowledge sharing between teams in PharmaScience. Most team members had regular communications with the team leader, and most of these communications took place face-to-face and via e-mail.

The key component of this communication structure was the strong support culture with the team leader in the centre. The majority of knowledge sharing was bi-directional between leader and team member, whereas there was little sharing between individual team members. Each team had shared databases, which were also used to codify and consolidate information for the team leader to access. Much of the knowledge transfer was one-directional from the team member to the team leader.

PharmaScience had a strong focus on codifying knowledge among team members and storing this information for the leader to access. The emphasis of the leader was then to apply this knowledge in order to produce valuable output. The value creation map of PharmaScience showed how the support culture strongly influences the people, especially the leaders, who then convert this gathered knowledge into intellectual property as well as directly into products and services, which generate financial success. The way team members interact is supported by practices and routines, such as regular meetings and shared databases. The physical infrastructure influences the wellbeing of the team members in PharmaScience.

Even though the resource base for PharmaLab was almost identical, the way R&D output was produced was very different. Creating the value creation map revealed that PharmaLab operated on a significantly different model to PharmaScience. Instead of having the strong support culture for the leaders, the teams in PharmaLab functioned as real teams and freely shared knowledge within the team, as well as with other teams in the organization. The culture was open and promoted the transfer of knowledge between internal and external stakeholders. This impacted the practices and routines and the way team members interacted. There were many more ad hoc meetings between team members, and outputs and solutions were developed in teams. Team leaders had more of a coordinating role and were less autocratic. Teams in PharmaLab developed output, which was then turned into processes, patented, and sold. Fewer services were delivered directly by the team leaders than at PharmaScience. The predominant value creation logic in PharmaLab was a much more collaborative R&D development that involved all members of the organization.

Once these differences became apparent, it was decided that a merger would not have been the best way forward. The value creation logics were too different and it was believed that trying to merge them would not work and, therefore, wouldn't deliver the desired economies of scope and scale. Instead, critical areas were identified and a joint venture approach was used to bring together some of the core competencies of the two organizations.

Post-merger integration

Once the merger or acquisition has taken place, good post-merger integration is fundamental to successful M&A activity. A recent survey by KPMG finds that two-thirds of the companies bought between 1996 and 1998 still need to be properly integrated.[31] However, as outlined above, the integration process should not be a 'salvage process'. It should be a planned process from the outset of the decision to do the deal, i.e. part of the due diligence process, or *pre*-merger integration planning.

The complexity, and so the difficulty, of integration tends to multiply with the size of the acquisition. At the lower end of the difficulty scale is the bolt-on acquisition. Here, there are usually earn-out clauses in the terms of the deal that help to retain the existing management team. Often, if the company being integrated is to remain a largely independent entity, there is not much more to do than to welcome them to the fraternity of the larger company, integrate their financial reporting and HR administration systems with that of the acquirer, and let them get on with what they do best, although opportunities for cross-selling of products or services should not be overlooked.

At the other end of the difficulty scale is the full-blown merger of two companies of roughly equal size and the reverse takeover of a larger company by a smaller one. The post-merger integration activity for these latter two categories can be highly complex and may demand the specialist expertise of an experienced team to help make the integration a successful one. But, as noted above, there is historically only a 50/50 chance of success. My view is that the earlier the integration planning process can start, the better the chances of succeeding.

Many types of mergers and acquisitions have economies of scale as their principal *raison d'être*. And so the realization of major cost savings opportunities will usually be of primary importance. Cost savings, of course, come principally from sales of businesses or other tangible assets, employee redundancies, enhanced purchasing power, and reductions in working capital. They can also come from redeploying resources to more productive uses. Recently-merged GlaxoSmithKline reckoned it could save $400 m a year just by combining its separate R&D operations and cutting out duplication – a saving, it claims, that it can then plough back into more productive R&D.

There is an enormous amount of work to do if the full potential (and that is usually what is promised) of the merger or acquisition is to be realized. This is a massive programme of activity that will certainly require a full-time project team for a period of several months or even years, with significant amounts of executive involvement, in order to deliver it. And, while all this is going on, the firm still needs to carry on its normal activities of delivering products and/or services to its customers. Savvy competitors won't stand still in the meantime either. It is little wonder, therefore, that many organizations fail to deliver the promised results within the anticipated timescales and budgets set at the outset. Let me give you an example of a typical large post-merger integration agenda:

- Integration of financial reporting and HR administration systems
- Redesign management structure
- Rationalization of overlapping functions (i.e. people)
- Rationalization of overlapping facilities (i.e. buildings and equipment)
- Rationalization of legal entities (i.e. subsidiaries)
- Sell-off of unwanted parts of the acquired company [?]
- Redundancy of excess people
- Retention of key customers
- Retention of key executives
- Relocation of retained executives/best managers [?]
- Avoid mass exodus of employees (communicate, communicate . . .)
- Integrate key internal operational functions (e.g. R&D, Marketing & Sales, Purchasing, Production, Distribution, etc.)
- Integrate corporate support functions (e.g. HR, Finance, IT, etc.)
- Integrate external supply chain components (e.g. dealers, distributors, suppliers)
- Integrate information technology systems (e.g. different operating systems)
- Leverage increased buying power
- Address regulatory compliance issues
- Redesign corporate identity (e.g. if name change)

and last, but by no means least. . .
- Unify internal culture of the merged company.

The last item requires some further explanation since this is one of the most important and distinctive intangible resources that an organization possesses. When you start to meld different cultures together in an M&A situation, there can be problems. Culture compatibility issues can be particularly complex for cross-border acquisitions where the values and practices of the different management teams can be at loggerheads, reflecting both their individual corporate cultures and their national cultures. The DaimlerChrysler 'merger' (really a takeover of the latter by the former) was a classic example of this, with massive differences in German and American attitudes to doing business that have taken several years to resolve.

With this in mind, therefore, it is an indispensable pre-deal planning process to ensure that an evaluation of organizational compatibility takes place. And the value creation maps can facilitate much of this work. This also allows you to take a view of the nature of the target organization's value proposition and relationships with its key stakeholders – for example, its investors, customers, intermediaries (dealers, distributors, retailers, etc.), employees, suppliers, regulators and the communities in which it operates. Not only is the way that these relationships are managed a good guide to the prevailing culture within the organization, but also this will highlight the importance of preserving (or improving) those relationships. It may be quite difficult to do so, for example, when substantial redundancies are planned as a part of the post-merger integration process.

Arguably then, better results should be achieved through better planning of post-merger integration activities prior to the deal being executed. However, this is not as easy as it might seem on the surface. Practically, the planned deal may not even happen because of the intervention of another bidder or through a regulatory blockage, and so the management preparation activity could be entirely wasted; and not many companies do enough serial major acquisitions to justify having a dedicated internal post-merger integration team in place ready to deploy their expertise (whereas a small team might be justifiable for an intended series of bolt-on acquisitions).

For merger and acquisition deals, the market-based view is most commonly necessary for selecting appropriate targets, but for post-merger integration it is the resource-based view that is paramount. All five categories of resources are vital components: monetary resources; physical resources; human resources; structural resources (such as cultures); and relational resources (in the context of a diverse set of stakeholders). It is these that will, or will not, deliver the ultimate value proposition. Both views need to be integrated for successful business combination outcomes but, in common practice, this is certainly not always the balance of priorities that is applied today.

References and endnotes

1   Heskett, J. L., Sasser, W. E. and Schlesinger, L. A. (1997). *The Service Profit Chain: How Leading Companies Link Profit and Growth to Loyalty, Satisfaction, and Value*. Simon & Schuster Inc.: New York.

2   See for example: Pisano, G., Shuen, A. and Teece, D. (1997). Dynamic Capabilities and Strategic Management. *Strategic Management Journal*, Vol. 18, No. 7, Aug, p. 509; or Eisenhardt, K. M. and Martin, J. A.

(2000). Dynamic Capabilities: What Are They? *Strategic Management Journal*, Vol. 21, No. 10/11, Oct/Nov, p. 1105.

3 Rindova, V. P. and Kotha, S. (2001). Continuous 'Morphing': Competing Through Dynamic Capabilities, Form, and Function. *Academy of Management Journal*, Vol. 44, No. 6, Dec, p. 1263.

4 I would like to thank Dr Karim Moustaghfir for the assistance in the work with Fujitsu, which earned him a Ph.D.

5 Preskill, H. and Torres, R. T. (1999). *Evaluative Inquiry for Learning in Organizations*. Sage: Thousand Oaks.

6 Ittner, C. D. and Larcker, D. F. (2003). Coming Up Short on Non-financial Performance Measurement. *Harvard Business Review*, Nov, pp. 88–95.

7 Argyris, C. (1991). 'Teaching Smart People to Learn'. *Harvard Business Review*, May/June, pp. 99–109.

8 Heskett, J., Sasser, E. and Schlesinger, L. (2003). *The Value Profit Chain*. Free Press, New York.

9 See for example: Kirn, S. P., Quinn, R. T. and Rucci, A. J. (1998). The Employee-Customer-Profit Chain at Sears. *Harvard Business Review*, Vol. 76, No. 1, pp. 83–97; or Ibid, Heskett, J. L., Sasser, W. E. and Schlesinger, L. A. (1997) (see note 1 above).

10 Heskett, J. L., Sasser, W. E. and Schlesinger, L. A. (2003). *The Value Profit Chain: Treat Employees Like Customers and Customers Like Employees*. Free Press: New York, NY, p. 250.

11 For the full case study see: Marr, B., Neely, A. and Schiuma, G. (2004). The Dynamics of Value Creation: Mapping Your Intellectual Performance Drivers. *Journal of Intellectual Capital*, Vol. 5, No. 2, pp. 312–25.

12 For more information see: Marr, B., Neely, A. and Schiuma, G. (2004). The Dynamics of Value Creation: Mapping Your Intellectual Performance Drivers. *Journal of Intellectual Capital*, Vol. 5, No. 2, pp. 312–25.

13 The data presented in this case study was collected in 1999 and 2000. The original case study was created with my colleagues Bruce Clark and Andy Neely, and presented at the 2002 PMA Conference in Boston.

14 Systems of regression equations were estimated econometrically and multiple estimation methods were used to test for sensitivity to assumptions (OLS, SUR, 2SLS, 3SLS).

15 I would like to thank my colleague Chris Adams for the valuable input into this section. Risk management is one of his areas of expertise.

16 Conducted by Marsh, the world's biggest insurance broker.

17 Hamel, G. and Prahalad, C. K. (1994). *Competing for the Future*. Harvard Business School Press: Boston, MA.

18 Goldratt, E. (1984). *The Goal*. North River Press: New York.

19 See for example: Kirn, S. P., Quinn, R. T. and Rucci, A. J. (1998). The Employee-Customer-Profit Chain at Sears. *Harvard Business Review*, Vol. 76, No. 1, pp. 83–97; or Heskett, J. L., Jones, T. O. and Loveman, G. W. (1994). Putting the Service-Profit Chain to Work. *Harvard Business Review*, Vol. 72, No. 2, p. 164; or Ibid, Heskett, J. L., Sasser, W. E. and Schlesinger, L. A. (2003) (see note 10 above).

20 National Retail Security survey.

21 Winter, G. (2000). Taking at the Office Reaches New Heights. *New York Times*, July 12.

22 Conducted by communications consultancy Hill & Knowlton and executive headhunters Korn/Ferry (Reported in *Financial Times*, 14 October 2003).

23 See for example: Drzik, J. and Slywotzky, A. J. (2005). Countering the Biggest Risk of All. *Harvard Business Review*, Vol. 83, No. 4, April, pp. 78–88.

24 Adapted from Adams, C. and Neely, A. (2000). *Measuring Business Combinations & Alliances*, white paper.

25 Adams, C. and Neely, A. (2000). The Performance Prism to Boost M&A Success. *Measuring Business Excellence*, 4, 3.

26 (1999). *The Economist*, January 9.

27 See for example: James, A. D., Georghiou, L. and Metcalfe, J. S. (1998). Integrating technology into merger and acquisition decision-making. *Technovation*, 18, 8/9, 563–73.

28 See for example: Sudarsanam, P. S. (1995). *The Essence of Mergers and Acquisitions*, Prentice Hall; or Harrison, J. S., Hitt, M. A. and Ireland, R. D. (2001). *Mergers and Acquisitions, A Guide to Creating Value for Stakeholders*. Oxford University Press.

29 For an interesting case example of an M&A assessment using the intellectual capital lens see for example: Gupta, O. and Roos, G. (2001). Mergers and Acquisitions Through an Intellectual Capital Perspective. *Journal of Intellectual Capital*, Vol. 2, No. 3, pp. 297–309.

30 For reasons of confidentiality I am unable to use their real names. For further information see also: Marr, B. (2004). Measuring and Benchmarking Intellectual Capital. *Benchmarking - An International Journal*, Vol. 11, No. 6, pp. 559–70.

31 See *Financial Times*, 22 February 2002.

Part III

Automation of Strategic Performance Management

Introduction to Part III: automation as enabler

So far in this book I have discussed how you create a strategic roadmap in the forms of value creation maps and value creation narratives. I looked at how to design relevant performance initiators and subsequently discussed how to analyse and interpret these in an enabled learning environment in order to gain management insights and to learn. Recent developments in the software world mean that this Strategic Performance Management process can be supported by software applications (see figure below). Many of the applications have been specifically designed for that purpose and, in this part of the

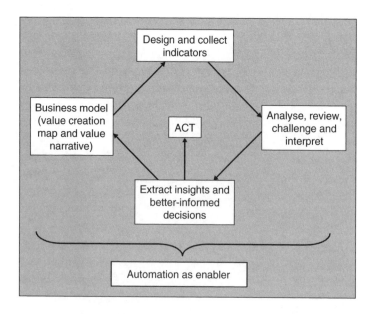

Automation as enabler

book, I will take a closer look at what these applications can and
can't do. Also, in the Appendix, I provide a framework that will help
you to select the most appropriate tool for your organization.

However, before I discuss the benefits of, and selection criteria for,
Strategic Performance Management software applications, I would like
to give you an important word of warning. Even though software applications can be a powerful enabler of the Performance Management
process, this does not mean that these applications can do the work for
you. The key is to design unique value creation logics and then develop
idiosyncratic indicators that help you make better strategic decisions.

There is no short cut to this. My advice would be to run away very
quickly if software salesmen are trying to tell you otherwise. There are
no industry templates and no magic off-the-shelf Strategic Performance
Management frameworks. And there are no lists of 10 key performance indicators that you can take off a database and then start your
Performance Management initiative.

However, implemented correctly and following the principles outlined in this book, automation will allow you to unleash the full power
of Strategic Performance Management. It will give all employees access
to customized Performance Management data in their preferred formats,
and it will allow collaborations, powerful analyses, and data integration to provide a single version of the truth.

I recently conducted a study of the current Strategic Performance
Management practices among the 5000 largest companies in the United
States.[1] This study confirmed the power of Strategic Performance Management applications. The study revealed that users of specialized
Strategic Performance Management applications were most satisfied;
whereas those organizations still using spreadsheets were the least satisfied. Many believed spreadsheets were inappropriate tools for Strategic
Performance Management. Shockingly, the study found that almost half
of the firms are still using spreadsheet applications, such as Microsoft
Excel, as their main tool for Strategic Performance Management. However, many organizations are realizing that those solutions are too
cumbersome, labour-intensive and unreliable. And many organizations are
currently looking for appropriate replacements. The major disadvantages
of spreadsheet-based Strategic Performance Management solutions are:[2]

1 No scalability. Systems quickly reach the capacity desktop spreadsheets can handle. Performance Management spreadsheets can grow
into big documents with colour coding, macros, calculations, etc.
I have seen various spreadsheet-based applications become slow and
prone to crashes. Often, there was just too much data and complexity
in the spreadsheet, which wasn't designed for that purpose.

2 Time-consuming to update. Spreadsheet-based solutions are usually manually fed and updated. In one organization that approached me, a business analyst spent about 2 months every quarter 'updating the spreadsheets'. This is not only slow but also leaves immense room for errors. A KPMG study conducted in 1997 found that over 90% of existing spreadsheets contain mistakes![3]

3 No collaboration and communication support. Information kept in individual spreadsheets is not designed for collaboration or communication. The spreadsheets are often scattered around on different machines, and it requires enormous discipline to work from the same spreadsheet.

4 Difficult analysis. Analysis is complicated for the reason that data is stored in individual spreadsheets; it is difficult and time-consuming to bring them together for analysis across more than one data-set.

Spreadsheet-based solutions are not really a workable option for any organization that is serious about Strategic Performance Management. For organizations that want to unleash the full potential of Strategic Performance Management, there is no alternative to installing purpose-built software applications. However, before I move on to discuss software application in more detail, it is important to note one other thing: implementing Strategic Performance Management is not an IT project! Turning it into one will jeopardize the entire development efforts.[4] Software will always only be an enabler and enhancer. This means that if the foundations of the Strategic Performance Management approach are weak, the automation will be too.

References and endnotes

1 Marr, B. (2004). *Business Performance Management – The State of the Art*. Hyperion Solutions and Cranfield School of Management: London.

2 Marr, B. and Neely, A. (2003). Automating Your Scorecard: The Balanced Scorecard Software Report. Stamford, CT: Gartner, Inc. and Cranfield School of Management; Marr, B. and Neely, A. (2001). The Balanced Scorecard Software Report. Stamford, CT: Gartner, Inc. and Cranfield School of Management.

3 See for example: http://www.kpmg.co.za

4 Marr, B. (2001). Scored for Life. *Financial Management*, 30 (1), April, pp. 14–17.

8

Benefits of automation

Implementing organization-wide Strategic Performance Management initiatives requires IT support. So-called Strategic Performance Management solutions help to integrate data from disparate sources, enable organizations to analyse the data across all strategic elements, and most importantly allow collaboration and communication of the strategic logic and key objectives organization-wide. This chapter discusses the benefits of implementing a software application and the subsequent appendix introduces a framework that will assist you in the selection process to find the most appropriate automation solution for you. Selecting the right application is critical for a successful implementation. However, the fact that there are many different vendors, who all offer quite diverse solutions, can make this a difficult task. Questions addressed in this chapter include:

- What are the benefits of Strategic Performance Management software applications?
- How can Strategic Performance Management software support collaboration and communication?
- How can Strategic Performance Management software support data analysis and extracting insights?
- How can Strategic Performance Management software help to integrate and manage data?

The software market for Strategic Performance Management applications is growing constantly. Today, there are many vendors trying to get their share of the multi-billion dollar analytic application market. Paper and pencil, or simple spreadsheet tools might be sufficient at the beginning when organizations start to design their Strategic Performance Management approaches. However, in order to make Strategic

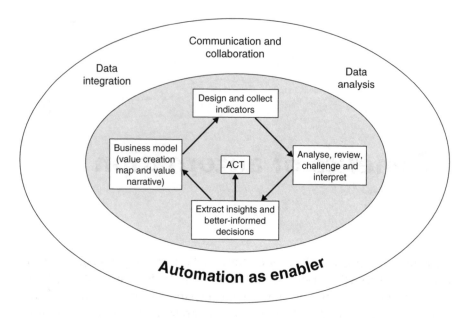

Figure 8.1 Benefits of automation

Performance Management an integral part of the organization, automation will usually be necessary.

According to André de Waal, one of the seven Performance Management challenges organizations need to address is to embrace information transparency in order to have the right information available at the right time, to make the best decisions, and to take actions.[1] Overall, I see improved data integration, improved data analysis capabilities and better communication and collaboration as the main benefits of Strategic Performance Management software application (see Figure 8.1). I will discuss each of the three areas in more detail.[2]

Communication/Collaboration

One of the key benefits of an automated solution is that it enables organizations to communicate strategic performance information to employees and other stakeholders. Communication enables dialogue, and dialogue enables learning. I discussed earlier how important it is that employees understand the strategic direction and how they are able to contribute to the strategic mission. Software solutions are able to display strategic performance information in various formats and personalized user interfaces. The same data can be visualized in a preferred format, for example, tables, graphs or speedometers.

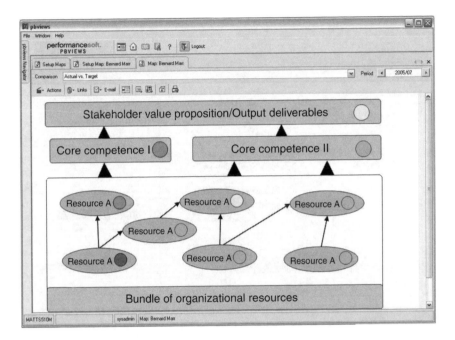

Figure 8.2 Screenshot: value creation map – PB views

Also, interactive value creation maps can easily be created. These allow employees to view the map and understand not only the strategic logic but the performance of the different elements too (see for example Figure 8.2). The elements of the value creation map are active and through a web-browser interface display the latest assessments in the form of, for example, traffic lights. Users can then click on these elements and see the underlying indicators, view descriptions and definitions as needed, and go on to analyse the data further.

Software applications not only provide the functionality to push data to users, but also enable them to provide feedback and comments, or even start discussion threads around specific topics. In addition, workflow capabilities can support initiatives and actions and provide a fast, automated (or ad-hoc) way of collaboration. Moreover, IT systems are able to provide automatically-triggered exception alerts. If, for example, a specific measure reaches a pre-defined threshold, automated e-mails or SMS messages could be sent to a group of people. Today, most applications are able to automatically and seamlessly support hundreds or thousands of linked value creation maps across heterogeneous organization structures.

Figure 8.3 provides another example of a value creation map, visualized in a tree diagram. Users can, for example, select different strategic elements and by clicking on them display their definition and

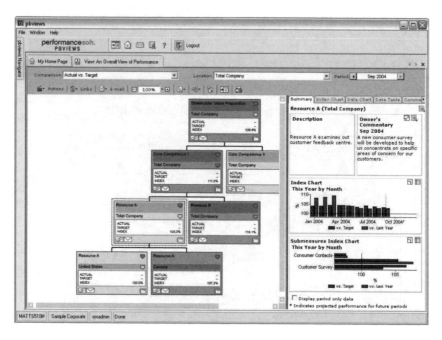

Figure 8.3 Screenshot: value creation map and indicators view – PB views

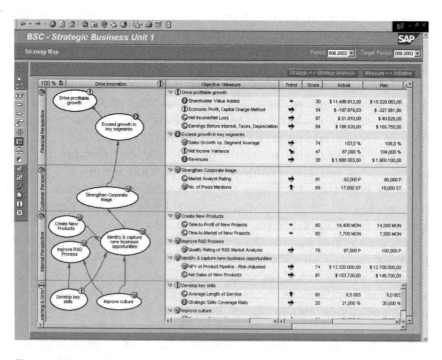

Figure 8.4 Screenshot: causal map and indicators – SAP strategic enterprise management

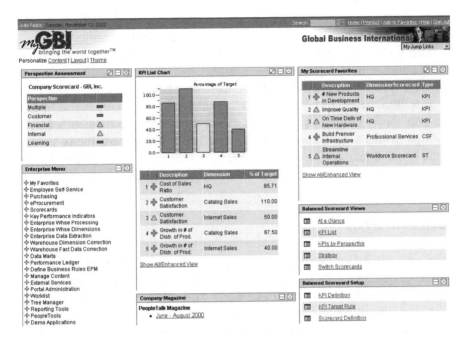

Figure 8.5 Screenshot: customized view – Oracle Peoplesoft Enterprise

indicators on the right-hand side of the screen. Views can be created to suit any requirements and any format. Here, the view includes a description of the resource, a comment by the owner, a bar chart showing the indicator data over the year (compared to last year), as well as a set of other useful indicators.

Figure 8.4 shows a similar view, where causal maps are shown on the left and the individual indicators for those on the right, together with targets, benchmarks, etc. It is also possible to create links to other documents, such as a value creation narrative to provide more contextual information about the map. From here, further drill-downs are possible to select an indicator view or a view of initiatives that are linked to strategic elements on the value creation map.

Instead of letting users click through the applications and explore performance interactively, it is also easy to create reports. These can take any form or shape and can be freely customized for specific users or group of users. Senior executives might want to see the value creation map overview and then a list of all indicators where the organizations is currently underperforming. An operations manager might see the cascaded value creation map and a set of key operations measures in a trend view. Figure 8.5 illustrates an example of a customized reporting view that was created for one specific user. Many applications also allow end users to create their own view which can then be set, for example, to the desired start page for whenever they enter the application.

The web-based format of these solutions allows access to the latest performance data from anywhere in the world where you have access to an internet browser. Security features such as usernames and passwords allow users to be identified. This also gives companies the option of only providing sub-sets of the entire performance data to selected groups in the organization. It would, for example, be possible to ensure that branch managers in New York can only view their branch data, and that the branch manager from London has no access to that data.

Data analysis

The second major benefit of Strategic Performance Management software applications is the ability to analyse performance data much more effectively and comprehensively. The interactive drill-down capabilities described above are the most intuitive way of exploring and analysing Strategic Performance data. However, many of the Strategic Performance Management software applications provide much more sophisticated analysis features, such as:

- Drill-downs
- Data visualization (including comprehensive graphing)
- Trend analysis
- Impact analysis
- Correlations and regression analysis
- Multidimensional OLAP analysis
- Simulation and scenario features.

Visualizing data in more graphical formats can be very powerful. In the section above I have described how entire interactive value creation maps can be visualized. Nowadays, many of the software applications come with powerful graphic capabilities that go far beyond what ordinary spreadsheet applications can deliver. Figure 8.6 shows, for example, an interactively colour-coded geographical map, indicating good performance in North America and Europe, and underperformance in Australia and South America.

The other important analysis is impact analysis or the assessment of correlations or regressions in causal models. If organizations have created causal value creation maps or other cause-and-effect logics, they are then able to use the data to 'test' and validate their assumed relationships as outlined in Chapter 7. Figure 8.7 and 8.8 both show ways

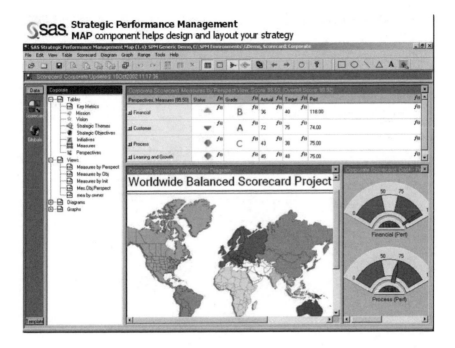

Figure 8.6 Screenshot: advanced visualization – SAS Strategic Performance Management

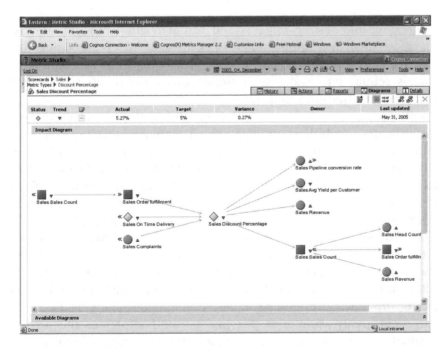

Figure 8.7 Screenshot: impact analysis – COGNOS 8

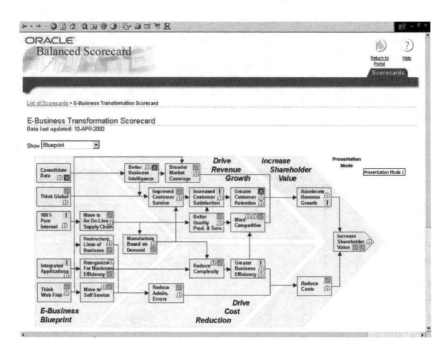

Figure 8.8   Screenshot: causal map – Oracle OBSC

of creating and testing impacts and causal relationships. In some of the more analytical applications users are able to create simulations based on their cause-and-effect logics. However, a lot of quantitative data is required to make such simulations meaningful, and in most cases I would question their value.

Often data has to be viewed from different perspectives and a sophisticated technique is needed to explore accumulated data. Multidimensional analysis tools usually perform this task. With them, data can be stored and examined in a multidimensional format similar to an ordinary spreadsheet, but in more than two dimensions.[3] These tools are linked to a graphical user interface (GUI) which provides the results on the computer screen presented in tables or graphs.

Multidimensional technology plays a significant role in business intelligence by enabling users to make business decisions by creating data models that reflect the complexities found in real-life structures and relationships. It consolidates and presents summarized corporate information from a multitude of sources. Multidimensionality as a concept can seem highly abstract at first but it simply expresses the way we naturally think. The best way to grasp the advantage of multidimensional viewing is to think of a three-dimensional cube. To understand

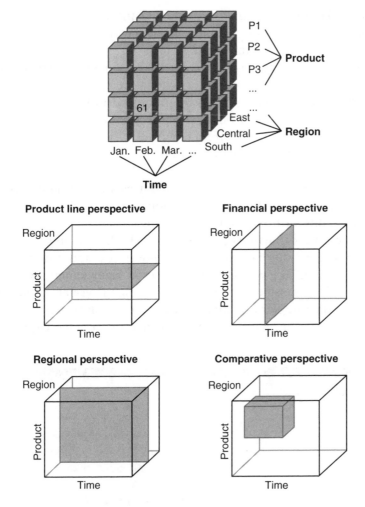

Figure 8.9 Multidimensional analysis

the benefit of the concept, I would like to provide the following practical example taken from a SAS Institute white paper (see also Figure 8.9).[4]

Users might be interested in the sales performance of the organization's products. Three dimensions (product sales, region and time) might all be of interest to a number of users, but each might want to view the data from a different perspective according to each user's function. Several examples follow:

■ A product manager might be interested in the performance of one particular product line in all regions over time (the 'product line perspective')

- A financial analyst might need to view the total sales results of all products in all regions within a particular timeframe, such as a calendar month (the 'financial perspective')
- A local manager might want information on sales results within a specific geographic region (the 'regional perspective')
- Finally, a market analyst might be interested in focusing on a single cell in the cube, a cell being the intersection of all dimensions at one point (the 'comparative perspective'). Typically, such an inquiry is undertaken for comparison purposes.

These examples look at the same data, but each has a unique perspective. Cutting through the multidimensional cube to reveal various perspectives is often called 'slicing and dicing'.

Another type of analysis is 'assessing risk'. In Chapter 7 I outlined how to use the value creation map to assess risk and how to create a risk log. Many of the Strategic Performance Management applications provide risk assessment tools. The advanced visualization of the Hyperion Strategic Performance Management application, for example, allows the creation of a risk or performance matrix (see Figure 8.10).

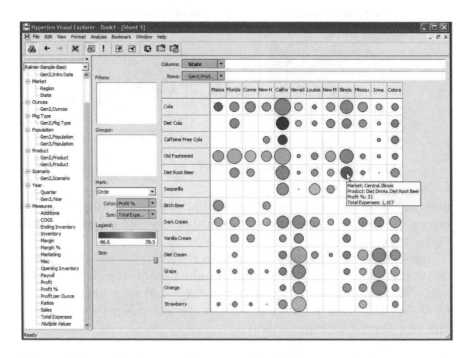

Figure 8.10   Screenshot: visual analysis – Hyperion Strategic Performance Management

Data integration and data management

The data issue is important in any comprehensive Performance Measurement system. Any Strategic Performance Management application must be fed with the relevant data. Since a Strategic Performance Management system provides a holistic view of performance, it needs to bring together data from very different organizational units and departments. A Strategic Performance Management software solution should work in harmony with existing data sources to fulfil its function as a data integrator.

Managers often believe that it is just a matter of connecting to the existing databases and then pulling out the data into the Strategic Performance Management application. However, the efforts necessary to integrate and collect data from disparate sources are often underestimated. And more importantly, a lot of the performance data required is not readily available in existing databases. From my experience, on average only about 20–30% of the required data is held in existing databases.

The first step, therefore, is to find out which information is relevant and required, whether the data already exists and, if so, where it is stored and how the data can be accessed. Most organizations have made significant investments in data warehouses, data marts and enterprise resource planning (ERP) systems, which means that a considerable portion of the required information can come directly from these back-office systems.

However, as mentioned above, a significant amount of information will usually come from office applications, such as Microsoft Excel, where the data is stored in spreadsheets. Increasingly there will also be data from third-party providers that has to be fed into an application. Third-parties could provide, for example, any benchmark information, customer satisfaction information, or brand and reputation data. Many organizations also outsource their employee satisfaction surveys. A large part of the organizational performance data may have to be entered manually into the system, either because it is non-existent or because it is not stored in the available IT systems. Tapping into different data sources and creating automated feeds is not a trivial task and it is important, therefore, to ask yourself whether it is really necessary (and economical) to connect databases.

For Strategic Performance Management, the data is usually integrated into a single database or data warehouse, and therefore this creates a single view of 'the truth'. The Strategic Performance Management solution, however, is more than just a data repository. It should be a tool to store and share information in order to turn it into knowledge and learning. In their book *Working Knowledge*, Tom Davenport and Larry Prusak distinguish between data, information and knowledge.[5] Data is just a structured record, with no meaning attached to it. Information, on the other hand, is a message that puts data into a context. It has a sender and a receiver and is meant to 'inform'. It therefore aims to influence or change the way the receiver perceives something. Knowledge is what we make of the information. When we take on information, we blend it with our experience and values in order to turn it into actionable routines, processes, practices or norms.

Strategic Performance Management solutions are not just a big database full of numbers. They also hold, for example, visualizations, definitions, descriptions, comments, discussion threads, and action plans. These provide the rich contextual information that allows us to make sense of the data and turn it into actionable knowledge and learning – which is the key objective of Strategic Performance Management.

In summary, Strategic Performance Management solutions help us to:

1 integrate data and manage data and information
2 analyse and visualize data in the most appropriate ways, and
3 facilitate communication and collaboration.

They therefore support Strategic Performance Management initiatives and facilitate better-informed decision-making and organizational learning.

References and endnotes

1 de Waal, A. A. (2001). *Power of Performance Measurement: How Leading Companies Create Sustained Value.* Wiley: New York.
2 Marr, B. and Neely, A. (2002). *Software for Measuring Performance.* In *Handbook of Performance Measurement*, 2nd edn, (M. Bourne, ed.) pp. 210–41, Gee: London.
3 Creeth, R. and Pendse, N. (1999). The OLAP Report. London: Business Intelligence.
4 King, R., McIntyre, J., Moormann, M., and Walker, E. (1996). A Formula of OLAP Success. www.sas.com
5 Davenport, T. H. and Prusak, L. (1998). *Working Knowledge: How Organizations Manage What They Know.* Harvard Business School Press: Boston, MA.

Appendix

Selecting the appropriate software solution[1]

The market for software solutions is growing rapidly. You only need to turn to the internet, search on Strategic Performance Management software solutions, and you will easily find in excess of 25 different vendors all of whom are willing to offer you a Performance Management application. Each vendor will claim unique advantages and features of their particular product, and each vendor will be able to provide credentials from satisfied users. Managers looking for an appropriate solution for their organization often have little to base their decision on or few tools to distinguish the various vendors. Here, I will address these issues and provide you with an overview of the application market as well as a framework of how to select the most suitable solution for your organization. Questions I will address in this appendix include:

- Is it better to buy a packaged solution or build your own?
- How can we distinguish between the different products?
- What credible vendors offer solutions?
- How can you create your own list of requirements?

One of the first questions you will be faced with is: do I buy a packaged application from a specialized vendor or do I build my own? Some organizations choose to develop their own software. The 'create your own' solution allows organizations to address their unique needs and objectives; however, it is generally more cost-effective to purchase a packaged application rather than to create your own.[2] Besides the cost factors, packaged applications are usually quicker to implement with vendors offering a wide variety of ancillary services such as conversion assistance, implementation training and system integration.

These packages also tend to represent the cumulative efforts of many individuals and organizations over a longer period of time, which usually results in better, more user-friendly applications than most first-time attempts to create 'home grown' applications.

DaimlerChrysler, for example, initially decided to develop their own solution. The problem was that it took 5–10 people over 18 months to develop the first, dubbed application. On the other hand, companies such as Skandia and Ericsson developed their own solutions and then later converted their developments into a product. Both have spun off a company which now sells the software solution to other organizations.

The various reasons for choosing a packaged application as opposed to "self-made" solutions are summarized below.[2]

Reasons for choosing a packaged application:

- When there is a packaged application that fits nicely with the functional requirements of your organization
- When there is no wish or no possibility to heavily rely on internal IT resources for creating a customized solution
- For prototyping, light-weight packaged applications can be used to 'test' different functionality before starting a full-blown automation.

Reasons for choosing a 'home-grown' solution:

- Functional criteria are not met by packaged applications
- There may be Business Intelligence software available within your organization that supports much of the functionality required
- A wish for total integration of the existing planning and control and/or knowledge management procedures, methodologies and tools within your organization.

Unless you have a lot of unused IT resources and an extremely good understanding of functionality I would always recommend going for a packaged application.

Once you have decided to go for a packaged application, there are some bigger choices to be made about:

- Implementation – what is your desired scope of the software implementation?
- Integration – how deeply do you want to integrate the software with operational and transactional systems?
- Customization and IT support/skills – to what extent do you need or want the software to be customized?

Scope of the implementation

The scope of the implementation can be very different and various vendors have different understandings of how much (or little) the scope of implementation should be. The smallest implementation scope would be an off-the-shelf point solution that runs as a stand-alone application on a PC and might replace an Excel spreadsheet by offering more specific functionality. These packages are usually quite inexpensive and can be bought ready to use. The advantage is that you can start using the software straight away, usually by inputting the data manually.

To increase the scope, vendors offer a broader set of applications which are likely to access a similar set of data. Those applications could, for example, include risk management, activity-based costing (ABC) or activity-based management (ABM) solutions, planning and budgeting application as well as solutions for stakeholder relationship management (SRM), process mapping, workflow management, customer relationship management (CRM) or business consolidation. The implementation scope broadens when companies also try to support some of the other applications or solutions. The broadest scope would be an integrated suite that offers all the functionality mentioned above. With an increasing implementation scope there is also a rising need for technical solutions like data warehouses or multidimensional databases that hold the data for the applications.

Organizations that are planning to purchase a software solution should consider the implementation scope, not only for the initial implementation but also taking into account future plans. You might want to start with simple reporting and analysis functionality but later expand the solution to additional functionality. For example, many organizations already have applications for planning and budgeting or CRM in place. In this case they might want to ensure that the new application they are purchasing is compatible with the applications already in place. Quite a few of the stand-alone solution providers have entered partnerships with other third-party vendors in order to be able to offer native links to products like ABM or CRM software.

Degree of integration

The degree of integration refers to how deeply the software is integrated with underlying operational systems like manufacturing systems, order entry, account systems, general ledger, purchasing, warehousing, human resource systems or general ERP systems.

The data required for the applications often resides in the underlying operational systems and databases. Full integration or 'closed-loop' integration would mean that the application is seamlessly integrated with the underlying operational systems and data can be fed automatically in either direction – from the underlying operational systems to the application and vice versa.

The products on offer vary in their integration ability. Basic standalone applications might offer no integration capabilities with underlying systems and are not designed for automated data feeds, but manual data transfer. These systems, however, might offer integration on an analytical level. This would mean users can analyse the existing data in the system through drill-downs, e.g. from an aggregate high-level performance indicator to underlying indicators, by querying a database. If the software application does not offer this capability it can be achieved by using Business Intelligence applications. Some applications offer integration with business intelligence tools. Other applications are designed for full integration and do not even allow manual data input. As discussed in Chapter 8, I think manual data input is usually required and you might not need a lot of integration. It is important to really think about the level of integration you require.

Required customization and IT support

You also need to look at the required customization and the required IT support. Not all products in the marketplace were developed as applications; some are more generic business intelligence tools that allow organizations to customize their applications. Some of the more advanced products offer things like wizards that guide users through parts of the design process for value creation maps or indicators. Other products offer little or no such guidance.

There are several issues you might want to consider before making the decision. The advantage of a ready-made application is that it includes all the methodological intelligence as well as the input of experts. The downside might be that the methodology does not 100% fit with the methodology your organization would like to implement. If your organization has specific requirements which cannot be found in any of the more advanced solutions it might be a reason for using more generic business intelligence tools. However, nowadays, most of the packaged applications offer enormous flexibility to be customized to your requirements.

Besides using more generic business intelligence applications to create customized solutions you can also use vendors or consultants to customize solutions for you. There are a few management consultancies that specialize in customizing applications by using their own or various third-party software components. This might be an option if an organization lacks internal expertise in methodology or has not got the internal IT resources to support the internal developments.

Having thought about all the above, you are still left with too many choices. So how do you know which of the different vendors to go with? How do you cut down the list from 25 to 3 that you might want to put on a shortlist? What is the process of making the right decision about selecting the appropriate solution? In the next section I will present a framework that will assist you in the decision process.

SOFTWARE SELECTION FRAMEWORK

Selecting the right software solution is a major decision for most organizations. The prices for software solutions vary enormously from a few thousand US dollars to far over a million US dollars. A realistic starting price lies at about $30 000 with typical spends in the region of $200 000 for reasonably sized organizations. Making the wrong decision, buying the wrong software, can not only result in a significant waste of time, energy and money, but can also undermine the entire effort and the credibility of the Performance Management system you are trying to put in place.

The starting point for any selection process has to be to recognize that each organization has a unique set of requirements for its approach. It is therefore not possible to provide a list of requirements that is appropriate for every organization. Organizations differ in terms of size, IT infrastructure, communication style, required level of security, cash position, strategic design, IT literacy, in-house capabilities, etc. All these aspects affect the selection criteria of an appropriate software solution. For the purpose of developing a selection framework this means that I can present the criteria you need to consider, but then you have to decide what you need and weigh each of the criteria to reflect your unique set of requirements.

Following the same logic, each of the different software solutions available has different strengths and weaknesses. Particular packages will be relevant for certain organizations, while they may be completely inappropriate for others.

It is therefore best to start with identifying what you really want and need and then see whether that is available from packaged applications. The easiest way to do this is to create a two-directional matrix in which you put weightings against each criteria. This matrix can then be used to compare available software products against the organizational requirements (for an example, see Figure 9.1). In the following sections I will define and explain each of the ten selection criteria you should think about before choosing a software application.

Company and product

First it is a good idea to check basic company information about the vendor as well as information about the software product. The main aspect here is the pricing, since prices as well as pricing models vary significantly. Here it is important to check not just license fees but also maintenance fees, which can fluctuate between 10–25% of the license fees. Software pricing is a complex issue and different pricing models might suit one organization better than others, e.g. pricing per user versus pricing per package. However, software companies are often flexible in their pricing and pricing models are subject to negotiation. It is also important to consider training and implementation costs as they can drastically increase the overall price of solutions, but often remain initially hidden.

As for the vendor company it might be good to understand the background of the company and the product, and how many people work on the solution. Very large software companies might have only a few people working on their application, which might be treated as a by-product. On the other hand, a small company that specializes in software might have more expertise and a larger client list. The size and global presence of a software vendor might be important if organizations plan to implement the application globally or across countries. Organizations might want to check the economic viability of the vendor considering recent collapses and mergers in this market.

Scalability

In order to assess the required scalability it is important to consider the final implementation scope. Companies might initially only automate one department or business unit but later plan to roll it out organization-wide. There are three aspects of scalability. (1) The application should be scalable in terms of programming. It should, for example, be easy to add new cascaded value creation maps. (2) The underlying database should be scalable since the amount of data and information accumulates quickly. (3) The communication approach should be scalable so that it is easy to disseminate the information through, for example, the Web browser. Language can also be an issue

Criteria	Required?	Weight	Product A	Product B	Product ...

Company/Product
   Sub-criteria I
   Sub-criteria II
   ...
	
	Yes/No
	Yes/No
		
		1–10
		1–10			

Scalability needs
   Sub-criteria I
   Sub-criteria II
   ...
	
	Yes/No
	Yes/No
		
		1–10
		1–10			

Flexibility needs
   Sub-criteria I
   Sub-criteria II
   ...
	
	Yes/No
	Yes/No
		
		1–10
		1–10			

Communication and
collaboration needs
   Sub-criteria I
   Sub-criteria II
   ...
	
	Yes/No
	Yes/No
		
		1–10
		1–10			

Security and access
control
   Sub-criteria I
   Sub-criteria II
   ...
	
	Yes/No
	Yes/No
		
		1–10
		1–10			

Technical needs
   Sub-criteria I
   Sub-criteria II
   ...
	
	Yes/No
	Yes/No
		
		1–10
		1–10			

User interface
   Sub-criteria I
   Sub-criteria II
   ...
	
	Yes/No
	Yes/No
		
		1–10
		1–10			

Analysis needs
   Sub-criteria I
   Sub-criteria II
   ...
	
	Yes/No
	Yes/No
		
		1–10
		1–10			

Service
requirements
   Sub-criteria I
   Sub-criteria II
   ...
	
	Yes/No
	Yes/No
		
		1–10
		1–10			

Future
developments
   Sub-criteria I
   Sub-criteria II
   ...
	
	Yes/No
	Yes/No
		
		1–10
		1–10			

Score:					

Figure 9.1 Software selection matrix

for international organizations and they might want to check whether the application comes in various languages.

Flexibility and customization

This is an important aspect and nowadays organizations are less willing to invest in applications that are not, for example, able to integrate with other applications. Many tools provide interfaces with reporting packages, activity-based costing solutions, CRM or planning tools. Flexibility should also be provided in terms of methodology support. Many organizations have multiple Performance Measurement and reporting needs; besides their strategic value creation map they might also want to use the software for frameworks such as other business scorecards or assessment frameworks (e.g. Baldrige National Quality Award, EFQM Award, Deming Prize, Investors in People, etc.). It usually makes sense to use the same application for all the Performance Measurement and reporting needs.

Communication and collaboration

The communication aspect of any implementation is key. Organizations have to address issues such as: do you want the software to be web-enabled, or even WAP enabled? Do you want users to be able to comment on any aspect of the strategy? Or do you want to restrict the commentary to any group, e.g. managers responsible for certain aspects in the strategy? For the majority of implementations it is important that the application integrates with the existing e-mail system so that alerts, reminders, assessments, and comments can be sent to specific users.

Most software solutions are able to trigger automated alerts, e-mails or SMS messages, which can be sent to individuals or groups indicating that certain areas of the business are under-performing and action is required. Most applications allow you to assign owners (and persons responsible for data entry) in order to automate the data collection and remind them if data, comments, or assessments have not been entered. You might want the software to support action and include activity or project management functionality that allows you to track progress against strategic objectives. Some organizations love and fully embrace this data-push concept and workflows, whereas others feel that such an approach is too intrusive and doesn't fit with their current culture. Sometimes it is a good idea to start without the automated e-mails and let people get used to the system and the information first.

Security and access control

You need to decide about the level of security needed in the system; some organizations are very open and openly share all aspects of their strategic performance with all employees; others require very tight security.

Technical specifications

The technical requirements depend on the existing information and communication infrastructure in your organization. Any new piece of software should support the existing desktop or network operating system. For an application it can be important to be able to extract data from existing data sources. This can be a major obstacle for any implementation. It is a good idea to involve the IT department in the discussion about technical requirements.

User interface/Data presentation

Here you have to decide about your visualization and data presentation needs. Applications vary between very graphical to more text and tables based. One of the most important aspects is the display of value creation maps and cause-and-effect relationships. I recommend going for interactive and dynamic visualizations, where the underlying data is linked to the different elements and where the connection means something. Some tools just display graphics without any real data, drill-down or impact analysis functionality. Dynamic maps allow you to use them as a powerful communication tool with traffic lighting and even the opportunity to mathematically test assumed relationships.

Analysis functionality

Tools offer different levels of analysis capabilities, stretching from simple drill-down capabilities to multidimensional analysis, complex statistical functionality, forecasting and even simulations. Organizations which require more complex analysis functionality often have tools for this already in place and have to decide whether to integrate or replace those. Analysis functionality also includes the number of graphical displays (from bar charts to advanced 3-D charts). Requirements in terms of charts and graphs depend on the indicators the organization tracks and their visualization requirements. It is especially important to include the business analysts in this discussion.

Service

Vendors offer different levels of service. Some offer no implementation support and instead partner with consulting companies to provide this. Other vendors offer comprehensive services including their own implementation service, consulting, international service hotlines, etc. Organizations need to be clear how much support they want and whether the vendor or their partners can deliver this.

Future

Here the future developments and release frequency of the product are addressed, which might indicate the vendor's attention and commitment to the product. It is also important to understand the future vision of the software vendor, which will influence the direction of any future product development. In an ideal case the future views of the vendor and your organization would be similar, in order to ensure future compatibility.

Overall, it is important to involve different people in the process of developing the requirements for your solution. Organizations often fail to involve all key functions and end up with a solution that matches only half of their organizational requirements. When only IT people are involved they typically look for the IT-specific capabilities and compatibility with the existing IT infrastructure. Finance people usually look for financial capabilities and possibly the most sensible economical solutions. Business analysts may look for the most comprehensive analysis capabilities, and general managers may look for a good user interface and ease of use. In order to address all requirements, it is therefore important to involve members of all four groups in the decision process. My experience has taught me that the selection process is best led by members of the management team in close collaboration with business analysts and the IT function.

Once you have developed your unique list of requirements, you can start to look for a suitable software solution that can deliver against those requirements and help to make your initiative a success. Below, in Figure 9.2, I present a list of the 25 leading vendors of software applications. A final tip once you have narrowed down possible vendors to a shortlist – ask for reference clients that have implemented

Company name	Product name	Website
ALG Software	EPO Performance Management Software	www.algsoftware.com
Active Strategy	ActiveStrategy Enterprise	www.activestrategy.com
Business Objects	Business Objects Enterprise Performance Management	www.businessobjects.com
Cartesis	Cartesis Suite	www.cartesis.com
Clarity Systems	Clarity Performance Management (CPM) suite	www.claritysystems.com
Cognos	Corporate Performance Management, Cognos 8 Business Intelligence	www.cognos.com
CorVu	CorVu 5 Performance Management Application	www.corvu.com
Geac	Geac Strategy Management	www.comshare.com
HostAnalytics	Business Performance Management (BPM)	www.hostanalytics.com
Hyperion	Business Performance Management Suite	www.hyperion.com
Information Builders	various products	www.informationbuilders.com
InPhase Software	Performance Plus	www.inphase.com
Lawson	Enterprise Performance Management	www.lawson.com
Microsoft	various products	www.microsoft.com
MicroStrategy	various products	www.microstrategy.com
Oracle	Oracle Enterprise Manager, PeopleSoft Enterprise	www.oracle.com
OutlookSoft	OutlookSoft Corporate Performance Management	www.outlooksoft.com
PerformanceSoft	PB views, Performance Management Software	www.performancesoft.com
Procos	Strat&Go Performance Management	www.procos.com
ProDacapo	various products	www.prodacapo.com
QPR Software	various products	www.qprsoftware.com
SAP	Strategic Enterprise Management (SEM)	www.sap.com
SAS Institute	SAS Strategic Performance Management	www.sas.com
Stratsys	various products	www.runyourcompany.com
Successfactors	SuccessFactor Performance Manager	www.successfactors.com

Figure 9.2   List of vendors and software products

applications of similar scope and scale, and contact them. Many will be happy to provide these and a visit or conference call with other customers can be useful for both sides.

References and endnotes

1 This appendix is based on: Marr, B. and Neely, A. (2003). *Automating Your Scorecard: The Balanced Scorecard Software Report*. Gartner and Cranfield School of Management: Stamford, CT.
2 See for example: Marr, B. and Neely, A. (2002). *Software for Measuring Performance*. In *Handbook of Performance Measurement*, 2nd edn. (M. Bourne, ed.) Gee: London.

Further reading on the topic

Readers who enjoyed this book might also be interested in another recent book by Bernard Marr. *Perspectives on Intellectual Capital: Multidisciplinary Insight into Management, Measurement and Reporting* focuses especially on the topics of intangible assets and intellectual capital in organizations today. With contributions from many leading experts in the field it provides a rich introduction and overview of the topic.

It is now widely recognized that intangible elements in organizations function as key differentiators and drivers of bottom-line performance. However, intangibles are encompassing many different constructs including competencies of employees, relationships with key stakeholders, well-designed processes, a strong brand image, or a positive organizational culture, among many others. This broad spectrum led to a truly multidisciplinary field. This book looks at each of the disciplinary views in more detail and, therefore, addresses questions such as:

- What is the economic impact of intellectual capital?
- What are the strategic roles of intangible value drivers?
- How can companies measure and report the value of their intangible assets?
- What are the accounting guidelines for intangibles?
- What is the latest thinking on intangibles in marketing or HR?
- And many more...

This edited book is the first to outline the current state of the art in managing, measuring, and reporting of intellectual capital from different disciplines and perspectives. It provides a well-grounded and comprehensive introduction to this fascinating topic.

Perspectives on Intellectual Capital by Bernard Marr
Published by Elsevier (2005)
ISBN 0-7506-7799-6

Index